AMERICAN BLINDSPOT

Also by Gerardo Martí

A Mosaic of Believers:
Diversity and Innovation in a Multiethnic Church

Hollywood Faith:
Holiness, Prosperity, and Ambition in a Los Angeles Church

Worship across the Racial Divide:
Religious Music and the Multiracial Church

The Deconstructed Church:
Understanding Emerging Christianity
(with Gladys Ganiel)

Latino Protestants in America:
Growing and Diverse
(with Mark T. Mulder and Aida I. Ramos)

The Glass Church:
Robert H. Schuller and the Strain of Megachurch Ministry
(with Mark T. Mulder)

AMERICAN BLINDSPOT

Race, Class, Religion, and the Trump Presidency

Gerardo Martí
Davidson College

ROWMAN & LITTLEFIELD
Lanham • Boulder • New York • London

Executive Editor: Nancy Roberts
Editorial Assistant: Courtney Packard
Channel Manager: Jonathan Raeder

Credits and acknowledgments for material borrowed from other sources, and reproduced with permission, appear on the appropriate page within the text.

Published by Rowman & Littlefield
An imprint of The Rowman & Littlefield Publishing Group, Inc.
4501 Forbes Boulevard, Suite 200, Lanham, Maryland 20706
www.rowman.com

6 Tinworth Street, London SE11 5AL, United Kingdom

British Library Cataloguing in Publication Information Available

Library of Congress Control Number:2019950637

ISBN 978-1-5381-1608-1 (cloth : alk. paper)
ISBN 978-1-5381-1609-8 (pbk. : alk. paper)
ISBN 978-1-5381-1610-4 (electronic)

♾ ™ The paper used in this publication meets the minimum requirements of American National Standard for Information Sciences Permanence of Paper for Printed Library Materials, ANSI/NISO Z39.48-1992.

As the son of immigrants to the United States of America, I dedicate this book to my parents.

To describe adequately recent and contemporary conceptions of what is political is a risky undertaking, full of
the pitfalls that come from standing so close to events
and interpretations of events. Accepting the risks, nevertheless, let us begin with some obvious remarks and
then try to see what their implications hold.
                    —Sheldon S. Wolin, *Politics and Vision*

CONTENTS

PREFACE

The purpose of this book is to examine the intersection of race and ethnicity, social class, and religion in America through the phenomenon of Donald J. Trump's election as the forty-fifth president of the United States. Overall, the book sidesteps the rancor and flash of emotional outbursts that are prevalent in op-ed pieces and social media. *American Blindspot* addresses the lack of historical understanding and provides information on the development of American society. Special focus is given to the workings of enslavement and territorial expansion in the development of American society, the complex history of Reconstruction, the changing approaches to immigration policy, the modern development of Christianity and business thinking, the intertwining of religious reasoning and economic policy, the intense disdain for President Obama, the differential effects of the Great Recession of 2007–2009, and the underlying base of white evangelical support for Trump and his presidency. Thus, although the themes of the book are selective, they involve the broader and complex processes of identity and race, politics and nationalism, faith and community, economics and financial pressures, citizenship and public life, and prejudice and discrimination, as well as charisma and symbolic leadership.

Let me be clear: this book is not an opportunity for the professor to air his opinions, and it does not focus on Trump's personality. Instead, the book constitutes an exploration of American society centering on racial, economic, and religious dynamics as they touch on the historical context of the Trump presidency—including discernment of the significance in his positions, policies, political appointments, and particular public statements (and those of his surrogates, supporters, and representatives) from a broader view of the history of the United States. Sociological sensitivity is embedded in my discernment of patterns of macro-change. For example, in my narrative, race and ethnicity are not biological, physiological, or genetic characteristics; they are social characteristics, legally enforced and socially sanctioned, and they develop over time. Social class is not merely determined by ambition, hard work, or "luck," but rather is associated with broader and historically situated opportunities for accumulation of privileges associated with beneficial social networks, the means to acquire material property, and the gleam of prestige associated with high social status. And religion is not merely a set of dogmatic beliefs or static church membership but also a set of "lived practices" that influence nonreligious activity in unanticipated ways. It is expected that many interests and questions will emerge to drive readers further into more specialized texts.

Davidson College provided a productive setting for teaching and writing, and this project would not have occurred without the intellectual freedom to pursue an expansive understanding of the sociopolitical development of the United States provided through our rigorous yet responsive curriculum. Thanks are due especially to my students at Davidson College who have engaged in so many fruitful readings and explorations of the "long view" on Trump's presidency. I am grateful that they have allowed me to work with their verbal comments and written materials in constructing this narrative. Thank you to Nicolo Agosta, Hannah Aronson, Louisa Bartkovich, Vivian Boe, Isabelle Bradberry, Daniel Brennan, Lauren Browne, Benjamin Caldwell, Caroline Coffey, Veronica De La Mora, Wesley Dugger, Eboni Freeman, Allegra Geanuracos, Abigail Giles, Jennifer Griffin, Grace Hall, Zoe Hall, Maribel Hernandez, Camille Herring, Henry Howell, James Hoyt, DaShanae Hughes, Alexander Jobe, Andrew Krueger, Sam Lucas, Adrian Macias, Idalina Pina, Courtney Potter, Daniel Rafla, Mary Margaret Robison, Snneha Saha, Leah Sarkisian, Emelyn Schaeffer, Jaelyn Taylor, Nellie Turnage, Amelia Twiss, Colby Wagner, Niara Webb, and William Yeo. Any mistakes committed in my sincere attempt to accurately convey some of our many insights over the multiple, layered structures of our American republic are solely my own. Thanks also to Dr. Lucretia Berry and the Brownicity team in the Charlotte area who provided me multiple opportunities to think through issues of race and immigration in the shaping of mainstream American culture through a series of workshops with adult learners. I appreciate Peter TeWinkle suggesting what became the main title of the book. I also extend deep gratitude to my wife, Laura, and our kids, Miranda, Zach, Nathan, and Genevieve, for their ongoing support of my development as a scholar.

An initial sketch of this book project was published in a chapter titled "The Legitimation of White Christian Libertarianism: Uncovering the Cultural Pillars of the Trump Presidency," in *Religion is Raced*, edited by Grace Yukich and Penny Edgell.[1] Portions of an article titled "The Unexpected Orthodoxy of Donald J Trump: White Evangelical Support for the 45th President of the United States," which was published in *Sociology of Religion*, are used especially in Chapter 9.[2] In writing about the expansion of the United States through the annexation of Mexican territory through the Treaty of Guadalupe-Hidalgo, I draw on jointly written publications stemming from research funded by Lilly Endowment with coauthors Mark T. Mulder and Aida I. Ramos, especially *Latino Protestants in America* published by Rowman & Littlefield.[3] I also draw on my thinking on white Christian Libertarianism through a book on the ministry of prominent megachurch pastor and televangelist Robert H. Schuller written with Mark T. Mulder titled *The Glass Church*.[4]

A note regarding endnotes: for some readers, there are too many citations; for others, not enough. Although my narrative includes many specific names, events, incidents, and statements, a choice was made to especially cite those items based on lesser known items or on arguments and information stemming from recent research. Other information deemed to be more broadly known, well established, or easily found using readily available research tools accessible from any public library have been left without a specific reference. It is hoped that readers will be encouraged to examine anything they come across that strikes their curiosity more intensely on their own. All errors are mine alone, and further development of scholarship will undoubtedly productively amend and expand assessments made throughout this narrative.

Sarah Stanton and, later, Rolf Janke, both wonderful editors at Rowman & Littlefield, were always efficient and gracious in working through all stages of the project. Special thanks to Courtney Packard and Alden Perkins who managed the complex processes largely invisible to authors yet essential for their published work.

Chapter 1

THE UNEXPECTED PRESIDENT

The 2016 Trump Election and
White Evangelical Support

No one, not even his most intimate campaign advisors, anticipated the election of Donald J. Trump as the forty-fifth president of the United States. Pollsters and professional political commentators expected a decisive loss, and journalists, policy wonks, and Washington insiders all prepared to usher in Hillary Clinton as the first female president of the United States. But as results trickled in state by state, the newspapers, TV news channels, and social media feeds took a turn in perspective as their predictions soured and recognition of decisive wins in the South, Midwest, and "rust belt" regions took hold. With more than enough electoral votes to claim victory, the brash, celebrity billionaire from New York was swept into the White House. The hours of waiting and final revelation resulted in wide-eyed, open-mouthed astonishment. Trump's political triumph exposed a shocking blind spot among political observers, even among the most seasoned political experts. What did they miss?

Soon, analysts and observers realized this: *Trump's election was not just a surprise, it was a revelation about our country.* Trump's "narrow path" of electoral victory was more than just successfully edging out his presumptive competitor; analysts and observers concluded that his gaining the presidency had pulled back the curtain on deep cultural strains among the American people. And although early commentators centered on the economic strains of the white working class or on "rural resentment," a closer look at the numbers resisted crediting the victory to any one marginalized group. Powerful undercurrents in American society were missed. Since then, social analysts like myself have been wrestling to grasp the profound cultural resonances that contributed to Trump's win in the 2016 presidential election.[1] I suspect we will continue to do so for a very long time.

As part of my own process toward understanding the meaning and implications of Trump's election, I decided to offer an undergraduate course in the fall of 2017 titled "Race, Religion, and Donald J. Trump." As a professor of sociology at Davidson College, a small, selective liberal arts college just north of Charlotte, North Carolina, my courses are "seminar style," which is best characterized as a cooperative process of critical thinking and analytical dialogue around shared readings. With every class, I have the privilege to think through important issues alongside intellectually curious students. This particular course was designed to avoid the unproductive exchange of uninformed opinions and instead to jointly pursue close appraisals of archival material and rigorous research. The goal of the course was clear: to nurture our historical and conceptual sophistication by uncovering underlying patterns and implications stemming from the Trump presidency. Resourcing the expertise from my own scholarship, the class centered on race and ethnicity, economic inequality, and religion.

This book is a direct outgrowth of that class. In preparation for the course, I spent several months (most intensely during the spring and summer of 2017) gathering materials, reading dozens of books, articles, and media posts in print and online, selecting sources, and eventually homing in on a manageable number of texts orienting around a set of key societal issues and historical processes. In the end, the sources I chose centered around several focal points that I found to be highly insightful for providing historical context to the forty-fifth presidency of the United States. My goal was not to be topically comprehensive (an impossible task) but to stimulate ideas, to accentuate abiding significance, to synthesize neglected knowledge, and to promote analytical depth. I favored peer-reviewed scholarly sources, which I supplemented with well-informed journalistic accounts from mainstream media sources. I also favored historical happenings that were less well known in the popular imagination or recently surfaced. I also challenged myself to broaden my learning by seeking sources outside my academic discipline and stretching the time horizon all the way back to the birth of the American republic. To my delight, I found that the majority of the readings I ultimately selected had been published since 2016—notable for the freshness of their perspective—and successfully extended the historical range of the course from the colonial period to the present day. In making these readings readily available to my class, the students and I jointly considered each source, talking and writing intensely about them week to week, cumulatively enlarging and deepening our learning over the semester, and finding more useful and relevant materials to share through group presentations. In constructing a synthetic narrative of our knowledge based on our class experience, I remained attentive to the questions and insights that came from my students. That initial class experience was repeated when I offered the course again in 2018 and twice again in 2019, reading and incorporating newly published sources as they became available. This book, then, is a synthetic attempt to bring together a cogent sample of our learning together.

In crafting my narrative, I am selective, sharing what students and I together found to be those aspects of American experience that most productively illuminate the historical and sociological context of the presidency of Donald J. Trump. The chapters compose a provocative, although admittedly not exhaustive, presentation of thought-inducing stepping stones for understanding. At Davidson I am fortunate to teach students who come highly prepared to succeed in college, and yet it was consistently evident to all of us—including the professor—how utterly uninformed we were regarding fundamental structures of our American society. We continued to find actions, policies, and statements that were historically and empirically true, yet none of our teachers, our extensive readings, or our broad media saturation had ever exposed us to understanding. Much about slavery in the United States was a blur. None of us recalled piecing together the tangle of events shaping the country during the Reconstruction period. And the closer we got to our own lifetimes following the Allied victories of World War II, the harder we worked to pull our fragmented information together. Amid our many eye-opening, "a-ha" experiences together, we progressed through our class often acknowledging that our understanding of Trump as a distinctly American phenomenon was limited and that rigorously analyzing more comprehensive information beyond opinion and rumor was difficult and time consuming. Although there surely must be a grounds-well of scholarly analysis happening right now that will provide much fuller context on this presidency, this book aims to fill significant gaps in our lack of understanding by looking backward, assessing our societal heritage, and cogently revealing neglected patterns from our shared past using some of the best existing scholarship on race, class, religion, and American history.

The book especially accentuates race and ethnicity, social class, and religion because they are critical—yet often misunderstood—dynamics implicit to our current political climate. They are also often controver-sial and explosive in our everyday conversations. The phenomenon of Trump is "huge" (as he himself might say), with considerable academic scrambling occurring as I write this. Through this project, I hope to convince readers of the importance of several heuristic touchpoints based in racial, economic, and religious structures. The following text will be useful not only for students but also for a growing number of scholars whose research agenda is taking shape now. Of course, in choosing to write during this historical moment, I cannot claim to be comprehensive in my assessments. In the spirit of sound scholarship, my narrative is open to expansions and corrections as they develop, serving as a platform for further thinking. We can expect that eventually we will have highly sophisticated analyses as more data are gathered, more sources are revealed, and greater historical perspective is achieved. Until then, this project resources and further stimulates lines of inquiry regarding the Trump presidency.

LEGITIMATION OF THE TRUMP PRESIDENCY

It was initially difficult to understand how someone who campaigned as a bullying strongman and deeply offended the sensibilities of so many people could become the president of the United States. Although many people felt sickened, angered, and fearful at the results of the election, it is important to remember that other groups of Americans were joyous. Trump was a proxy for values and initiatives those groups felt had been devalued by mainstream American politics. Although some were quick to place the blame on Hillary Clinton's unsecured email server, or working-class identity politics, or low voter turnout, a fuller examination is more intriguing. The truth is that an underlying American ethos was the most salient dynamic shaping the election, one that fueled Trump's core supporters, motivating them to come out to the polls and to continue to express satisfaction with his performance in office. Even if many believe that Trump did not actually "win" the presidency because of Russian interference or the fact that he did not actually win the popular vote, the question should be posed as to how Trump was seen as a viable candidate for the presidency in the first place.

In short, to understand the 2016 election and the subsequent support for his presidency, one must understand why so much of the American population is willing to legitimate Trump to occupy the highest elected office in the United States, viewing his policies and pronouncements as good, right, and true. The concept of legitimation draws from the theoretical work of Max Weber who wrote extensively about the dynamics of power and politics in *Economy and Society*.[2] The essays compiled in this posthumous work describes *legitimation* as the foundation of power, indicating that power is based not on coercion (you must obey or you will be hurt) or interest (if you obey you will receive good things in return) but rather on a bundle of beliefs and attitudes held by a people that predispose them to accept the exercise of power as good and proper or, alternatively, to accept the will of an authority as that to which others ought to defer (obey because it is the right thing to do). When an authority is legitimated, one is ethically bound to follow; as such, legitimation represents a core aspect of power in that it represents the assent of a group in giving authority to another who is entrusted with the ability to make executive decisions without the need for each individual in the group to assent. The one who has legitimate power is given permission to exercise authority. The obligation of obedience is inherent to legitimate power, not because obedience is demanded, but because the authority is deserving of our obedience.

Discerning the underlying social legitimation that propelled and empowers Donald J. Trump in his presidency remains an ongoing topic of conversation—whether with the policy analyst on cable news or with my neighbor next door. Some simply assert that Trump represents what many viewed as the end goal of the American dream. Trump's family originally came from Germany and the Scottish Isles. Although they were immigrants, they were the right kind of immigrants, Northern European, and they changed their name from Drumpf to Trump and gave up their ancestral identity. German "Teutons" supposedly possessed great intelligence, independence, love of liberty and order, and patriotism. Eventually, the aspiration to become president came to this white, blond, alpha male whose family had climbed up the economic ladder to become extremely wealthy and who had himself achieved an outstanding level of popular celebrity. A vote for Trump was a vote for the faith in the meritocracy of the United States. As attractive as such an explanation might be to some, the workings of legitimacy go much deeper than such superficial analysis.

Trump is often said to "lead by his instincts," and his instincts reflect a long historical development. Even cursory attention to the debates surrounding the Trump presidency provides some awareness of the more substantive elements of popular resonance generated by Trump's stance on issues. For example, Donald Trump was able to tap into the fears of whites, Christians, and conservatives over the changing demographics of the country. For many Americans in the twenty-first century, the more visible presence of immigrants and minorities constituted an ominous cloud, appearing to demand concessions on their cultural presumptions, pulling attention and dominance away from "true" Americans. In the 1990s and into the 2000s, it appeared that America was embracing multiculturalism, and the mainstream discourse on diversity implied that those who did not accept the value of diversity in every sphere of life were un-American, which angered and rallied the many fractured groups aligning with a white-superior agenda. Whether intended or not, Trump became an ally of white nationalists who recognized in him a race-based warrior and hero. Even among whites who did not associate with such groups, the shift from a primarily white society to a mixed-ancestry society was unsettling, even intimidating. Sensitivity to new traditions, new languages, new religious sensibilities, and new social cues were felt as a burden. Trump invigorated xenophobic passions among those who still believe that the American national identity is inherently white and conventionally Christian.

Trump resonated with many disillusioned white Americans, presenting himself as a defender of the everyman and promising a return to a conservative Christian–friendly, patriotic, civic nationalism. Trump connected with an audience that was fearful of the change the greater ethnic, racial, and religious diversity would bring. Trump rejected "political correctness," refusing to fake sentiments of equal dignity and equality in favor of warning of the dangers of foreign immigration and taking advantage of racial resentment, fear of marginalization, and the perceived economic and safety threat of immigrants among a predominately white evangelical voter base.

The resonance contributing to the legitimation of Trump's presidency also involves emergent ideologies regarding the ideal workings of the American economy. Critically, it is important to see that beliefs in white superiority do not automatically result in all whites experiencing wealth, income mobility, high-prestige occupations, or even tangible results like Ivy League college degrees and home ownership. Whiteness does not automatically grant wealth or status, yet comparatively speaking, the difference between the experience and opportunities afforded by being designated as "white" is starkly different from that of blacks, Latinos, and Asians (with the exception of income among some highly educated and well-resourced Asian subgroups).[3] Whiteness is indisputably associated with privilege in American society—even when most whites still feel financial pressures or inability to advance in their overall well-being.[4]

Even more, white Christian conservatives now align with free-market libertarians. Today, conservative economic and conservative evangelical Christians' beliefs have fused into strong political support for the presidency of Donald Trump because wealthy elites allowed their neoliberal economic and political ideals of individual liberty to converge with the evangelical conviction that the United States is a nation founded on Christian values. More than 70 percent of conservative evangelicals believe that the Constitution created a Christian state,[5] and 57 percent believe that to be considered American, one must be a Christian.[6] Neoliberals harnessed the power of Christian nationalist morality to promote a platform that promoted low government interference, restraining the government from interfering in civic affairs, except in pursuit of national security (e.g., keeping dangerous immigrants out of the country) and enforcement of traditional "family values" (e.g., limiting access to abortion and restricting LGBT persons in the military). Trump was accepted as embodying the fusing of religious and economic ideals neoliberals felt were best expressed in the Reagan presidency.

So, although not everyone voted for Trump, understanding the attitudinal commitments of those who did is instructive for understanding the sources of legitimation for his candidacy. Trump's victory was widely considered an "upset." Conservatives and liberals alike were surprised that a platform as polarizing and unsophisticated as Trump's (or a person as morally dubious as Trump) could win over so many among the electorate—especially those who considered themselves to be highly religious. Although Trump did not earn the affection of the general population, he did secure the overwhelming support of white conservative evangelicals.

Exit polls from the voting booth revealed a key factor: Trump received majority support from only one racial group, whites (58 percent), and overwhelming support from one significant religious group, white evangelical or "born-again" Christians (81 percent).[7] Conservative white evangelicals felt that their interests were excluded from the Obama presidency[8] and that their religious convictions were under attack, especially with new initiatives on gay marriage and the open welcome of gay and transgender persons into the military. Further examination of Trump voter attitudes affirmed foundational racial and religious connections between Trump and his political base. When asked what religious group faced the most discrimination in America, 54 percent of Trump voters said Christians followed by 22 percent for Muslims and 12 percent for Jews.[9] Conservative Christians believed their "religious freedom" was under threat. Prominent voices in the evangelical community, like Franklin Graham, Jerry Falwell Jr., and Robert Jeffress, stand behind Trump's isolationist foreign policies, even when they appear prejudicial and xenophobic.

Addressing a values voter summit, the forty-fifth president of the United States declared, "We don't worship government. We worship God." His statement highlights the enduring link between Christianity and American politics. From the outset, the United States has had a complicated relationship with religion; although ordained by Congress in the mid-1950s as "one nation under God," politicians simultaneously insisted on the separation between the structures of church life and state policies. Among the contentions over the role of religion, conservative white evangelicals had long vocalized their desire to highlight their religious orientation in the public sphere. For many conservatives, Trump was a means to preserve a more Christian and socially conservative America. Combined with their support for capitalism and assurance of divinely bestowed economic success, white evangelicals backed Trump as a presidential candidate and ultimately as president.

Evangelicalism is a subsection of Christianity (under the broad umbrella of Protestantism) that is generally distinguished from mainline Christianity by two fundamental beliefs. The first is the assumption of a radical conversion experience by which a believer's life is personally and permanently transformed by God into a spiritually upright person, and the second is the assumption that the Bible is not only a timeless guidebook for virtuous Christian life but also the ultimate source of religious truth.[10] Evangelicals are committed to a more literal interpretation of the Bible than Mainline Protestants, and more "liberal" practices—like ordaining women to ministry and sanctioning same-sex marriages—are not evident among conservative evangelical churches.[11] Evangelicals are proud in proclaiming their belief that their religious orientation is free of historical baggage. But this ahistorical claim is misguided. Not only does evangelicalism have a substantial history, its past informs the contemporary practices of mixing religious conviction into participation in the political realm.

Following their Calvinist roots, early American evangelicals viewed the fledgling United States as God's chosen nation, believing that political participation was ordained by God to usher in his Kingdom on earth.[12] We readily find that many early evangelicals were fervent patriots and tireless activists. Revivalist preacher Charles Finney wrote that Christians are "bound to exert their influence to secure a legislation that is in accordance with the law of God."[13] They campaigned against Thomas Jefferson in 1800 for his deist philosophy, claiming that he was not "qualified to govern Christians."[14] Evangelicals were the foundation of the religious abolitionist movement and helped transform Northern conceptions of slavery from an economic problem to a violation of morality. Throughout the nineteenth century, evangelicals took on a wide variety of secular social ills such as alcoholism and prostitution.

Although these historic religious imperatives are important, they neglect other aspects of evangelical Christianity over the past two centuries. Evangelicals have long found identity in religious defiance against the status quo, whether through rejection of the denominational structure of Mainline churches or the interminable agitation against the secular evils of society. And yet, looking at their actions, evangelicals for the majority of American history have sided with wealthy elites and, as stated by the prominent historian George Marsden, "reflected fairly closely the patterns and shifts of the political thought of the times, often providing their own Christian version of prevailing trends."[15] Support for the institution of slavery is a prominent example, but certainly not the only one. At the turn of the twentieth century, that ready correspondence with mainstream culture came to an end. Evangelicals found themselves on the defensive in a society that was rapidly secularizing, and the American political atmosphere seemed to be trending irreparably away from their ideals. Legislative efforts became more hostile and protective, a shift that was most visible in their vehement opposition to the public school system. Evangelicals believed public schools infringed on biblical values when they publicly sanctioned the teaching of evolution and removed prayer in schools. Wealthy evangelical conservatives funded networks of private schools and colleges where they could educate their children in accordance with their own beliefs, free from secular government involvement. These private schools also came to represent protection from feminism, homosexuality, and other nontraditional sentiments on sexuality and the structure of the family. Coincidentally, these beliefs ran parallel to many of those held by small-government economic conservatives who detested the post–World War I liberalization of American polity. Once this parallelism was realized, it was carefully synthesized into something greater than an accidental alignment: a political juggernaut that sought to preserve an idealized Christian America, a vast mobilization of forces powered by wealthy businessmen, charismatic leaders, and a perception of God's blessing.

The successful passage of progressive political policies in the New Deal largely contributed to the emergence of the Christian Right. The National Labor Relations Act, the Works Progress Administration relief program, and the Social Security Act were considered "un-American" by conservative Christians because they provided aid that negated the work ethic conservative Christians believed was based in the Bible.[16] Conservative Christians believed that poverty is the "natural condition" of the social world and that it is a curse by God to punish the rebellious.[17] Policies that alleviate the natural condition of poverty go against the social justice of God. It is a form of social Darwinism assuming that those who suffer economically are damned by God. Moreover, equality in America is undesirable, unbiblical, and unrealistic.[18] The Bible indicates a clear difference between followers and those who lead. Relief programs challenged such ideas.

In reaction to progressive social policies between 1940 and 1970, economic conservatives and evangelicals formed a powerful alliance. Both used moralistic messages to endorse conservative ideals. A philosophy of "Christian economics" emerged, which upheld capitalism as an inherently virtuous system. For evangelicals, free-market capitalism allowed a person to put one's fate in God's hands, whereas New Deal–era government influence represented the human usurpation of God's role in the economy. Neoliberal economists endorsed a capitalistic and individualistic reading of the Bible, and both pulpits and secular media were used to broadly promote this approach. In the 1940s, leaders of financial movements such as Spiritual Mobilization placed economics and politics in a moral framework, marginalizing dissenting liberal voices within evangelicalism.[19] Later, in the 1970s, conservative talk radio advocated social and political stances as religious convictions. For example, during this time James Dobson inaugurated his highly influential radio broadcast *Focus on the Family*, which presented what appeared to be a unified voice for an increasingly right-leaning and Republican-supporting white evangelicalism.

Meanwhile, church leaders promoted a conservative Christian nationalism, cultivating a tension between their congregations and liberal ideals. This entailed striving against the threats of socialism, multiculturalism, and secularism. Nationalism pervaded these evangelicals' ingrained patriotism and "America-first" rhetoric as congregations decisively aligned themselves with the Republican Party. Church leaders drew tacit boundaries between liberalism and Christianity, blaming liberals for the moral degradation of society. As sociologist Lydia Bean stated, they "enforced an implicit consensus that voting Republican on 'moral issues' was an essential part of the evangelical identity."[20] Christian businessmen, those underscoring evangelical support for capitalism, were encouraged to take on leadership positions in local churches, lending their voices to fiscally concerned conservative causes.[21] Evangelicals came to see that being faithful followers of God entailed supporting candidates and policies for socially conservative morality alongside capitalist principles.

In 1979, Jerry Falwell, head of the Moral Majority, was one of many
Christian leaders who turned both abortion and restriction of federal
government interference with religious freedom into primary targets
for evangelical political action.[22] As the movement moved into the
1980s, these sentiments played an enormous role in the election of
Ronald Reagan. In his run for the presidency, Reagan ran a campaign
based on conservative social and economic reform. Christian conservatives abandoned President Jimmy Carter, a self-professed "born-again"
evangelical whose religious convictions aligned closely with their own.
But President Carter had not taken a strong enough stance against
abortion in the aftermath of Jerry Falwell's campaign against *Roe v.
Wade*, the 1973 Supreme Court decision that removed many restrictions on abortion.[23] Moreover, Carter supported sanctions by the Internal Revenue Service to remove tax-exemption from private schools refusing to abide by Civil Rights legislation and racially desegregate.[24]
Later, Falwell's son, Jerry Falwell Jr., who took over as president of his
father's Liberty University, accentuated the importance of politics over
faith in his support of Donald Trump, saying, "We're not electing a
pastor. We're electing a president." Falwell Jr. went on to state that the
parables of Jesus demonstrated his support of cutting taxes and deregulating business. More importantly, by publicly stating that the president
does not have to be religiously sound, and that conservative Republican
policies of tax cuts and deregulation were preached by Jesus, Falwell Jr.
demonstrates how right-wing evangelicals believed Trump to be God's
candidate.

Reagan's success was indicative of the widespread assimilation of
many evangelicals into economic conservatism, which made up a far
larger portion of Reagan's platform than social reform did. Moreover,
Reagan's strong stance against communism appealed to the nationalism
that had become so ingrained within conservative Christianity. In later
elections, this "new Christian right" rallied behind George H. W. Bush
on the basis of his Republicanism, not his religious conviction.[25] Bush's
son, George W. Bush, formed strong bonds with evangelical leaders
during his father's presidency, which helped garner support during
George W. Bush's 2000 and 2004 election campaigns.

In the waning years of President Barack Obama's second term, the
political atmosphere was tense and increasingly polarized. Evangelicals
in 2015 remained a significant part of the American population (24.4

percent)[26] and had grown tired of the incumbent administration's liberal ideology. Many of these voters found solace within conservative movements such as the Tea Party. As analyzed by Scott Clement and John C. Green, "[T]he Tea Party [draws] disproportionate support from the ranks of white evangelical protestants."[27] Similar to Donald Trump, the Tea Party excuses their racism, sexism, Islamophobia, and other bigotries with alleged patriotism, a strategy used by every right-wing movement that conceals discriminatory practices. And statements conveying religious conviction often buttress their assertions. For example, their racism centers around a belief that "blacks are in violation of the Protestant ethic."[28] Even though the Tea Party views itself as "a color-blind movement," the title "color-blind" betrays their neglect of societal structures and policies that work against racial minorities.[29]

Recent surveys reveal a waning in the significance of conservative Christianity in American culture,[30] but the significance of this voting block has asserted itself in distinctively racial rather than religious terms. For example, white Republicans' approval of Donald Trump rose in tandem with the intensity of their white racial identification; more specifically, the data from the 2016 American National Election Studies Pilot Study reveals a steeply sloped bar graph depicting a clear pattern: the greater the saliency of a person's racial identity as "white," the more likely that person was to vote for Trump.[31] Eight months into Trump's presidency—after months of controversy and increasing critique from conservatives and other Republicans—Trump voters continue to skew toward greater concern with whiteness alongside their concern for Christianity. Specifically, asked what *racial group* they think faces the most discrimination in America, 45 percent of Trump voters say white people, a significant percentage gap compared with other groups (17 percent of Trump voters identify Native Americans as the group facing the most discrimination; 16 percent, African Americans; and 5 percent, Latinos).[32] And despite a number of contentious decisions from the Trump administration reflecting racial bias (e.g., the ban on Muslim refugees from entering the United States, lack of criticism for white supremacists, Immigration and Customs Enforcement detentions and family separations of Latin Americans seeking asylum at the southern border, continued push for building "The Wall" bordering the United States and Mexico), evangelicals' white racial identity remains highly mobilized for aggressive support of this president. As recently as

August 2019, white evangelical support for President Trump was at an all-time high, with 77 percent holding a favorable view.[33] Those who report attending church weekly were more likely to approve than those who attend less often, 81 percent versus 73 percent. The profound support for Trump among white evangelicals has remained remarkably consistent amid an unprecedented barrage of controversies, criticisms, and scandals. Even with the start of impeachment hearings, job approval remained high at 71 percent.[34] This support is historically rooted—so much so that white evangelicals have difficulty discerning the sources among themselves.

RACE, WEALTH, OWNERSHIP, AND OPPORTUNITY IN AMERICA

Perhaps those with a keener sense of American history or a better sense of the intertwining of race, economics, and religion would not have been surprised that 81 percent of white evangelicals would vote for Trump. At face value, he benefitted from party allegiance. Many conservatives could justify their vote on the basis of his GOP nomination. Yet Trump's appeal among evangelicals goes much deeper than mere partisanship. He appealed to a moralistic view of contemporary issues such as immigration, economics, abortion, and family values. He also used nationalistic rhetoric, asserting the moral and economic degradation of America. He also stressed a "right versus wrong" orientation to nearly everything, a binary judgment that pulled more moderate evangelicals into making a stark choice in their vote. The racial component cannot be denied: more than 76 percent of evangelicals are white.[35] Trump's xenophobic stances on immigration and Islam were far more likely to appeal to a white American audience. And consistent with the gender ideology found among evangelicals, Trump's personal "authoritarian machismo is right in step with a long Evangelical tradition of pastor-overlords."[36]

Whatever the social sentiments buttressing the election of this president may be, they surely did not emerge overnight. Therefore, much thought is being invested in trying to discern the most salient historical forces supporting the authority of this president. Our explanations falter simply because they are so poorly resourced: some aspects of the

Trump presidency gain attention, while others are left ignored, unexamined, or unexplained. To understand the legitimation of the Trump presidency, which has turned the nation toward divisive conversations on religion, racism, white supremacy, and economic inequality, one must understand the history those conversations are built upon. Despite many who believe differently, history shows that there has often been an intentional plan enacted through public policy to subvert minorities, enforcing a racial hierarchy that keeps them as a permanent lower class compared with whites.[37]

One hundred days into Donald Trump's presidency, the Pew Research Center conducted a poll measuring approval of Trump's job performance. Whereas only 39 percent of the general public was pleased with Trump's performance (a number that compares to 60 percent to 70 percent of recent presidents in the same time frame), white evangelical support was a whopping 78 percent.[38] Even as of January 2019, 70 percent of church-going white evangelicals approved of Trump, with just a little less approval, 65 percent, from infrequent attenders.[39] Some Americans may be inclined to believe that Trump's support from white evangelicals can be attributed to increased racial tensions in America as manifested by greater attention to police shootings of unarmed blacks or advocacy against oppression from groups like the #BlackLivesMatter movement. Yet at least equally important are Trump's economic sentiments based on the assumption of individual entrepreneurship, which resonates with the economic orientation among evangelicals. Businessmen have long been involved in conservative Christianity, connecting ideals of religious freedom with economic freedom. For example, Spiritual Mobilization, a large, conservative organization founded in 1935, had as its mission connecting Christianity with conservative politics, emphasizing in one of their magazines that "all we [Christians] can do, consonant with our Christian political responsibility, is to minimize the power and size of our government."[40] Advocating limited government, conservatives promote freedom to accumulate unregulated wealth. Generally speaking, conservatives frame economic freedom as the opportunity to rise to higher economic classes. Evangelical leaders connect the desire for economic freedom with that of religious freedom by arguing that limited government intervention allows for a strong religious presence in America. Such economic ideals among evangelicals largely favor the policies historically put in place by Republican politicians.

It has been said that "Christian conservatives are Christian capitalists" and that "Christians should not be satisfied with being second class."[41] Pat Robertson, conservative Christian, CEO of Regent University, television personality, and 1988 Republican presidential candidate, believes that "God encourages profit and in fact expects people to seek as much of it as possible, using wealth to create more wealth."[42] Ultrawealthy and influential Americans like Charles Koch and James Buchanan have brought Christian economics to center stage, convincing them that a representative government ruins capitalism by pulling money away from wealthy elites who have their interests in limited government in mind.[43] Conservative Christians believe capitalism, not social programs giving money to the needy, promotes hard work and toughness, values important among contemporary evangelicals.[44] Together with their libertarian allies, conservative Christians advocate for reduced government, leaving economic outcomes to the effort of individuals and the will of God. These business-oriented Christians believe Jesus supports profit and greed as avenues for individualism and freedom. The intertwining of limited government and the belief in the influence of God fosters the alliance between religious and economic conservatives.

One of the fundamental beliefs of the evangelical political movement is the notion of freedom, specifically religious freedom.[45] Among white evangelicals, religion is assumed to have a central role in politics, but not just religion in any sense; in America, that religion is the Christian faith. Religious freedom is the assertion of a singular religion, not the accommodation and promotion of religious pluralism. Similarly, conservative evangelicals' opposition to liberal social policies, like direct payments that assist the impoverished, reveals a contradiction to evangelical commitment to the common good. In this orientation, "true" Americans are Christian, hardworking individuals operating within the capitalist system and supportive of conservative social policies.

If the economically successful are favored by God, then the poor are assumed to have committed a moral failing. As a result, evangelicals often do not support social policies such as welfare that would reduce inequality,[46] believing them to be "the product of social coercion."[47] The intervention of government obscures the authentic nature of generating wealth and the consequences of those who cannot support themselves. A major impulse within Christianity is the need to be charitable, which can be seen in myriad religiously affiliated nonprofits and relief organizations in the United States. Occasional Christian charity may be appropriate for the poor, and it is preferred in lieu of state-sponsored programs.[48] These are selective, operate within particularistic social networks, and tend to provide short-term assistance for individuals, not long-term challenges to structural imbalances. Charity is advocated to come from individuals, not the government. Ultimately, in regard to social policy, the virtue of occasional charity is overshadowed by the orientation to capitalist principles. The best charity helps individuals make themselves appropriately marketable, hopefully attaining a lucrative position of great responsibility based on hard work and talent. Wealthy elites are believed to possess commendable character and therefore should take on the responsibility of stewardship to society; they are entrusted by God to lead our nation.

Capitalism is associated with competition and individual responsibility, and some of its staunchest supporters are white evangelicals. Success in business is itself a commendable achievement among evangelicals. Having achieved astronomical success as a real estate tycoon in the capitalist system, Trump was able to appeal to evangelical voters who associate economic prowess with divine favor. The support for capitalism was built among Christian evangelicals in the twentieth century. Conservative Christians support business-friendly platforms, but they "consciously [choose] a moralistic message, not an economic one."[49] It was said, "A system that provides so much for the common good and happiness must flourish under the force of the Almighty."[50] This statement implies that all Americans benefit from capitalism; yet white evangelicals ignore the radical inequities in wealth distribution in the United States.

The degree of wealth inequality that pervades American history is astounding. Economic inequality in the United States is prevalent despite, or perhaps because of, the financial workings of the capitalist system. For example, the wealthiest Americans, dubbed the "one percent," monopolize more than 40 percent of the nation's wealth. And money plays a bigger role in our political system than is often believed, especially as wealthy elites intentionally mobilize themselves to influence policies and elections. Similarly, the amount of influence corporations and the wealthy elite have had over political and economic systems is as pervasive as it is often hidden. With these factors in mind, we must question whether capitalism truly benefits the common good as conservative evangelicals claim.

A blunt truth addressed in this book is that America was founded on racist ideals, which led to a national identity that aligned with these principles. Knowledge of the legitimation of white superiority and the persistence of a racial hierarchy throughout the history of the United States are critical for understanding the social and political mechanisms for racial inequality in wealth. In evaluating the historical understanding of who is considered "American," how "American" is defined and who defined it, and recognizing that this question has persisted throughout and evolved in response to history, we are better able to appreciate how white superiority and a racial hierarchy have been legitimized and contribute to an environment in which interests are aligned in such a way that Trump could become president.

Attempts to define a "true" American extend back to the Declaration of Independence, the document that essentially founded our country and captures its highest ideals. As a consequence of defining a new country, the document also defined citizens of this new country. When Thomas Jefferson famously said all men are created equal, he envisioned that this would be true of all citizens of our new nation. However, knowing Jefferson's other writings, we know Jefferson did not intend for this ideal of citizenship to encompass blacks, a group he thought to be inferior, or to Native Americans, whose various tribal nations were considered savages who wandered the wilderness and were unlikely to be ready for civilization anytime soon.[51] Grounded in such judgments, along with other pronouncements and practices at the beginning of our country, white men such as Jefferson provided an initial classification of who was American, initiating the legitimization of white settler superiority and the establishment of a clear racial hierarchy.

Race, despite Jefferson, is not a biological fact but an ideational construct, and thus, above all, a historical artifact.[52] By taking blacks to be inferior to whites and indigenous peoples as uncivilized, Jefferson and others in early America both affirmed and further developed racialized notions that would continue to predominate in our American culture not only because they expressed these beliefs but also, and more importantly, because they instituted policies and enacted structures that took abstract presumptions and concertized them into the immersive experiences affecting everyone in daily life. So, although America was not founded *for* the purpose of extending racialized notions, it was nonetheless founded *with* presumptive ideas of race, assuming white superiority, which affected who could be considered an American. These ideas were foundational to the inception of our republic, and there has never ceased to be a time in our country's existence that they did not exert a profound influence. More specifically, the exclusion of blacks and Native Americans was not an isolated phenomenon but rather a constant theme throughout American history. Furthermore, this early history had immediate consequences for others deemed "not white" like Asians (Chinese, Japanese, etc.), Latinos (Mexicans, Puerto Ricans, etc.), and, more recently, those from the Middle East (including those not geographically located in the Middle East like ethnic Pakistanis and Muslims from all nations).

Donald Trump announced his candidacy in June 2015 with a rousing nationalistic speech at his New York property, Trump Tower. He spoke of the imminent dangers of immigrants, unfair trade, and the moral and economic degradation of the United States. His message was so hyperbolic that he was written off by many Americans, including leaders within the Republican Party. He was considered a joke, and his campaign was thought to be a giant advertising campaign to give attention to the Trump brand. However, his message resonated with conservative evangelicals who believed in his promise to "Make America Great Again." Although questions about the sincerity of his religious convictions would be debated, the no-nonsense bluster was taken to be a form of authenticity. He was not a politician, but a businessman. He appeared to care deeply about his country, and his nostalgic vision of a strong America, bolstered by strong critiques of the Obama administration, won him many admirers. He also cozied up to evangelicals, appearing unashamed to be around them and affirming of their social anxieties. His sentiments, his political style, and his constellation of support for an array of concerns proved strong enough to win him both the Republican nomination and the 2016 presidential election.

In launching his presidential campaign, Trump famously talked about Mexicans coming across the border "bringing drugs, bringing crime," who were "rapists," such that Mexico was "sending us not the right people." Such statements are part of a larger American tradition of discriminating and disenfranchising Mexican immigrants. Ever since the 1848 Treaty of Guadalupe Hidalgo, which gave the United States much of its western territory, including parts of Arizona, Utah, Nevada, California, and New Mexico, the place of Mexicans in America has been contested. Language in the treaty providing them citizenship and property rights was largely ignored and promises were reversed. Since 1848, Mexican natives and Mexican immigrants have not fitted into America's national identity. Further, the relationships between cross-border migrants, the economic interests of business owners, and government policies have been convoluted.

The nativism—favoring long-established white families over recent immigrants of color—represented in Trump's remarks was equally evident in his many statements regarding the birthplace of Barack Obama. Since Obama's first presidential campaign in 2008, Trump has questioned where Obama was born, thereby questioning his legitimacy as a presidential candidate. Trump fueled and stoked the flames of the "birther" controversy, claiming that Obama was born in Kenya and raised in Indonesia, and that he is Muslim. The fact that President Obama is half white and half black did not matter as he has always been and indisputably still remains within the category of "black"—reflecting the long-held "one-drop rule" indicating that any "tainting" of a person's ancestry with black parentage puts that person in the black column. The inflammatory assertion that Obama is Muslim further accentuated his disqualification among many white Americans who, since the terrorist attacks of September 11, 2001, have turned decisively against Muslims. Many white Americans believe that Muslims' real allegiance is to a jihadist Allah of the Quran, which insists that they violently overthrow Western traditions in favor of an oppressive, Islamically based state guided by Sharia law; thus Muslims are not to be trusted. Over time, it seemed that Trump's constant and ill-informed assertions would delegitimize his own candidacy; instead, many still side with Trump and see such racialized comments as permissible and commendable.

Trump has talked a lot about race, although he is not interested in a full conversation on race. Through his recension of the Obama administration's Deferred Action for Childhood Arrivals program, his championing of the Muslim ban, his tepid response to hurricane damage in Puerto Rico, or his aggressive efforts to limit all foreign migration and to fund "The Wall" to prevent immigrants from crossing the southern border, Trump's assumptions regarding the racial profile of "America" became clearer. Through Trump's policies and priorities, the remnants of debates on slavery, colonization, immigration, and racial exploitation are made manifest, revealing political wrangling that is embedded in our national identity. Trump supporters repeatedly brush off complaints regarding his rhetoric as overly sensitive; negative characterizations of Trump are countered with claims of liberal propaganda and "fake news." Dismissals on the one hand contradict the support for Trump's perspective on such matters on the other hand.

The reluctance of the Trump administration to provide assistance to refugees and foreign countries is similarly tied to racialized notions of God's favor. The White House intends to operate on an "America First" foreign policy, one that implies an alignment with white evangelicals who believe the United States to be God's favored country. The idea of who is a "true American" plays a central role in Trump's administration. Xenophobic nationalism and neoliberal capitalism supplement white conservative evangelical stances on issues like abortion and same-sex marriage. And wealthy Americans bond with evangelicals through their shared desire for limited government, lower taxes, and an America based on values of individual conviction and freedom. Together, these attitudes and the social structures that carry them have deep consequences for the political and economic opportunity for ethnoracial groups in America, accelerating and expanding opportunity for some groups while intentionally leaving others behind.

UNDERSTANDING TRUMP SUPPORT REQUIRES A LONGER TIME FRAME OF OBSERVATION

To the unwary citizen and the untrained observer, Trump's election seemed unlikely, even impossible, based on day-to-day poll numbers. But observation across a longer time frame might have predicted his victory based on the strong undercurrents of American society. As John Fea wrote, "As a historian studying religion and politics, I should have seen this coming."[53] The history discussed in this book is not hidden but neglected. The history taught in schools across America has often neglected much of this American history—especially those aspects of history that are less pleasant to the mythic image of American images of equality, opportunity, and success. Race, labor, economics, and religion are simply left out. Reviewing neglected aspects of American history provides insight into persistent notions of identity and the consequences that extend from long-held values and beliefs.

Donald Trump did not coerce people to vote for him. Instead, he tapped into profound sentiments in his statements, made promises that appealed to them, and reflected a persona that was in keeping with their desires. No single individual is powerful enough to change people's minds; instead, politicians resonate with their audience and use that resonance to gain political power. Therefore, Trump's election does not reflect change but a powerful movement to maintain the status quo of privilege and familiar prejudices. Although Trump's win was unexpected even in the final hours of live reporting of the election results, understanding the sentiments that carried the election reveal long-standing threads of American culture. The election of Donald Trump was made possible by the sentiments embedded in the racial, economic, and religious history of the United States.

Trump was a legitimate candidate who became a legitimate president because of the historical pattern that buttresses the legitimacy for his stances. Racial dynamics dating back to the founding of the United States are still evident in today's political and social discourse. Race is ingrained in the history of our nation and reflected in the policies established by our government. One cannot fully understand modern American politics without learning the history of American racism. Racialized sentiments reflecting white superiority are engrained in white society, including those who became accepted as "white" over time (Irish, Italians, Jews, etc.), such that it has become normalized, assumed, and largely unspoken. Donald Trump was implicitly understood to restore such white-favoring racial dynamics after the Obama presidency, helping subdue the fear of radicalism in racial (blacks and immigrants) and religious (Muslim) politics, combining bigotry and Islamophobia that swayed people toward his election.

The election of President Trump was also layered into a presumed American identity through a white conservative Christian lens. Religion is not separate from politics, and learning about evangelical support for Trump allows a better appreciation for the centrality of white identity to contemporary evangelicalism. The evangelical vote for Trump stems from a theologically slanted, libertarian view of economics, especially notions of work and reward, as well as the reverence given to free-market capitalism. The language of Christian white nationalism is laced into his rhetoric, such that Trump is viewed as a restorer of proper racial (white) and religious (Christian) foundation who would guarantee the financial prosperity of our capitalist system.

It can be argued that, in the end, Trump was not an unlikely candidate after all, especially given the many ways he appealed to the sentiments of white evangelical voters. His success is indicative of the ongoing influence of race, class, and religion in the shaping of American politics. Trump's personal stances are neither idiosyncratic nor original, reflecting a long historical development that continues to have implications on the treatment and opportunities afforded nonwhites in the United States. He presented a campaign platform to a group of voters among whom it already resonated, a resonance that continues despite his blunders and offenses in office. Despite the underlying history accounting for the win of Donald Trump, many Americans are still caught off guard in explaining how he won the presidency and still garners strong support from his political base. It may be a signal that the subversive conservative power influencing American politics today to enforce conservative Christian morals through State mechanisms and exaggerate further the wealth of the elite may continue to go largely unnoticed, and therefore unchecked, by the American people.

Chapter 2

DEEP CULTURAL BACKGROUND ON RACIAL INEQUALITY

Slavery and Territorial Expansion in Early America

The United States is built on a paradox. Our Founding Fathers are the celebrated statesmen of America's Revolutionary generation who are credited together with a successful war for autonomy from Britain, with creation of the republican form of government ratified in the Constitution, and with the liberal ideas of the Declaration of Independence that affirmed that "all men are created equal." Yet the majority of them, including such iconic figures as George Washington, Thomas Jefferson, Benjamin Franklin, James Madison, Patrick Henry, and John Hancock, all owned slaves. Those slaves were denied their own autonomy and the sacred dignity of "life, liberty, and the pursuit of happiness." In the Founding Fathers' America, all people did not deserve the dignity of equality, a fact enshrined in the infamous "Three-Fifths Clause" enacted by the Constitutional Convention of 1787, which counted the enslaved as three-fifths of a person.

The scope of the physical and emotional chains that bound blacks in slavery for so long are hard for most Americans today to grasp. Forcibly brought to the continent for their labor, Africans from a variety of nations and tribes were not just denied political participation in the states that governed them (as were women, most propertyless white men, and most "free" blacks), but also the basic autonomies of property, consumer choice, and free association with others. Even in an age when brutality was pervasive, most Americans recognized the basic cruelty of enslavement, a cruelty evident from slaves' precarious journey as cargo on ships through the Middle Passage to the auction block and continuing to a diminished life expectancy under white ownership. Throughout their bondage, enslaved blacks were not passive but asserted their agency, rebelling against their circumstances rather than accepting them as an inevitability.[1] Nevertheless, they still faced radical restrictions on their ability to work, travel, marry, or even express a hint of desire for such freedoms.

By the early 1800s, although the enslaved accounted for as much as 80 percent of the gross domestic product of the U.S. economy,[2] many Americans concluded that slavery was no longer morally justifiable and agreed that the peculiar institution should end. Those who benefited from slavery considered it to be a "gift from God," deliberately and divinely bestowed for the prosperity of white people. But Northern whites and poor Southern whites knew that much of the wealth generated by slavery remained among the "plantocracy," the shrinking minority of elite slave owners who took over more and more of the share of slave labor and the property and profits that came with their use. The "free labor" movement—the notion that whites should be able to own their own land and make a modest living from the fruits of their own labor—continued to grow and was a fundamental motivation for the fight against the institution of slavery as represented by the Confederate States in the Civil War.[3] The fight against the slave economy and the concern for the plight of unfree blacks grew alongside each other.

Various motives emerged to remove slavery, yet few were concerned with the condition of oppression among slaves. Even those who most desired to grant the enslaved their freedom ran against a new problem. The morality of slavery was never adequately addressed in early America because of the question that would inevitably follow: what would happen to whites if slaves were suddenly set free? Even antislavery, "liberal" whites who held notions of fairness, dignity, and equality did not expect blacks to integrate into their white society as peers. And if blacks remained within the confines of the continent, how would whites exercise control over an expansive population who were no longer bound to their white masters?

As early as the founding of the United States, there has always been resistance against blacks being fully integrated into the new nation. As

Nicholas Guyatt writes in *Bind Us Apart: How Enlightened Americans Invented Racial Segregation*, "Even slaveholders were aware of a contradiction between the nation's founding principles and the practice of holding human beings in bondage."[4] This is significant because the pattern of injustices inflicted on blacks in the earliest moments of our American history created a precedent for the treatment of other racial and ethnic groups later in our history.

The white European immigrants who settled in North America exploited the bodies of enslaved Africans. This practice expanded to the violent expulsion of native tribes and, later, the denial of promised benefits to indigenous people still living in recently conquered lands following the Mexican American War. There persisted a contradiction between the principles of freedom and equality lauded by the Founding Fathers and the cruelty inflicted on people of color through the failure to see them as potentially equal participants with the full benefits of citizenship and self-determination.

WHEN SLAVES BECAME BLACK

Historians and social scientists have repeatedly shown that neither blackness nor whiteness are biological but a result of social and political mechanisms used to distinguish opportunities, privileges, and status between white and nonwhite.[5] The lack of freedom among slaves became associated with *blackness*, but slaves were not necessarily black. For example, American history includes a long history of white indentured servanthood and white slavery. Aristotle believed slavery was determined by innate character, not biological race. White slavery survived for centuries, with early European raids gathering and selling white slaves since at least the Viking conquests, moving massive numbers of people around the world. The Irish-Catholic St. Patrick, whose March 17 saint day is celebrated as St. Patrick's Day, may be the most famous white slave in history. By the eleventh century, one in ten Anglo Saxons were enslaved.[6] Whites were even willing to enslave themselves, with an epidemic of self-slavery occurring among the poor of Europe. White slavery was only displaced with the expansion and conquest of colonial powers in foreign continents in the sixteenth century. So although Americans have immortalized enslaved people as black, the

African slave trade is relatively recent in world history and, unknown to most of white America, evolved from white slavery. Over time, after establishing an entirely new industry of black slave trading and black slave breeding, the privilege of whiteness erased the shame of white slavery, making whiteness and blackness opposing symbols of freedom and slavery. Once this distinction was established, those who ascribe to whiteness became imbued with moral and ethical superiority.

The birth of the American republic coincided with intense economic competition between wealthy, seafaring nations (especially competition for the British, Dutch, French, and Iberian slave trade) that fought aggressively to secure ownership of vast territory and material resources. America was not founded on immigration, but rather as an extension of British colonialism. Colonists moved to another part of their own country, and with them came "vagrant minors, kidnapped persons, convicts, and indentured servants" as their slaves.[7] One-half to two-thirds of people who came to the western hemisphere (about three hundred thousand to four hundred thousand people) were unfree laborers.[8] The 1790 census includes the category of "free whites," demonstrating that "free" was not yet synonymous with "white."[9]

The expansion of African-based slavery and its organization into the plantation system efficiently mobilized unpaid labor, resulting in a massive economic windfall to America. The system of commodifying the enslaved body was increasingly racialized such that slavery became an inherently black characteristic, supposedly based on black genetic dispositions. This is because, although blacks had inferior status, they were believed to be stronger and hardier and thus better suited to the strenuous labor expected of them, compared with Native Americans who quickly perished in enslavement. As black slavery expanded, a distinction between races had to be made.

The slave trade did not respect national or tribal boundaries among Africans but forcibly bound members of disparate tribes and nations together. Although originating from the same continent, they did not all share a common language, religion, or ancestral heritage. Blacks who survived being shipped as cargo to American shores were diverse in origin but became synthesized into a singular "race" in the process of enslavement. Indeed, it was a system of Christian slavery that initially distinguished Christians from pagans in local records on the assumption that all Africans were pagan. Yet Christian masters and colonial leaders came under pressure to evangelize slaves (some from their own conscience). Compelled to convert, a practical question emerged regarding slaves' consequent status as converts. African slaves joining the community of the saved prompted changes in distinguishing between "whites" and "blacks," which solidified race as the criteria for separating persons by their status rather than their religion. Thus blacks could become Christians like their white masters, but their social status would not be equal. In fact, when the enslaved were baptized, the liturgy of conversion read during the service explicitly stated that their newfound freedom was only a spiritual one; their Christian duty to their masters required them to remain submissive.[10] Although the conversion of slaves could have upset the entire social order, church leaders and slave owners colluded together to make clear that, theologically, slavery was part of God's order.

THE WHITE PROBLEM WITH BLACK LIVES

The implications of freedom and equality for the enslaved persisted. In his *Notes on the State of Virginia*, published in full in 1785, Thomas Jefferson openly speculated about the capacity of people of color to self-govern in this new land. He wondered: could "savage" people ever fully participate as equals in American society? In writing out his conclusions, Jefferson saw potential in Native Americans to become civilized, and he was impressed with a quality of nobility that he discerned among them. However, he candidly suspected that blacks simply could not achieve the same standing. His suggestions (discussed later in this chapter) about what to do with blacks further articulated his pessimistic view. Later, when Jefferson signed the Abolition of the Slave Trade Act of 1807—the bill that prohibited the importation of slaves and ended American participation in the slave trade—he left unresolved the question of what to do with enslaved blacks already in the United States. Ultimately, his assessments of their suitability for participating in civilized society remained unchanged.

Although the abolition of the slave trade might be celebrated as a triumph against the expropriation of labor, in actuality, the scope of slavery greatly expanded in the United States after cutting off the international slave trade. Simply stated, the institution of slavery expanded because slave *owners* became slave *breeders*. Intentionally ignoring cultural and national backgrounds of individual slaves in favor of simply multiplying the number of productive and profitable black bodies, the number of slaves grew dramatically as a source of labor and as a source of capital. Blacks lacked legal status as persons, but they were quite valuable, not only to be bought and sold but also as assets that owners could borrow money against; they could be used as collateral to take out mortgages or to advance and leverage lines of credit. Thus, following the forcible and involuntary importation of Africans, the intentional breeding of black bodies solidified the perception of a large, singular racial group who were *blacks* or *negroes* or *African Americans*, bodies that were financially valuable but that supposedly shared a particular genetic composition and a decidedly inferior standing.

Jefferson's opinion regarding the inferiority of blacks was not an exception. At the time, the description commonly applied to blacks was *degraded*. The term was used by slave owners and abolitionists alike; it was generally believed that enslavement was associated with the deterioration of the best, most humane qualities of a group. Those of African descent were not equal to even the poorest white person because they were degraded. And yet there was disagreement as to the cause of this degraded condition. What was the source of their degradation? (Ironically, slave owners argued that to be forced to relinquish their "rightful property" would be an act of degradation against the white race.)

Many intellectual and influential "enlightened" white men (the majority of them Christian) thought much about the personhood of blacks and saw the capacities of black bodies as diminished. For them, the degraded condition of blacks in America was not rooted in their biology. Rather, their degradation was a result of their extended period of enslavement. Their condition was a product of their environment, and therefore potentially correctable. Nevertheless, few expressed confidence that blacks would someday exercise the independent intelligence and self-discipline required to become trusted equals in a democratic American society.

In the 1780s, Johann Friedrich Blumenbach, a German intellectual, divided the human race into five variant species: white, yellow, copper color, tawny, and jet-black. He derived the term *Caucasian* to describe the ideal beauty of whiteness. A made-up phrase stemming back to the land of Caucasus, where Greeks placed the setting for their myths, he stated Caucasians were the "colour white, cheeks rosy; hair brown or chestnut colored," or, as we know it today, the Aryan race.[11] Around the same time, Christopher Meiners, another German scholar of the late eighteenth century, drew on travel reports and unsupported claims to assert that the inferiority of nonwhite people required their enslavement. For him, Germans (of course) were the most beautiful and pure of blood and needed to be protected from non-German "dirty whites."[12] The ideal white became Germanic people who inhabited Britain, known as *Anglo Saxons*.[13] The American philosopher Ralph Waldo Emerson spent the 1800s connecting Americans with Britains and then Britains with Saxons.[14] Saxons were viewed as occupying the top of the racial hierarchy, never having been enslaved. The reason was evident from their murderous history, showing the Saxons could overpower any enemy using their "gorgeous male energy."[15] In America, where only free men could prosper, to be American meant to be Saxon.[16]

Belief in the degradation of blacks, having developed over generations, was now so deeply absorbed among the American white elite that no quick change to effect the condition of blacks was likely. In this way, prejudice against blacks in the nineteenth century was not solely perpetuated by poor white Southerners or the white Southern plantation aristocracy. It also persisted among the most educated and progressive whites, whose notions of blacks' racial inferiority were grounded in a matrix of intellectual and theological speculations on the origins of their state of being.

The debate regarding the source of degradation among blacks came to be based on an irresolvable set of convictions: either enslaved blacks were inherently inferior or the condition of slavery resulted in their degradation. Either way, blacks were relegated to a subordinate status that justified the deprivation of freedoms accorded whites. Even those leaders who earnestly sought to properly assimilate blacks into mainstream white society argued this only insofar as they could ensure themselves and their audiences that blacks could be useful, productive civilians who would not disrupt the established workings of mainstream, white-based society.

What of "free" blacks? Were they entrusted with a greater sense of humanity and equality than enslaved blacks? Closer examination of blacks who were not someone's property, many of whom were in the northern states of the American Republic, still experienced deprivation because of widespread notions alleging their inferior status. Some might mistakenly believe that freed blacks—those who were not enslaved—experienced political rights and freedom of movement, but the reality is that they faced significant prejudice and curtailment of power and opportunity. They were restricted in where they lived, the occupations they held, the schools they attended, and the civil rights they were afforded. Blacks were not allowed to serve on juries, nor were many among them allowed to represent black clients in court. Consequently, they were especially vulnerable both to prosecution and conviction by the white-dominated justice system.[17] So it was not only slaves but also free blacks who were denied equality, constrained by prejudicial beliefs that marred their image among Americans. Even prominent political figures like Noah Webster believed that "free blacks" were disproportionately responsible for "burglaries, rapes, or murders."[18]

Such notions regarding the untrustworthiness and savagery of all blacks were explicitly stated and widely shared. After emancipation, laws that freed blacks from white ownership did not specify rights of citizenship, and legislators left many loopholes open to abuse. Anxieties of a violent slave rebellion lingered, and whites feared that blacks would attempt to overthrow the government. To counteract the imagined terror of former slaves, whites invoked their own capricious acts of intimidation and terror. Freed blacks posed a novel threat to the white dominance of society as they began to enter classrooms, compete for jobs, spend their money at consumer establishments, and generally interact outside of their own race as equal members of society. Restrictions on blacks, formal and informal, grew. Slave codes were amended to become black codes (which eventually developed into what are now known as *Jim Crow laws*; see Chapter 3). The pervasive belief in the degraded condition of African Americans confined blacks to a permanent second-class status—whether slave or free.

WHITE WOMEN AND BLACK SLAVERY

A common misconception is that women did not own slaves, and that their treatment of slaves reflected their stereotypical place in American households: nurturing and maternal. Despite white stereotypes of genteel, ladylike Southern belles, white women played an integral part in the institution of slavery and the slaves they owned.[19] Some white women were given slaves as young children by their families, and others were given slaves in preparation for marriage.[20] Owning slaves made women more appealing to possible suitors because it allowed men to acquire more property and increase their social standings.[21] Marriage legally included the practice of coverture, meaning that brides lost their independent identity and all property transferred to their husband's control.[22] However, women devised strategies to circumvent coverture and continue sole ownership of their slaves after marriage, which included devising marriage contracts that granted wives control over all the property she already owned or might gain during her marriage.[23] If husbands violated these contracts, they would be taken to court, and their wives often won.[24]

Women were not merely given slaves, they also acquired them through buying and selling in slave markets and were well-acquainted with the economic workings of slavery.[25] Women did not avoid the harsh environments of slave markets but attended public auctions and had direct interactions with slave traders in their own homes.[26] The violence of slavery was carried into the intimacy of their homes, where slaves were racially and sexually exploited. For example, some slave-owning women used enslaved women as wet nurses for their babies. This meant the enslaved women were continually conceiving so they could lactate. The use of women as nursemaids was frequently entangled with acts of rape, and family separation of black mothers from their own children so black women could act as nursemaids for white mothers was common.[27]

White women could be just as brutal as men in how they treated their slaves, in contrast with the notion that white women were nurturing toward enslaved people, an image they themselves helped to curate after the Civil War.[28] Growing up, girls watched how slave-owning adults treated enslaved people, and this influenced how they treated their own slaves.[29] This also ingrained in them a sense of their own superiority over people of African descent, which desensitized them to the cruelty of slavery.[30] Although sometimes women delegated the responsibility of oversight and discipline to others, it should not be mistaken as a sign of discomfort with brutality. Instead, it allowed them to maintain their "reputations as members of the southern gentility while preserving their authority."[31]

A benefit of the institution of slavery to slave-owning women is that it provided a potent avenue for the exercise and expression of power.[32] Slavery allowed white women to access economic power and independence that they were otherwise denied, which contributes to an explanation of why so many were so devastated with the end of slavery. The freedom that white women experienced via slavery was not a part of a "grand scheme to secure women's rights or gender equality."[33] They did not push for equality with men in all aspects of life but merely wanted rights over those slaves they saw as their personal property as such property rights secured a place for them in the American societal hierarchy. Therefore, emancipation not only took away a source of wealth, it also destabilized the "respect and legal and economic autonomy [they held] within their households and wider communities."[34] In rewriting the history of slavery, white women claimed to believe that they were helping an inferior people become civilized in the name of God; in actuality, these women supported slavery because it was in their economic and social interests to do so.[35] Following the Civil War, white women continued to uphold a "white-supremacist order" because they saw how slavery had directly benefited their own status.

ARGUMENTS FOR THE INTEGRATION OF BLACKS

Long before the signing of the Emancipation Proclamation, white intellectuals proposed alternatives for black integration into white society. These considerations whirled among those who envisioned an integrated black-white society in which all blacks would be free to become full-fledged American citizens. However, among those who supported the integration of enslaved blacks into mainstream white society, proposals on the means by which that process might be carried out were not at all clear, involving contradictions and complications, and no consensus ever emerged.

The most radical liberals speaking out on the possibility of black-white integration in the early American Republic, like Samuel Stanhope Smith and the Marquis de Chastellux, supported *amalgamation*, that is, the gradual mixing of races through intermarriage until biological distinctions between them ceased to exist. Specifically, some reformers believed prejudice might be overcome through caring physical interactions in the most intimate of settings. Other reformers viewed intermarriage as a clever strategy for consolidation and control. The majority of those holding this view simply believed that intermarriage (euphemistically indicating permissible sexual relations between the races) encouraged by the government would result in the emergence of a new race of *mulattos*, who themselves would produce *Quarterons*, until distinctions of color would be removed.[36] As one promoter of amalgamation said, "The only way to scale up this tactic of racial passing and to realize black equality on a sweeping scale would be to make interracial sex the cornerstone of social relations in the South."[37]

The notion of amalgamation was revolutionary and seemingly based on notions of equality. But the promotion of racial mixing through intermarriage implied that blacks in America could not be fully accepted in America on their own. Their eventual acceptance would come about only by eliminating the distinctiveness of their existence and absorbing them into the more mainstream white population. In amalgamation, whiteness was instituted as the norm. To accomplish the goal of amalgamation, their children (or grandchildren) would need to pass as white. Amalgamation would mix enough whiteness into the American population such that blackness would simply disappear. Of course, thanks to long-held prejudices against blacks, the hidden biology of a plausible white-passing child would always be tainted by suspicion of his or her African parentage.

The plausibility of suggesting intermarriage as a broad-scale initiative was rejected. The great majority of white Americans recoiled at the suggestion of legitimating sexual relations between the races. White slaveholders used the threat of a mixed-race population as an argument to perpetuate the institution of slavery. For many whites, even the thought of racial intermarriage provoked disgust. For example, Benjamin Rush, a Founding Father and prominent physician from Philadelphia, considered black skin to be an "ailment," a "modification of that disease which is known by the name of Leprosy."[38] In contrast with these early Americans, leaders of other white European empires can be found encouraging racial intermarriage. The British encouraged racial mixing in India, the French used intermarriage to build strong relations with the fur-trading Natives in Canada, and the Spanish mixed with slaves and indigenous peoples in the Caribbean to produce a race of *mestizos*. These colonizing nations assumed that the emergence of a multiracial society in newly conquered lands was inevitable. Intermarriage was thought to create stronger relations with natives and to increase the overall colonial population. But any early enthusiasm for race-mixing in America quickly dissolved after the Revolutionary War, in great part because of the economic power inherent to the institution of slavery.

For the exceptional couples who did intermarry within these nascent United States, the legal recognition of their black-white marriages was messy and inconsistent. State governments were given the authority to determine regulations within their borders, and the federal government exercised oversight over territories; however, the laws regarding interracial relationships (involving sex, marriage, and procreation) differed greatly by state and territory. For example, marriage between blacks and whites was banned entirely in Virginia, but it was legal (and conventional) for white men to have sex with their female slaves. Meanwhile, in South Carolina, such marriages were legal, but any mixed offspring that resulted from the union would be enslaved. Some states did not even bother to make intermarriage illegal because it was so difficult to imagine that black-white unions would ever become acceptable. Massachusetts, which styled itself as the vanguard of Northern antislavery efforts, passed a ban on intermarriage in 1786. Even Abraham Lincoln publicly stated that he did not require a law to resist the temptation of marrying a black woman.[39] The idea of racial intermarriage was so taboo and the resulting mixed-race children caused such great anxiety that black-white marriage was eventually outlawed altogether.

Critics of intermarriage believed that any potential "betterment" of the black race through racial mixing would go hand in hand with the permanent "degradation" of the white race. The most extreme of critics would not accept that whiteness could ever wash out blackness. Instead, blackness soon would overwhelm the white population. The rejection of amalgamation was rooted in the supposed inferiority of blacks. Neither biblical scriptures nor advances in science at the time readily concluded that nonwhites were inferior to whites; eminent men like Noah Webster conceded that black and white people were both "creatures of God." Yet even those who opposed slavery seemed unwilling to live among freed blacks. Thus, after slaves were emancipated, a *second* and quite different emancipation was required: white people would need to be freed from having to be in the presence of free blacks. Racial intermingling was much more likely between Native Americans and western settlers than among eastern seaboard whites and free blacks.

Much of the concern regarding the potential for integrating blacks into white-dominant society revolved around how quickly the integration could occur. The issue of *timing*—gradual versus immediate emancipation—was a significant aspect of the social and political debate regarding the future of American slavery. For example, for some, the lack of education among the enslaved population was a significant barrier to admitting them to full citizenship. However, the prospect of educating slaves created apprehensions among whites because they believed literacy and free discussion could inspire a revolt. Gabriel Prosser, a slave from Virginia who was partially inspired by the rhetoric of the American Revolution and the Haitian revolution, famously rallied dozens of other slaves to rebel in 1800. Although he and most of his coconspirators were caught, tried, and hanged, Gabriel's rebellion became a vivid example of what might occur should slaves be trusted with even a modicum of freedom. And because Gabriel was well-educated, education itself was seen as disruptive of the normalized relations between whites and enslaved blacks, further complicating ideas that educating slaves would contribute to the peace and prosperity of blacks and whites alike. Later, the rebellion of Bible-reading Nat Turner (whose Bible can be seen in the National Museum of African American History and Culture in Washington, DC) further accentuated this sentiment, greatly widening the rift between white Christians and black Christians. The fear of slaves violently seeking their freedom before whites felt they were ready for it directly contributed to delaying initiatives toward emancipation.

The consequences of emancipation were reduced to either *benevolence* or *burden*. Either free blacks would require the generosity of whites, or they would become a burden to be borne by whites for an indefinite time. Neither were seen as optimal, because both would require enormous assistance to blacks at the expense of whites. As a result, most educated Christian white men viewed slavery as wrong in principle but also saw it as a necessary evil, because the economic backbone of a strong nation necessitated the perpetuation of "the peculiar institution." Their abhorrence of the tortuous treatment of slaves was overshadowed by concern for the deeply rooted financial structure of slavery—not only for the plantation economy but also for the many occupations centered on the slave trade industry, including auctioneers, boatmen, man hunters, and more. Blacks had built up the economic power of the United States through their physical and intellectual labor, and any disruption would have dire consequences for both the North and the South. Most lawmakers concluded that abolition would result in dramatic social upheaval, prohibiting emancipation from being put into practice, or even taken into serious consideration. The moral dilemmas of slavery were thereby swept away in favor of political and economic stability. Today this might reasonably be framed as the self-preservation of white privilege. All thought of amalgamation between blacks and whites had been rejected, so the initiatives on what to do with emancipated blacks tended to center on how best to effect a complete separation of blacks from the white population.

ARGUMENTS FOR THE EXPULSION OF BLACKS

Conversations continued back and forth over decades on the potential for emancipation. Fear of revolution was only one factor among many that spurred anxiety about such a large community being freed from bondage. Abolishing slavery without a plan to effectively integrate blacks was deeply problematic, and most believed blacks could not suddenly be ready to integrate adequately. Even the most progressive of reformers realized that if the emancipated were offered equal rights they would represent a significant new voter base that could radically disrupt the political and economic status quo. Even more, some speculated that if formerly enslaved blacks achieve greater wealth and higher skills, poor whites could become indentured, turning the racial hierarchy upside down. Any sort of feasible, gradual plan to avoid the social disorder of abolition remained elusive. And yet if blacks were not given equal rights, they would become a substantial encumbrance on the fledgling government of the United States. Unable and unwilling to rationalize any emancipation plan, early Americans continued searching for alternatives.

One radical option evaded the problem of race mixing and racial integration altogether: *colonization*. Up until the end of the Civil War, many of the most iconic public figures in the United States addressed the fear of racial amalgamation by committing themselves to the idea of colonization. Colonization was not just a fanciful idea. It was a highly esteemed, financially sanctioned, and well-organized effort among white elites. They held themselves accountable for reversing the degradation of blacks because they were the only members of society powerful enough to create the conditions under which blacks could someday develop their own humanity. Once the benefits of resettlement were realized, it was thought that blacks would willingly leave the United States. The American Colonization Society (ACS) was formed in 1816 as a charitable organization with this goal in mind, and it boasted a distinguished list of members. Managed by prominent Americans and generously supported through donations, the ACS represented the most popular solution among whites—both progressive and discriminatory—to the threat of black integration to society. Although proposals for establishing an independent, black-led nation within the borders of the continental United States were entertained, their ambitions eventually took them overseas. The ACS funded and founded the country of Liberia in West Africa as a destination for freed slaves. James Monroe, both as president of the United States and as the head of the ACS, founded the colony of Liberia and named its capital after himself: Monrovia.

Colonization became the most prominent proposal for how to deal with freed blacks, a solution that itself had its own history. Many of the Founding Fathers supported colonization. In *Notes on Virginia* (the same work containing the suspicion that blacks would not be able to adequately civilize themselves), Thomas Jefferson advocated for colonization in part so that blacks would be "removed beyond the reach of mixture."[40] He believed that if fully integrated, blacks would be a detriment to society, especially given the "habits of vice" that the conditions of slavery had damned them with for so long.[41] Jefferson "urged a different solution: slaves should be freed gradually and on the condition that they leave the United States."[42] This was reinforced in his personal correspondence. Edward Cole, who served as secretary to President James Madison, wrote to Jefferson about his plan to take the slaves he inherited from his father to western colonies to set them free and live among them. Jefferson urged against such action and rejected any notion of *miscegenation* (interbreeding between races), asserting that slaves should be gradually released only on the condition that they relocate outside the United States.

For Jefferson and many of his contemporaries, the prevailing solution for the issue of how to proceed with the gradual emancipation of slaves was to resettle and colonize them outside the boundaries of America. Colonization—the structured removal of all blacks to a separate land, preferably off the American continent—was for a time the most "enlightened" solution to the perceived difficulty of integrating such a large number of blacks effectively into American society. The initiative garnered huge support. Even Abraham Lincoln openly advocated for colonization, saying that blacks who insisted on staying in the United States had "an extremely selfish view of the case," eventually commissioning his own attempt with several hundred blacks on the coast of South Carolina, an experiment under white leaders that failed miserably amid death and disease.

The backing of the plan for colonization by the most liberal thinkers of the day clearly indicated that blacks were ultimately viewed as lacking any viable role as American citizens. Colonization initiatives further established that it was impossible to imagine their full integration into US society. Although colonization was framed as a charitable act, it cannot be ignored that such efforts were ultimately rooted in the belief that blacks were less than fully human and could never truly "fit" into America. For example, Benjamin Franklin surmised that the entire race had been "degraded into perpetual bondage," and lamented that they required white superiors to govern them.[43] With colonization, freed blacks would be relocated to form a colony of their own, away from whites, under their own government. Even if the most progressive among them believed that blacks were not permanently inferior, they were unwilling to put into action plans that would end their presumed degradation and permit their participation in American society. Proponents of colonization concealed their fears of integration behind concerns that blacks could not achieve their "natural potential" or "equal citizenship" among wealthier, freer, and more established whites. Therefore, white "liberals" and enlightenment thinkers believed removal and colonization offered blacks an opportunity to live in a civilized society of their own making, so it was widely considered a positive and charitable solution to genuinely help them. Proposals for sites included the African coast and land in Central America. These white liberals believed blacks could only "realize their innate potential through separation" in a homogenous space where eventually, through hard work and self-development, they would prosper.[44] The colonization scheme resembled Indian Removal, the forced relocation of a much smaller and more highly segregated nonwhite population. Theoretically, Indian Removal served to foster two homogenous communities that would live alongside one another to mutual benefit, thus bypassing the assumed detrimental effects of a mixed-race population. The acceptance of colonization as a solution to sidestep the challenges of integrating society was the moment that the notion of "separate but equal" entered our national consciousness. After all, colonization was essentially racialized segregation.

Colonization conveniently relieved liberal whites of the challenges of integration. When blacks colonized, whites would become free of any obligation for them. Many in power would ultimately help themselves by assisting blacks to self-segregate by voluntarily leaving the American continent. Even Samuel Hopkins's missionary scheme to take freed slaves to the West African coast to "spread the gospel" was actually a veiled colonization attempt under the guise of Christian morals. Colonization effectively removed all notions of integration. Although there were blacks, like David Walker, who resisted colonization on the principle that America "is as much ours as it is the whites,"[45] pressure was brought to bear on free blacks to leave.

In short, white elites' refusal to accept that blacks and whites could coexist and cohabitate left only one viable option: the total expulsion of blacks from the American continent. Had these liberal white elites figured out the means to accomplish this bold task, their "benevolent" desire to relocate blacks would surely have resulted in blacks' forced removal. However, the logistical challenges of colonization proved too difficult to conquer. Just as attempts to "civilize" Native Americans had failed, efforts to elevate former slaves through relocation fell flat. What lingered from this effort in American society is the fundamental conclusion that blacks could not successfully integrate into an established white-dominant society. And the corresponding refusal of whites to entertain such a prospect led to the ongoing practice of racial segregation.

FROM FAILED EXPULSION TO EFFECTIVE SEGREGATION

It became apparent that even the most racially progressive early
Americans did not want to live in an integrated, multiracial, and mixed-
ancestry society. These "liberals" of the day concluded that a profound
inferiority, whether brought on by debasement in slavery or inherent to
their biological makeup, made black people less valuable than their
white superiors. The logistical failure of colonization transformed into
more pragmatic efforts to institutionalize segregation, thereby creating
conditions that had prolonged effects throughout American history.
The federal government had little power to enforce laws in the early
American Republic (the expansion of federal power was to come later
during the Civil War under President Lincoln), and individual states
found ways to reinforce racial hierarchies, often by promoting proslavery and prosegregation laws and taking advantage of legal loopholes and
trapdoors to prohibit blacks from gaining access to even the most basic
of human rights. Rather than expulsion, the systematic separation of
blacks from whites inevitably entailed barring blacks from the mobility,
opportunity, and social ease embedded in the ethos of white superiority. In the end, ongoing segregation was a direct consequence of the
failure to integrate emancipated slaves.

The debates, delays, and ultimate failure to institute any plan for the
liberation and elevation of blacks paved the way for the deeply rooted
racialized structures we know today. In the North, once slaves were
freed, they encountered the same roadblocks "free" blacks had faced in
much of the country, North and South alike: the lack of available jobs,
the lack of citizenship, and the lack of laws enforcing equality. On the
contrary, new laws were instituted that even more deliberately excluded
blacks from political and economic participation (see Chapter 3). After
emancipation, the legal responsibility for safeguarding the few rights
that were afforded to blacks was foolishly left to the states. In the South,
whites simply amended *slave* codes to become *black* codes, crafting
new laws to restrict the freedom of blacks and encouraging white authorities to catch them in acts considered criminal in order to effectively reenslave them through imprisonment. Furthermore, blacks were
terrorized by newly formed white-power groups, some of which, like
the Ku Klux Klan, were more organized and others that simply partici-

pated in spontaneous mob violence. Both resulted in ongoing and un-punished abuse, rape, burnings, and lynching of blacks by whites.

As black migrants surged northward and westward to escape the oppression of former slave states, they posed a threat to the wavering tolerance of blacks among whites in formerly "free states," a tolerance that had grown thin in even the most socially progressive cities in favor of extending more opportunities to unpropertied whites. States deliber-ately imposed restrictions on education, occupation, and housing. Tak-en all together, the end of the Civil War did not create a pathway toward successful integration. Rather, widespread neglect for black rights further exacerbated prejudicial attitudes that laid the foundations for new forms of systematic discrimination and oppression.

NATIVE AMERICANS AND WHITE SETTLER COLONIALISM

The impoverished condition of blacks in America would not have ex-isted without the colonial settlement and economic ambitions of white Europeans. The extraction of black *labor* was preceded by the expropri-ation of *land* taken from Native American nations.[46] Through a steady progression of aggressive enlargement of US territory by white settler colonizers from the 1600s through the 1800s, Americans claimed land as rightfully theirs by enacting the belief that forcible occupation of land grants ownership, especially when those living on the land were not using it properly. Indigenous people occupied the land, but it ap-peared to white colonists that they were not accomplishing anything productive with it. The land was "empty" or uncultivated.[47] White colo-nial settlement and Native American dispossession were both aspects of the same activity.[48] So, whereas the logics of racial enslavement and hierarchies of privilege were based on anthropological notions of inferi-ority and superiority, the logics of white settler colonialism and indige-nous dispossession were based on notions of empty and unused space.[49]

The new American government's rationale for expropriating indige-nous land was established as early as 1789 during George Washington's first presidential term.[50] He initially instructed US officials to negotiate with Native American nations (and their tribal coalitions) to establish trade agreements, which would lead to further negotiations for the purchase of their lands. Washington made clear to US officials that if the Indians rejected "reasonable terms" (a stipulation always assessed by the Americans themselves), it might become necessary "to punish them with severity."[51] From the start of their commission, US officials expressed strong doubts regarding the trustworthiness of Native Americans, claiming deceptive practices among the leaders they encountered. They conveyed their suspicions in reports back to the federal government and indicated their plans to conduct military expeditions against ostensibly recalcitrant Indians, which Washington approved. In these and other communications regarding American Indians, the word *extirpation* ("to do away with," "remove," "totally destroy") was interchangeable with *extermination*.

Years before, Washington had already expressed in a personal letter his preference for taking indigenous land by force rather than by purchase, comparing Indians with wolves such that getting rid of them "is like driving [out] the Wild Beasts of the Forest."[52] Although the United States never officially declared a "just and lawful war" that encompassed all Native American communities across the continent, federal officials would authorize and endorse violence against Indian groups interpreted as resisting US armed forces. By 1790, the federal government had accepted in principle the use of devastating military force to weaken and subdue Native American tribes, which sanctioned not only the dispossession of Indian land but also the genocide of whole Native American peoples.[53]

American leaders most immediately accessed their principles of conquest of Indian land through the work of Swiss jurist Emmerich de Vattel, whose book *Law of Nations*, published in 1758, was highly influential among US founders. According to Vattel, the people of Europe were "pent up" amid an already "well cultivated" land. In contrast, the "savages" of the American continent "stood in no particular need" of the land and "made no actual or constant use" of it. Indeed, those "who inhabit fertile countries but disdain to cultivate their lands and chuse rather to live by plunder . . . deserve to be extirpated as savage and pernicious beasts." Hence, white Europeans "were lawfully entitled to take possession of it and settle it with colonies."[54] In short, the white settlers to the American continent viewed Native American land as uncultivated, therefore unused, and populated by savages who had no need for it. As former Europeans, they not only desired land to relieve their cramped places of origin but also saw themselves as capable and civilized people who know how best to cultivate it. This development of the 1493 Doctrine of Discovery—the well-established legal justification for colonization and seizure of land that accompanied the first wave of conquest to the "New World"—provided the legal argument for white settler colonialism in America and justified the extirpation and extermination of indigenous groups occupying they land white settlers sought to productively exploit.

Remember that Jefferson had contrasted the potential civilization of Native Americans with blacks, tentatively arguing that the personhood of Native Americans could be cultivated and, eventually, they could become a welcome partner to the newly established United States. Yet his interactions with Indians revealed his deeper conviction regarding their inherent racial inferiority. During his presidency, Jefferson may have believed that civilization among such people was possible, but that possibility was deferred to a distant future. So although he had speculated on their future condition, he also initiated specific policies to persuade eastern Indians to uproot their dwellings and settle westward.[55] Jefferson's disingenuous wording regarding the possible equal dignity of Native Americans belied his underscoring of the image of their savagery in earlier writings (he once referred to "the wilds of America")[56] and his later attempts to move these supposedly wandering tribes through policies aimed at their relocation to remoter regions of the west. Even more, Jefferson believed the inherited traditions of indigenous peoples preserved ancestral customs, invoking the aristocratic conservatism of European feudal society, which ran counter to his understanding of democracy.[57] By continuing the federal government's clearing of Native Americans' space for occupation by white settlers, Jefferson's policies anticipated the far more comprehensive policy of Indian Removal that would be enacted by Andrew Jackson.

With his characteristic brusqueness, Jackson urged President-Elect James Monroe in 1817 to stop negotiating treaties with Indians as if they were independent nations, a notion he found preposterous.[58] For Jackson, Indians could not own land; they occupied the land, but they could not *possess* it. Native Americans were subject to US sovereignty, and the federal government had full authority to regulate such groups, which included the distribution and dispossession of land. Jackson was not alone in this judgment. Indeed, the Supreme Court of the United

States agreed. Drawing on the Doctrine of Discovery as a legal foundation to establish validity, Chief Justice John Marshall argued in the decision of *Johnson v. M'Intosh* in 1823 that American and European governments had "ultimate dominion" that included the "exclusive right to extinguish the Indian title of occupancy, either by purchase or by conquest."[59] Once again, Indians were characterized in the wording of this decision as "fierce savages," further reinforcing their inability to stake claims on the land. The following year, President Monroe stated in his 1824 message to Congress, "unless the tribes be civilized, they can never be incorporated into our system [of government] in any form whatever."

Over the years of treaties and negotiations between the American government and Native American nations, offers of purchase were made at times, but the terms of purchase were solely set by government officials who reserved the right to determine if the offer was fair. If terms of payment were refused, then violence was enacted to force concessions. The giving up of Native American lands, whether through negotiated payment or sheer force, was determined almost exclusively by coercion exerted by the United States.[60]

When Andrew Jackson entered the presidency, his approach to dispossession proved to be decisive. In his 1830 State of the Union Address, he referred to his policy of Indian Removal as a "benevolent policy."[61] He asked, "Can it be cruel . . . to give him a new and extensive territory, to pay the expense of his removal, and support him a year in his new abode? How many thousands of our own people would gladly embrace the opportunity of removing to the West on such conditions!" Jackson's actions led to great suffering and misery according to various "Trail of Tears" accounts from Native American nations subject to removal.[62] Looking to the great expanse of territory recently opened to the United States, Jackson used this speech to contrast the "wandering savage" from the "settled, civilized Christian" (note the presumption of white settlers as Christian). Specifically, he argued that a "few savage hunters" would be replaced through his policy by "a dense and civilized population," which would allow "settlements of whites" to "advance rapidly in population, wealth, and power." According to Jackson:

> [I]t will separate the Indians from immediate contact with settle
> ments of whites; free them from the power of the States; enable

them to pursue happiness in their own way and under their own rude institutions; will retard the progress of decay, which is lessening their numbers, and perhaps cause them gradually, under the protection of the Government and through the influence of good counsels, to cast off their savage habits and become an interesting, civilized, and Christian community. . . . Toward the aborigines of the country no one can indulge a more friendly feeling than myself, or would go further in attempting to reclaim them from their wandering habits and make them a happy, prosperous people.

It is a remarkable speech for its candor. Jackson not only contrasts wandering savages with civilized Christians but also explains that the removal of Native Americans is merely a continuation of a natural historical process. He bases his understanding on a mythology commonly held at the time (e.g., as reported by Alexis de Tocqueville in *Democracy in America*)[63] that the American continent had previously been occupied by an ancient and superior race:

In the monuments and fortifications of an unknown people, spread over the extensive regions of the West, we behold the memorials of a once powerful race, which was exterminated or has disappeared to make room for the existing savage tribes. . . . The present policy of the Government is but a continuation of the same progressive change by a milder process.

For Jackson, this distant, superior race now lost in antiquity but for their prehistoric remains had died or been killed off, making room for the "existing savage." Now, Native Americans in turn would be swept away by a new superior race "to make room for the whites" through the gentle hand of his government.

Through the expulsion of Native Americans to a smaller, segregated, and sequestered territory, Jackson made explicit a deeply held presumption that the white settlers of the United States consisted of a sovereign, civilized, and Christian people who required territorial expansion for the development of their prosperity and the exercise of their egalitarian democracy.[64] This powerful framing of American nationalism presumed both whiteness and Christianity. Settlers shared a common racial and religious identity, forming a base of affinity that would allow for mutual assent to shared decision-making. In contrast, as de Tocqueville reflected on indigenous tribes on the American continent around this time, "The Indian . . . attaches himself to barbarism as a distinctive sign of his race, and he repels civilization."[65]

A profound review of the United States's establishment of "civilized" democracy through colonial expansion is found in Adam Dahl's book, *Empire of the People: Settler Colonialism and the Foundations of Modern Democratic Thought.*[66] In this rendering of the founding ideals of the United States, Dahl explains that the white settler colonialism of America is based on the dream of establishing an empire, one that features the contradictions of an egalitarian system that promotes the advancement of its own people while excluding those deemed unfit to partake of this privileged system of equality. According to Dahl, "the language of empire permeated the constitutional debates of the 1780s," and "James Madison approvingly recorded the common sentiment that the men present had convened for the purposes of 'laying the foundation for a great empire.'"[67] Writing under the pen name *Publius*, John Jay conveyed the shared sentiment that Providence had abundantly blessed these newly independent Americans with a bounty of soils and streams, of plants and animals, for both the provision and enjoyment of its new inhabitants.[68] Dahl summarizes, "By expanding westward and conquering foreign populations along the way, American settlers were carrying out the will of God."[69]

As demonstrated in the American experience, white settler colonialism is a process of dispossession, appropriating native land, labor, and other resources to build a white, utopian society. Spatial mobility is viewed as necessary for social mobility. Indeed, the expansiveness of land and the verdant bounty available to all would avoid excessive competition, social antagonisms, and the gross deprivations of class warfare. Working together, white settlers forge a new constitutional arrangement by which they rule themselves while subduing others and eliminating all competing forms of sovereignty.[70] As the country sought to expand further westward, the Founders expressed concern that their nation could not maintain its unity across such a broad expanse of space. Yet their concern was mitigated by inaugurating a democracy that declined to sanction the absolutist dictates of a centralized state. The Founders ordained a republican system of government—a federation of states—that entrusted decentralized power to white settler sovereigns who would rule themselves and whose joint citizenship would preserve their borders and secure their unity. So, rather than establishing a rule of colonial administration over native peoples, the United States chose a policy of exclusion and appropriated their land, which set the conditions for recruiting even more white settlers while exploiting the labor of imported peoples, both of which further spurred the desire for territorial expansion.

THE US CONQUEST OF THE SOUTHWEST

Simultaneous with the developments of relations with blacks in the eastward states and with Native American nations scattered across the continent was the increasing salience of the western frontier in the national consciousness. Initial calls for the creation of a black colony in the West fell by the wayside in the rush to settle new lands, and new settlers were enjoined to clear territory of indigenous peoples. After the Louisiana Purchase, the most significant westward expansion of the United States was accomplished by outright conquest. Indeed, the conviction grew that the "the historical development of civilization has a spatial direction: human progress moves westward."[71]

Mexico had been a territory of Spain, but in 1821 it won its own war for independence. Although the region north of the Rio Grande was populated by Mexicans living in small, rural communities, war had exhausted the young nation's resources, and it was unable to properly secure the borders of its northern territories. Land was cheap, government oversight was negligible, and people living there were vulnerable to attacks from Native American tribes.[72] Mexico's General Law of Colonization of 1824 was intended to encourage colonization under Mexican rule, providing Mexican citizens, Christianized Native Americans, and white Americans the means to take possession of land, with the hope that growing communities would better protect Mexican territory against Comanche and Apache raids.[73] In the process, many white settlers, most of whom were Protestants seeking opportunity, migrated into Mexican territory, especially Texas.[74] Consequently, the white population grew and by 1830 outnumbered the Mexican population. Although Mexico had antislavery laws, whites ignored them, and many across the South and in Congress fought desperately to expand slavery to these newly settled areas.[75] The exhaustion of soil in the South further motivated slave owners to move into this largely unused territory, expanding slavery to expand their productive capacity and leverage potential economic opportunity.

The Mexican government struggled against the stream of white settlers, fighting to restrict immigration to their country and enacting legislation to require slaveholders to release their slaves. However, newfound independence and a heightened sense of self-importance among white immigrants inspired unrest among this newly settled population. Protestant Texas rebels embraced their claim to racial and religious superiority over Mexican Catholics and sought to overthrow them.[76] White Texans went to war alongside Tejanos (Mexican Texans) against the Mexican government, forming an independent nation in 1836, which would be annexed to the United States as the state of Texas in 1845. This annexation was in part responsible for the border disputes that led to the Mexican-American War. Less than two years later, the American army under command of General Winfield Scott invaded Mexico, took control of the capital, Mexico City, and forced a surrender.

Subsequent negotiations between the United States and the Mexican government in 1848 resulted in the Treaty of Guadalupe Hidalgo. Under this treaty, Mexico surrendered more than five hundred thousand miles of territory. This massive region included most of what is now known as Arizona, California, Colorado, Nevada, New Mexico, Utah, and Wyoming, and extended as far north as modern-day Canada.[77] The sudden transfer of ownership of this territory to the United States had grim socioeconomic effects for those living within it. All at once, more than one hundred thousand Mexican citizens became aliens on their own land.[78]

Although the treaty pledged to ensure former Mexican citizens the same rights and privileges as US citizens and the ability to retain ownership of their land,[79] many Mexicans in these newly added territories lacked official papers certifying their proof of ownership. Former Mexicans, now supposedly American citizens, had difficulty keeping land and maintaining their ranching lifestyles. When suing for ownership, Mexicans frequently lost in US courts to claims by whites.[80] Vagaries of weather, increased competition with white settlers, and the inability to secure loans to obtain access to credit for their business activity resulted in loss of wealth and property.[81] With the invention of barbed wire and new initiatives to limit access by fencing in private land that had been given away or sold off by the federal government, those Mexican Americans retaining some land abruptly lost access to water and grazing fields for their livestock and agricultural needs; unable to readily assimilate as white Americans, they found themselves thrust into a new American racial hierarchy as second-class citizens.

Although Spanish Catholics had built mission settlements throughout the southwest, they had focused on the conversion of Native Americans since the conquests of the late 1500s. With American annexation, Protestant missionary activity in the territory was a relatively new phenomenon. Since at least 1830, white missionaries from all major Protestant denominations worked to convert Mexicans to Protestantism.[82] These missionaries incorporated indigenous Mexicans into their racial hierarchies, which included notions of criminality, hygiene, intelligence, sexual propensities, and motivation for honest work. Mexican Catholic communities were compared with "Sodom and Gomorrah," biblical cities that God annihilated in retribution for the magnitude of their sins.[83] The mixed racial ancestry of Mexicans (European and indigenous groups), along with their Catholic faith, was fodder for explaining their inferiorities.[84] In practice, white Protestant missionaries had ambitions far beyond Mexican Americans' religious conversion. Their efforts at evangelization comprised an exhaustive effort to civilize and "Americanize" former Mexicans.[85] Racial prejudice was inherent to efforts toward Mexicans and contributed to the failure of effectively evangelizing the region.[86]

After the annexation of Mexican territory, racist arguments about inferiority based on skin color were used to justify their domination.[87] Mexican Americans experienced threats, racial violence, and state-sanctioned killings by Texas Rangers.[88] Refused their rights as citizens, and despite promises to the contrary, many moved south of the newly established Mexican border to evade the consequences of federally sanctioned white repossession of their land.[89] The imposition of "foreignness" continues to affect Mexican Americans today—as well as Latin Americans from Central and South America—and remains even among generations of Mexican Americans whose local heritage predates that of the descendants of white European immigrants to the United States. In the latter part of the nineteenth century, when native white resistance to Irish and Italian immigration on the eastern seaboard occurred, it was resolved through newcomers' ability to become accepted under the racial category of white, a process never granted to Mexican Americans (see Chapter 4).

RACIAL EQUALITY AND EARLY AMERICA

The vestiges of bygone colonization linger on in this crucial respect: a wide swath of whites still consider African Americans to be incapable of integrating widely into mainstream American society. Through neighborhood-level segregation, exclusion from certain educational institutions and professions, and the sidelining of concerns for their interests and often their own visibility, much of white-dominant America effectively chooses segregation and exclusion as a way to address the contemporary oppression of blacks in our country. Similarly, the legacy of expulsion and conquest remains in the continued prejudice still experienced by Native Americans and Latinos today. White European migration from East to West is the favored narrative for describing the evolution of the United States, rather than recognizing that a significant portion of America's development is better understood as a sudden adoption of the southwest to the northeast. Native Americans were steadily relocated to segregated regions; however, the US takeover of formerly Mexican territories meant that Mexican Americans suddenly *found* themselves in a new country without ever having migrated. Mexicans were abruptly and unexpectedly racialized to be indigenous peoples and became subject to the same justifications for land dispossession that had been imposed for decades on Native Americans.[90] Even today, there are many multigenerational Mexican-American families who lived in America before it was considered "America." Their land was considered vacant, and the legality of private property enforced to push them out such that individualized settler land rights were given priority over communal Mexican entitlements. Moreover, the long-standing permeability of what was once an effectively arbitrary border became consequential for the ongoing challenges of managing the circular movement of people North and South, informing contemporary immigration policy and Trump's political demand to build "The Wall." Unsurprisingly, the Mexican border has remained a contested zone, and attitudes toward Mexicans vary based on discrimination and economic necessity. The experiences of Mexican Americans are only one window into broader attitudes toward Latino groups in the United States (including Puerto Ricans and Central Americans, especially those from Honduras, El Salvador, Guatemala, and Nicaragua), each of which is informed by the degree of interference on their behalf by the American government.

Overall, the historical circumstances of bondage, conquest, and complex migration patterns manifest themselves to this day in the resulting power conflicts and ethnoracial tensions of the United States. The past experiences of enslaved blacks, dispossessed Native Americans, and conquered Mexican Americans have shaped the present contours and constraints of their social strata in the United States. The assertion of white superiority over these populations set a precedent in which race was a leading candidate for reaping the benefits of an expanding American society. Diligent, institutional perpetuation of hierarchies between those assumed to be native white and those deemed to be of lesser status because of their "color" necessitated either strict governance or total expulsion. All of these developments served to protect and perpetuate the integrity of native "whiteness" as the ultimate defining component of an emergent American national identity.

Chapter 3

RACIALIZED POWER AND CONSTRAINTS OF FREEDOM AFTER SLAVERY

Failure of Reconstruction

The Emancipation Proclamation signed by Abraham Lincoln in 1863 threatened to compromise the black-white racial separation that had been long established in the United States and since before the founding of the American Republic. Most feared by whites during and after the Civil War was *racial mixing*, which meant more than just the close social interaction between blacks and whites but also their sexual intimacies and the mixed-race children who would inevitably result. Interracial marriage was soon illegal in most states, and where it was not illegal it was simply because a legally recognized union between whites and blacks was inconceivable. Segregated churches, schools, and public spaces were organized to separate groups and thereby avoid the risk of racial mixing.

The social practices and societal institutions of racial separation innovated after the Civil War reflected beliefs about free blacks' capacity to achieve status equal to whites. In contrast, white political leaders initially held Native Americans in much greater esteem, and their policies reflected it. Early American officials viewed themselves as national protectors of the Indians, entering into negotiations with various tribes and nations, and considering ways to establish a relationship that respected their sovereignty—even as the American government continued to expand further into the frontier, signing treaties they never intended to respect with more than four hundred separate nations. Although the United States failed to honor these agreements and soon thought of indigenous people as "wandering tribes" with no rights to land, initially Native Americans were thought to be "in body and mind equal to the white man," as Thomas Jefferson wrote in his *Notes on the State of Virginia.* In contrast, he believed that blacks forcibly brought to America did not constitute a cohesive, self-sustaining civilization, and were therefore unworthy of governmental respect or support. Basing his opinions on beliefs about the physiological inferiority of blacks, Jefferson was among many who supported the expulsion of blacks to their own independent colonies overseas, in the hope that physical removal and resettlement would free white America from the dangers of black assimilation.

Later, Abraham Lincoln echoed similar sentiments regarding the subcivilized status of blacks, justifying his views on the exclusion of blacks from public life and intermarriage with a belief in their biological inferiority. In his presidential debates with Stephen Douglas in September 1858, Lincoln stated:

> I am not, nor ever have been in favor of bringing about in any way
> the social and political equality of the white and black races, that I
> am not nor ever have been in favor of making voters or jurors of
> negroes, nor of qualifying them to hold office, nor to intermarry with
> white people; and I will say in addition to this that there is a physical
> difference between the white and black races which I believe will
> forever forbid the two races living together in terms of social and
> political equality. And inasmuch as they cannot so live, while they do
> remain together there must be the position of superior and inferior,
> and I as much as any other man am in favor of having the superior
> position assigned to the white race.

By the time of Lincoln's speech, racism was so embedded in American society that his explicitly racist statements were not only accepted but commended. Today, Americans who see Lincoln as the Great Emancipator are shocked to discover that he boldly asserted such racist views.

Shortly before signing the Emancipation Proclamation, President Lincoln had sought to remove black people through colonization (see Chapter 2).[1] Using his executive power, the federal government sought to create colonies, transporting thousands of ex-slaves to places in Central America like Belize and Panama. Yet the removal of blacks from the United States through colonization never came to fruition. The impracticality of the idea became strikingly evident in the radical failure of his 1862 initiative to establish a colony in Île à Vache, Haiti. Under Lincoln's command, the federal government partnered with New York financiers to send five hundred recently freed slaves to colonize the small island of Île à Vache. Intending to grow the black population to five thousand, the colony was to be made into a profitable workforce funded and controlled by white American capitalists. But the experiment barely lasted a year. These newly free blacks found themselves subjected to bondage once again. After suffering from disease and neglect, a lack of basic necessities (like food, medicine, and building materials), and the gross incompetency of management from local white overseers and their far-off white American patrons, they revolted. The spectacular failure of this colonization effort ended any further attempts to colonize blacks, and federal attention shifted toward recruiting blacks to the Union Army as well as employing them (and recent immigrants) in the newly expanding railroad lines.[2]

Free blacks would now live among whites in the continental United States. Across America, once former slaves were freed, the question of integration became even more urgent: how were "uncivilized" blacks supposed to integrate into "civilized" white society? Most dismissed the assumption behind the question, believing black freedom simply would not happen. But when the institution of slavery was removed, prominent white political and economic elites still agreed that blacks could not simply enter white political, economic, and social structures as equals. And so, despite the dissolution of slavery and the failure of colonization, an inferior status clung to blacks as they were freed from enslavement.

By the end of the Civil War, Native Americans had been largely subdued and sequestered, and, following the 1848 Treaty of Guadalupe Hidalgo, Mexican Americans had been racialized as indigenous people subject to the same controls and dispossession as Native Americans. Yet the issue of black racial integration persisted, especially as blacks made up a significant demographic of the U.S. population and their numbers were factored into the political representation of each state. The question evolved from one that worked toward equal status for blacks to one that insisted on developing new forms of control. At the federal, state, and local level, white elites began to ask: How will whites regulate free blacks who are no longer enslaved? For many, the question boiled down to this: how do whites exercise control over black people they no longer own? How do whites continue to exercise control over a black population that is now free? In answer to these questions, the United States established new processes for systematically discrediting and dehumanizing blacks in America.

NO RIGHTS WHITES WERE BOUND TO RESPECT

The great majority of whites in the United States, North and South, never questioned that blacks were not truly American and therefore did not deserve the same level of dignity as white Americans. This implicit assumption was formally established by law in a legal decision that predated the Civil War. In 1857, just four years before the start of the Civil War, the Supreme Court of the United States ruled in the Dred Scott case, a landmark legal judgment that resulted in the total abandonment of the rights of *all* blacks, both slave and free.

Remember that before the Civil War, America distinguished between states where slave ownership was permitted and those where it was denied. As Andrew Delbanco writes in *The War before the War: Fugitive Slaves and the Struggle for America's Soul from the Revolution to the Civil War*, slave owners had long been concerned that fugitive slaves who fled to "free states"—states that did not permit slavery within their borders—would nullify their slave status and become free.[3] The issue even entered the debates in drafting the Constitution where representatives of "slave" states continually fought to extend slavery into newly formed states and new territories.[4] And although the Constitution never uses the words *slave* or *slavery*, the Fugitive Slave Clause (Article IV, Section 2, Clause 3) is universally understood as a commitment on the part of the federal government to enforce the return of fugitive slaves to their owners. Politically, Southern slave owners kept pushing to further extend the "benefits" of slavery throughout the expanding territories and newly formed states of the continent. A series of negotiations and compromises in government accumulated, none solving the issue to anyone's satisfaction, with anxiety and frustration growing. With *Dred Scott v. Sandford*, the Supreme Court justices hoped to settle the issues of enslavement, citizenship, and property rights of slave owners in the developing nation with one sweeping judgment.[5]

Dred Scott had been a slave, but he spent several years (along with his enslaved wife) in the free states of Illinois and Wisconsin. When his original owner died, the widow attempted to hire Scott and his wife out to another white person. Scott attempted to formally purchase his freedom for $300, but the widow refused, so Scott decided to sue for his freedom—and won. Yet lawsuits continued for years on appeal to higher courts. Ten years later, after the appealing and overturning of lower court rulings granting Scott and his family freedom, a proslavery Supreme Court in a spectacular upset ruled against Scott. The consequences of the case went far beyond Scott and his wife.

The ambitious judges of the Supreme Court in 1857, under the leadership of Chief Justice Roger B. Taney, intentionally elevated the significance of the Dred Scott case. On the surface, the court affirmed the right of slave owners to take their slaves (i.e., their property) into western territories without worry that freedom would be granted simply by crossing state lines. But the real consequence of the court's decision was the removal of every free state's sovereignty to determine the legality of slavery for themselves. Because the property status of slaves could not be changed when occupying free states, slave owners could now exercise their ownership of slaves anywhere in America. The decision essentially declared the Missouri Compromise of 1820, which had been forged to intentionally limit the spread of slave states into new territories, unconstitutional. The United States was now declared open for the expansion of slave ownership, slave breeding, and domestic slave trading everywhere. Slave owners rejoiced.

As much as slave owners cheered, the wording of the decision was disastrously harmful to the well-being of blacks in America. In the Dred Scott case, the Supreme Court explicitly stated that *no black, whether slave or free*, could claim US citizenship, declaring that African Americans, even if emancipated and living in a "free state," were not and could never become citizens. Specifically, the majority opinion written by Chief Justice Taney affirmed a widely understood notion that Scott was not considered a legal person under the US Constitution. This is because, in the opinion of the justices, black people were not recognized as citizens when the Constitution was drafted in 1787 (although the text of the Constitution itself is ambiguous, and there were indeed free blacks recognized as citizens of states within the United States in 1787, granting them certain privileges). Scott was black and therefore could not be a US citizen. Not being a citizen, Scott was not a legally recognized person and had no right to sue at all. In short, blacks could not be American citizens, so blacks were not eligible for rights that pertain only to citizens of the United States.

The decision was rooted in the belief of the inherent inferiority of blacks. This is clear from the wording of the judgment provided with the decision. Chief Justice Taney, reading from the Court's opinion, said that blacks "had for more than a century before been regarded as beings of an inferior order, and altogether unfit to associate with the white race, either in social or political relations; and, so far inferior, that *they had no rights which the white man was bound to respect*" [emphasis mine]. With this decision, formerly "free" black citizens became even more vulnerable regardless of where they lived, leaving them unable to purchase property, obtain passports to travel internationally, or have access to the court system to address injuries or injustices.

Today, we condemn the judgment of the court, and many consider this decision to be the worst in its history. Yet, as problematic as it was, the sentiments embedded in the judgment were broadly shared. Not only did the Dred Scott decision nullify the 1820 Missouri Compromise, but the 1860 convention of the Democratic Party debated the adoption of a national slave code based on the decision. Northern delegates rejected the explicitly proslavery platform, and the resulting fracture among Democrats regarding the treatment of blacks contributed to the successful election of the Republican candidate, Abraham Lincoln.

Legally, the Dred Scott decision was overturned at the end of the Civil War when, in 1865, Congress passed the Thirteenth Amendment to the Constitution abolishing slavery and, in 1868, it passed the Fourteenth Amendment granting citizenship to all persons born or naturalized in the United States (including former slaves). These momentous decisions transformed slaves into citizens, but in crafting the amendments, the legislators neglected to specify processes to protect and enforce widely anticipated privileges assumed to be associated with American citizenship. With little to no compensation given for the years of labor taken from them, and no assets to draw on for building a new life, freedom alone was not enough to overcome the dramatically disadvantaged position of the formerly enslaved. Another shortcoming of the provision of freedom for blacks is the weakness of the Fifteenth Amendment. This amendment granted all male citizens, including blacks, the right to vote. However, although the amendment was passed to extend rights and citizenship to former slaves, it left enforcement of that right to the states, allowing states to establish their own criteria and oversight for voting. So although James A. Garfield spoke in favor the amendment, saying that it finally "confer[ed] upon the African race the care of its own destiny," in actuality blacks were provided suffrage without the backing of federal enforcement.[6] The power to manage race-based issues was entrusted to the same white-supremacist regimes that had fought against the freedom of blacks, leaving the formerly enslaved subject to former Confederate leaders who remained committed to their inferiority.

Yes, blacks could be citizens, but the actual substance of their rights was far from settled. Moreover, the ability to exercise their freedom was severely limited. Instead of promoting mobility and opportunity, those in control of economic and political forces soon implemented a series of laws, crafted new institutions, and extended racialized cultural practices to define true (or deserved) citizenship as belonging to long-standing, native white populations—and to selective groups of European immigrants from foreign countries whose peoples were deemed to be "white" (see Chapter 4). So, as the initial thrill of Emancipation passed, blacks would find their supposedly free status trod over not only by ex-slaveholders but also by poor whites without property. And when a wave of foreign immigration hit the American continent, even the poorest immigrants—whites recruited and welcomed from overseas to populate the expanding Western frontier—experienced more welcome, more assistance, and more opportunity than American-born, formerly enslaved blacks.

SLAVERY, NOT STATES' RIGHTS: MOTIVATION FOR THE CIVIL WAR

To further grasp the significance of the regulations of black bodies after emancipation, the larger narrative of "states' rights" should be properly contextualized. A common argument today is that the Civil War was based on a fight for the rights of states to determine their own policies. This is true only to the extent that the assertion of states' rights was motivated by an insistence on asserting their right to enslave blacks as a legitimate system of economic organization, one that is based on the absolute and nonnegotiable oppression of blacks. The assertion of states' rights therefore centered on the push for continued profits by a steadily declining number of white owners who were extracting labor and credit from their black property.

That the slave economy was the core justification for the secession of the states is written into the fabric of the documents proclaiming the founding principles of the rebel Confederate government. Every secession document describes the preservation of slavery as an essential reason for establishing the Confederacy. For example, in March 1861, the vice president of the Confederate States of America, Alexander A. Stephens, delivered a speech in Savannah, Georgia, describing the new Constitution, which detailed the moral code that undergirded the Confederacy. The "Cornerstone Speech" is remarkable for its clarity and transparency. In this speech, Stephens stated that the foundation of the Confederacy denied the principles held by many under the "old" Constitution because those ideas "were fundamentally wrong. They rested upon the assumption of the equality of races. This was an error. . . . They assume that the negro is equal, and hence conclude that he is entitled to equal privileges and rights with the white man." Instead, "[o]ur new government is founded upon exactly the opposite idea; its foundations are laid, the corner-stone rests, upon the great truth that the negro is not equal to the white man; that slavery subordination to the superior race is his natural and normal condition."

The disruption of not allowing Southern slave holders to do what they wished with "their property" is fundamental to the motivation for secession. In the same year as Stephen's famous speech, the state of Georgia approved a long declaration justifying secession, stating that the North had disrupted "safeguards for our liberty, equality, security, and tranquility," specifically "by their declared principles and policy they have outlawed $3,000,000,000 of our property." The Alabama legislature resolved to secede because of "assaults upon the institution of slavery" by Union fanatics. And Louisiana Commissioner George Williamson wrote an impassioned plea to the secession convention of

Texas urging their lawmakers to do as his state had done, to secede in order "to preserve the blessings of African slavery."

Such direct statements (and many others) documenting the motivation for secession are in contrast with later romanticized narratives lamenting the Lost Cause of the South.[7] Accounts of the Lost Cause— which were more than just family stories but often written into state-approved textbooks for school children—stressed the honor and nobility of the South and its leaders, asserting that slavery was a benevolent institution characterized by kindness and loyalty, and emphasizing the chivalry of Southern gentlemen; the virtue of Southern women; and the natural order, legitimated by the Bible, of black enslavement. Slave society was presented as imbued with good morals and civic order where blacks were comfortable and content.[8] Secession of the Southern states was only a justified response to the Northern assault against the Southern way of life. Despite the pervasiveness of these sentimentalities, the larger historical record betrays such a benign view.

The slave states of the South sought to claim independence to determine slavery as a prerogative to ensure the continued flow of wealth being wrung from their black property. The preservation of the economic structure of slavery was foremost among their motivations. During the Confederacy, the desire to further expand the institution of slavery and make their slave-based economy more sustainable motivated diplomatic initiatives to create economic alliances with the remaining slave nations of the Caribbean (Cuba, Puerto Rico, and Netherlands Antilles). The connections between states' rights, economic wealth, and slavery were so densely intertwined that Confederate bank notes made it central to their symbolism, placing pictures of contented slaves hoeing soil, loading cotton bales, and working in front of plantation houses on their paper currency. By presenting these dark-skinned workers as happy and productive on their Confederate dollars used to buy and sell daily necessities, the South boldly proclaimed in their day-to-day commercial interactions that enslavement was the foundation of their natural and God-ordained way of life.

Although notions of black inferiority and the denial of equality for blacks are usually associated with the Confederacy, it should be noted that these core ideas were held widely outside of the South. As indicated earlier, the parallels between Lincoln's personal convictions and the tenets on which the Confederate States of America were founded are striking: both North and South believed that equality between whites and blacks was unachievable because of basic, biological differences. Both agreed that blacks were inherently inferior to whites. It follows then that both asserted that American society should be organized, with privileges and responsibilities distributed, according to a white-black racial hierarchy. In short, the idea that blacks were biologically inferior to whites was intrinsic to the structure of race relations for both the North and the South in America before the Civil War. It was the central justification for the secession that initiated the Civil War; therefore it is not surprising that these notions continued to shape the experience of blacks well after the Civil War.

A COUNTRY FOR WHITE MEN: EMANCIPATION AND THE BEGINNING OF THE BLACK CODES

Although the intent of the Emancipation Proclamation issued by Abraham Lincoln was not decisively achieved until passage of the Thirteenth Amendment to the Constitution ("Neither slavery nor involuntary servitude, except as a punishment for crime whereof the party shall have been duly convicted, shall exist within the United States, or any place subject to their jurisdiction"), this bold move initiated the "free" status of more than three million blacks. As sweeping as this was, it must be noted that presidential proclamations and constitutional amendments did not in themselves change widely held sentiments that slavery was a justified, God-given blessing, a practice ordained by God obviously legitimated by the visible prosperity it produced.

Some of the most powerful arguments for slavery were produced *after* the end of the Civil War, especially *A Defense of Virginia and the South* by Presbyterian pastor, professor of theology, and Confederate States Army chaplain Robert L. Dabney. In his densely written tome of more than 350 pages published in 1867, Dabney emphatically wrote that slavery was not only lawful but also protected by the Constitution, promoted the well-being of "Africans," and was sanctioned by God.[9] In arguing for "the righteousness of slavery," Dabney insisted that he took "no extreme positions" and that his position was supported by the law and, "above all, by the Word of God."[10] Of course, the Bible was central to his exposition: "The principles of scriptural exposition are simply those of common sense; and it will be the writer's aim so to explain them that they shall commend themselves to every honest mind, and to rid them of the sophisms of the Abolitionists."[11] Yet, despite the reliance on scripture, a cornerstone of his argument was rooted in ostensibly scientific notions of biological inferiority:

> [W]hile we believe that "God made of one blood all nations of men to dwell under the whole heavens," we know that the African has become, according to a well-known law of natural history, by the manifold influences of the ages, a different, fixed species of the race, separated from the white man by traits bodily, mental, and moral.

Buttressed by such arguments, blacks continued to be viewed by Southern whites—and many Northern whites as well—as undeserving of their newfound autonomy. Many believed that blacks should now earn their freedom by demonstrating their merit and proving their worthiness to remain in mainstream American society. The discriminatory pressure on blacks was only accentuated by the generous manner in which the federal government treated formerly rebellious states after the war.

Abraham Lincoln fought the Civil War not for the freedom of a people enslaved but to preserve the Union. An 1882 letter written in the midst of the war to Horace Greeley, editor of the New York *Tribune*, makes this clear:

> My paramount object in this struggle *is* to save the Union, and is *not* either to save or to destroy slavery. If I could save the Union without freeing *any* slave I would do it, and if I could save it by freeing *all* the slaves I would do it; and if I could save it by freeing some and leaving others alone I would also do that. What I do about slavery, and the colored race, I do because I believe it helps to save the Union.

Lincoln had not advocated for the rights of blacks or in favor of making voters or jurors of blacks, nor of qualifying them to hold elected office. So, although Lincoln fought for the survival of America, he did not believe the full and equal participation of black people was essential to it. Instead of working for the rights of blacks, Lincoln earnestly worked so that there would be no animosity between opposing sides of the war.

Reconstruction initially included initiatives to bolster and stabilize the well-being of former slaves; yet, in practice, the main concern of the federal government during Reconstruction was in reintegrating the formerly treasonous Southern states. To accomplish this, Lincoln believed that no retribution should be sought against former Confederates—even when their actions were condemned as crimes to prevent similar acts in the future. Pardons were liberally granted to prevent administering consequences to the Confederates, which allowed the reinstatement of the antebellum Southern governments that had been so viciously opposed to the abolition of slavery. By Executive Order, in 1863 President Lincoln required only 10 percent of seceded state voters (eligible white males) to take an oath of loyalty to rejoin Union. Although the "Radical Republicans" wanted a majority of former Confederates to make a loyalty oath to the Union, Lincoln was anxious to reunify and prevented such efforts. When taking into account the public and primary reason for forming the Confederacy—the extraction of wealth from the enslavement of blacks, which was claimed as a God-ordained blessing—90 percent of white eligible male voters were allowed to hold to that ideology. The rest of the population was not even asked.

Lincoln's vice president and successor, Andrew Johnson, said, "This is a country for white men and by God, as long as I am president, it shall be a government for white men." After Lincoln's assassination, Johnson gave out massive numbers of pardons to the defeated leaders of the Confederate States of America. He also returned land to Southern plantation owners who had abandoned them, confiscating lands that were intended to be used to support the beginnings of black economic independence. Blacks who had begun tilling lands they had thought were theirs were forced to relinquish them; they now had to hire themselves to the white landowners with year-long contracts at low wages. Even more, the same leaders of the Confederacy were reinstalled into their roles as government leaders at local, state, and federal levels. Johnson enforced the abolition of slavery but offered no solutions regarding the treatment of these newly feed blacks, claiming it was up to the newly reinstated antebellum Southern governments to instate their own racial relations. And he openly impeded the improvement of the status of blacks. The enforcement of new protections and privileges for blacks were left to the States; those intended protections did not fully materialize.

So, although the end of the Civil War ended black enslavement, the eagerness of the federal government to "heal" a divided nation allowed the former states of the Confederacy to fold themselves back into the United States. At the same time, the formerly enslaved were granted rights on paper, but federal government leaders insisted that it was up to them to deal with their issues of power, status, and opportunity on their own. [12] Blamed for their own problems, the formerly enslaved were expected to discipline themselves and work within the system with even more strenuous effort, making the problem of racial inequality a *personal* one rather than a *systemic* one.

Structural institutions shifted from structures supporting enslavement to a generalized diminishment of black dignity and economic independence to perpetuate their subordination. As a consequence, bold plans intended for the betterment of blacks among abolitionists and Radical Republicans quickly faltered. Nearly all of the federal government's initiatives for work, housing, and education on behalf of newly free blacks were neglected or intentionally dismantled. One example is the failure of the Freedmen's Bank.

The Freedmen's Savings Bank was established as part of the Freedmen's Bureau (Bureau of Freedom, Refugees, and Abandoned Lands), a "first-draft" structure for shaping the freedom of blacks through welfare, employment, and land redistribution, including pensions and other forms of financial aid. The Bureau established hospitals, improved educational opportunities, and banks—which failed disastrously. [13] The Freedmen's Bank was intended to increase black wealth, and freed slaves poured in most of their limited savings and income into this new institution. Yet it was not a true bank in that it did not extend credit to blacks or find productive ways to invest and expand the small savings individuals had entrusted to the bank. Instead, the Freedmen's Bank was set up like a "large piggy bank," where the money just sat. The growth of the assets was too tempting for white overseers who saw only an unused cache of wealth. When the chairman, Henry Cooke, revised the charter to allow loans, those bank investments were based on nepotism, political favor, and sheer recklessness. By the end of Cooke's tenure, the bank had lost $75 million dollars that had been placed in the bank by blacks (worth $1.5 billion today), overextending and bankrupting the bank. [14] And even though the federal government oversaw the Freedmen's Bank, they did not take responsibility for its performance, and they did not return the irresponsible losses on bank member savings, wiping out a lifetime of funds of formerly enslaved who had been encouraged to place their earnings there. The failure of the Freedman's Bank affected trust between blacks and the growing banking system of the United States for generations.

Even with poor management and failed initiatives, the Freedmen's Bureau was widely construed as an unearned, racially biased effort against whites. The new president, Andrew Johnson, had openly racist ideas and actively opposed the Bureau, believing that blacks did not deserve such benefits. The Freedmen's Bureau was seen as a system of giving free money to "undeserving poor." The work of the Freedmen's Bureau was therefore subverted, with whites saying that blacks were taking undue advantage of the government's benevolence. The Freedmen's Bureau was terminated within a few years of its creation in 1869.

Besides the lack of practical help, the supposed freedom of blacks was accompanied by radical limits. Blacks were neglected by law; often faced murder, rape, and assault from white supremacist groups; and were subject to newly conceived "black codes" (which later became Jim Crow laws) that enforced segregation of public facilities under the guise of "separate but equal" philosophy, a concept that had gained traction within the colonization movement (see Chapter 2). Black codes were purportedly set in place "to stop vagrancy and put an end to the undeniable evils of idleness and pauperism arising from the sudden emancipation of slaves."[15] But whites already believed that blacks were naturally ignorant, lazy, and criminal. Andrew Johnson called them "immoral, drunken sluggards." Black codes were intended to catch blacks under legal pretense, keeping them as propertyless, rural laborers under strict controls without access to political or other legal rights. Even "free" states had antiblack laws despite their being cast as havens of freedom and equality.

The Reconstruction period therefore continued the oppression of the slave-holding era, this time leaving blacks to fend for themselves. At the same time, whites formed new social structures (informal and encoded, organized and impulsive) for continuing marginalization, exclusion, and outright oppression. The black codes of Southern states restricted civil rights, preventing blacks from owning land or voting, and requiring them to bind themselves in strict legal contracts to white employers. Blacks could only work with plantation, mill, or mine owners, and black women could only work as domestic help. Not only were they largely stuck in the South, most often black workers were commonly and legally bound a year at a time to labor under white farmers and business owners. Blacks had to sign contracts at the beginning of each year, and if they could not prove their gainful employment, they were "charged with vagrancy and put on the auction block."[16] This ambiguity in the status of free blacks is manifested in an economic system that forced them back into bondage to employers, sometimes in the very same fields in which they had been enslaved. Even children were not exempt from these policies and were apprenticed as orphans. Although such policies were intended to prevent blacks form becoming a burden to society as vagrant wanderers, they also prevented blacks from enjoying many types of leisure activities and barred them from hunting or fishing, often unknowingly, in waters designated as private property or from working independently, for example, using skills like blacksmithing that had been learned while enslaved.

Blacks were no longer possessions of white owners, but the white population scrutinized them and rejected the extension of opportunities for their advancement. Blacks were kept from voting (we still deal with voter disenfranchisement today),[17] so elected leaders felt little need to honor black interests. Because blacks had no collateral and were believed to be weak in character, banks did not lend them money, and black business owners were not extended credit. Black mobility to other states was hindered. States like California, Illinois, Iowa, Michigan, and Wisconsin had long been unwelcoming to free blacks, and Oregon barred residence or even extended travel altogether. Among these "free" states, the resistance to the institution of slavery had been accompanied with a resistance to free blacks as well, making their states intentionally prowhite settler states.[18] And nearly every state had "sundown towns" that excluded blacks (and other nonwhites) from any lengthy stay in their cities through a combination of discriminatory local laws, intimidation, and outright violence.[19]

In the end, free blacks attempted to enter the marketplace as wage earners but were limited in their suffrage, deprived of access to capital, and denied mobility. As demonstrated in Mehrsa Baradaran's book *The Color of Money: Black Banks and the Racial Wealth Gap*, their supposed economic "risk" caused by their supposed inferiority put them in jeopardy of obtaining credit, having higher interest rates, and being denied access to education and training requiring more intensive skill or expertise. Although they attempted to enter the economy of the United States, the formerly enslaved were systematically deprived of opportunity, with no political power to change it.[20]

Poor whites also lacked the leverage of wealth, but they had an advantage blacks did not: poor whites leveraged the value placed on their whiteness. As Kenneth Stampp writes,

> For the low-status white man the essential fact of life was the color of his skin. "I may be poor and my manners may be crude," he told the world, "but I am a white man. And because I am a white man, I have the right to be treated with respect by Negroes. That I am poor is not as important as that I am a *white* man; and no Negro is ever going to forget that he is *not* a white man."[21]

Sharecropping provided land, tools, and animals for blacks, but the circumstances were arranged such that blacks had to pay back the owner for the use of all those tools, leaving sharecroppers poor and perpetually in debt. Whites refused to rent or sell properties to blacks. Wages among all blacks were kept below subsistence level. The deep process of dehumanization sustained notions buttressed by such cruel practices, and those beliefs did not dissipate with the end of the Civil War.

Deprived of property and rights, the condition of free blacks worsened even more with the intentional violence committed against them. The end of the Civil War brought the start of hate groups asserting a brutal form of white-based identity politics. These violent groups, most prominently the Ku Klux Klan (KKK), turned against the few protections afforded blacks by the federal government, believing that the state was now oppressing their own interests as white people. Because the state had abandoned them, the loosely structured gangs of white supremacist groups like the KKK enacted a belief that only violence would preserve the racialized moral order of the South. As with the institution of slavery, whiteness remained rooted in violence to forcefully maintain an unjust racial hierarchy. The Klan viewed itself as a moral guardian, restoring Christianity and civilization, with preachers claiming that the Klan was God's instrument for rescuing the South from the chaos brought by Reconstruction.[22]

In the formation of white-power groups, blacks were targeted and terrorized, at times through activity organized by groups like the KKK, at other times through spontaneous mobs. Thus blacks were not just denied access to certain privileges, they also suffered the onset of racially motivated violence, a horrific period of ongoing abuse, rape, burnings, and lynching. Secret social groups like the KKK and the White Camellia, alongside the White League and Red Shirts, intimidated blacks with such severity that they effectively ended any attempts at Reconstruction. When the KKK targeted local Republican leaders, superficial support for political initiatives to benefit blacks quickly waned. The disintegration of Republican efforts toward newly freed blacks revealed that their outreach toward black voters was based more on breaking the cotton monopoly and the power of Southern Democrats than on any principle of racial equality.[23] The Compromise of 1876, which appointed Rutherford B. Hayes as president of the United States, brought an abrupt end to Reconstruction initiatives, involving a negotiated agreement to curtail federal efforts toward black civil and political advancement. Jim Crow structures quenching the ambitions of blacks went unchallenged and perpetuated segregation, a societal arrangement that was officially sanctioned in *Plessy v. Ferguson*, the 1896 Supreme Court case that enshrined "separate but equal" in law.[24]

SANCTIFYING THE MEMORY OF THE SOUTHERN CONFEDERACY

The Confederacy ended with the Civil War, but romanticized notions of the Confederacy continued to live on and still continue into the twenty-first century. After losing the Civil War, the South needed to rebuild itself. Through glorifying the Confederacy, the South created a mythology that asserted the its moral victory over the North's material victory.[25] The religions and rituals of the Lost Cause are based first in villainizing the North as "satanic," especially as a result of its apparent benevolence toward blacks, because slavery was a God-ordained institution. Ministers went so far as to describe the North's victory as the beginning of the apocalypse, likening it to the vivid cataclysms on earth as described in the biblical book of Revelation.[26]

Known to scholars as the "Religion of the Lost Cause," the Lost Cause is an idealized version of Southern heritage, a sacred designation of a cultivated historical memory, a glorification of the "war against

Northern aggression" that demands from white Americans a duty to respect the Confederate soldiers; the Confederate flag; and the ideals of family, sacrifice, and honor said to be embedded in Confederate society. The war was portrayed as a holy war and was centered around "the myth of the Crusading Confederates";[27] this portrayal was especially effective because it moved the war from being about politics and economics to one of morality and religion. These notions did not coalesce until after the establishment of Jim Crow and involves a selective reconstruction of collective memory.

The most tangible tributes to the Lost Cause narrative are Confederate monuments.[28] The timing of the building of Confederate monuments is especially interesting. Built mostly in the late nineteenth century, and then later in the early twentieth century after the *Brown v. Board* decision that demanded the racial integration of public schools, these statues were built to mirror those of existing statues of American Revolutionary War heroes like George Washington. Now, Stonewall Jackson, Robert E. Lee, Jefferson Davis, and countless others are memorialized. Monuments to Confederate soldiers joined these illustrious predecessors in "immortality"; their bases often included inscriptions of biblical verses and the designation "Good Christian," while the figures themselves would often hold Bibles alongside their guns or while dressed in full military regalia.[29]

Alongside these physical dedications to fallen heroes, the South created its own holidays to remember its dead. Jefferson Davis's birthday became Memorial Day and he was depicted as the Christ-like martyr of the war. Southern ministers spoke of Robert E. Lee as a "Christian knight" who led his people much as how Moses led the Israelites out of Egypt in the book of Exodus.[30] Stonewall Jackson, with his plain and direct military style, was the embodiment of the early holy prophets of the Old Testament, and his coincidental death on a Sabbath day solidified his place within the mythology. And Confederate General Robert E. Lee surrendered to Union General Ulysses S. Grant on April 9, 1865—Palm Sunday—which motivated spiritual comparisons with Jesus entering into Jerusalem in triumph before his crucifixion. Ministers and political figures of the time went so far as to change the lyrics of popular spiritual hymns and scriptures themselves to support the glorification of the Civil War.[31]

Interestingly, Robert E. Lee opposed Civil War monuments and memorials. In 1866 he wrote,

> As regards the erection of such a monument as is contemplated, my conviction is, that however grateful it would be to the feelings of the South, the attempt in the present condition of the country would have the effect of retarding, instead of accelerating its accomplishment, and of continuing, if not adding to, the difficulties under which the Southern people labour.

Despite his misgivings, a movement to overcome the shame and stigma of the Confederacy mobilized funding to build an extensive series of monuments over the next several decades.

It remains ironic that Americans are still often defined by the successes of meritorious whites, forgetting that the country is built on land taken from indigenous peoples and benefited so greatly from labor extracted by forcibly migrated Africans. In the romanticized memory of the Confederacy, this boiled down to the Southern belief that whites, specifically the Anglo-Saxon whites of the South, were at the top of a properly instituted racial hierarchy that was steadily being weakened and needed to be saved at any cost. The Lost Cause received legitimation from religious leaders—some monuments are placed on church grounds—as the Reverend R. Lin Cave noted in 1896: "The preservation of the American government is in the hands of the South because Southern blood is purely American." Southern religious leaders after 1900 shared the belief that this pure blood was being contaminated. Blacks were not the only danger. In 1918, the Southern Presbyterian Assembly noted the post-1900 arrival of European immigrants in Southern cities "had almost overnight changed the complexion of our people and modified our claim to Anglo-Saxon exclusiveness."[32] The influx of Southern and Eastern Europeans also threatened the integrity of whiteness (see Chapter 4). The blatant association of Anglo-Saxon whiteness with a racialized Christianity set the stage for the reemergence of the KKK in the 1920s and 1930s as a broad-based and family-friendly movement to restore the goodness of true Americans.[33]

THE WESTWARD EXPANSION OF A
WHITE SETTLER NATION

Slavery was officially abolished in 1865 with the end of the Civil War and the Thirteenth Amendment to the Constitution. But chains do not come only in physical forms; they also persist through racial dynamics that maintain a white-privileged racial hierarchy. As sociologist George Fredrickson wrote, "a slaveholding mentality remained the wellspring of white supremacist thought and action long after the institution that originally sustained it had been relegated to the dustbin of history."[34] The prejudices held by whites at the end of slavery informed the reception of newly freed blacks. And because it was widely believed that blacks did not earn their freedom by demonstrating their qualifications to integrate into civilized white society, they were not accepted as proper Americans—a sentiment made abundantly clear by the series of initiatives taken by white Americans against newly freed blacks.

Stressing the primacy of biological differences, whites could hold on to a white settler sentiment that they participated as equals in a democratic system while being racially exclusive (see Chapter 2). This *Herrenvolk* ("master race") democracy assigns primacy and power to the majority racial group while being untroubled by the disenfranchisement of "lesser" groups. As historian Richard White notes, both Jeffersonian and Jacksonian visions of society "could tolerate gross inequality as long as that inequality did not threaten white men."[35] Now in the transition out of the institution of slavery, not only did whites resent the freeing of slaves, they formed new codes and laws to restrict the freedom of blacks, to catch them in acts considered criminal (which led to imprisonment, effectively reenslaving them), and to block their best interests from being served. The supervision of black rights encoded into law was unwisely left to the states that had so strenuously fought to uphold black enslavement.

Southern whites found themselves in a rapidly changing economy and were forced to deal with the new status for former slaves. The years of Reconstruction encompassed significant social changes, much of which involved reinscribing a racial hierarchy as well as the tremendous building of wealth, resulting in astounding gaps of inequality. But as the Reconstruction period transitioned into the Gilded Age, Republican politicians of the northeast who had forcefully advocated for the well-being for emancipated blacks—the Radical Republicans—lost their influence, and their political advocacy was seen as a hindrance to looming concerns for the success of the party as a whole. As Lawrence Goldstone writes, "The radical generation was passing, eclipsed by politicos [and] 'the struggle over the Negro' the party's rising leaders believed, must give way to economic concerns."[36]

Reconstruction gave way to the expansive industrialization of the later nineteenth century, a time of new farmlands, intensive resource extraction, and the completion of the transatlantic railroad. Northern investors who had placed nearly all of their funds into the cotton industry took their expansive assets and sought new investments, moving capital to new industries springing up in the expanding West, putting money in extraction industries like drilling and mining, processing industries in meatpacking and manufacturing, and distribution networks like regional railroads. Indeed, the movement of capital from East to West was instrumental in the expansion of the financial industry and created the investment banking system that became so powerful throughout the twentieth century.[37]

As the US economy expanded during the Gilded Age and well into the twentieth century, new forms of racial suppression that held out the promise of liberty to blacks but actually revealed multiple new racial structures to hinder and obstruct economic mobility and political empowerment in favor of white settlers were also fostered. Political movements in Southern states remained focused on inhibiting the rights of the black population, with continued fighting against Northern efforts, until Republicans acceded to the need to appeal to white Southern voters. The political push against racial oppression became less insistent and more accommodating. Southern Democrats persisted in their resistance to Civil Rights legislation for blacks, blocking all maneuvers to give attention or be responsive to the plight of blacks and intentionally dismantling what were perceived as unfair advantages against whites. Southern states resisted black suffrage, equal education, access to civic and leisure amenities (like hotels and restaurants), and, really, all considerations of black economic advancement.

Congress did little to limit the abuses against blacks, and a succession of presidents ignored the issue. For example, when Mississippi convened a convention to revise their constitution to bar blacks from voting while granting the same rights to illiterate whites, this explicitly

racist action prevailing against the spirit of the Fourteenth and Fifteenth Amendments went unchallenged. Other states took notice, and
their white leaders "understood they had been handed a recipe for
success."[38] Thanks to the large contingent from the South in Congress,
all racial initiatives were essentially vetoed by Southern Democrats. The
Southern intolerance for racial equality was the limit for public policy
for the nation, which meant that the United States remained for almost
the entirety of the next one hundred years "a Southern nation."[39]

It was not just former Confederate states that pushed back against
opportunity and mobility for free blacks. The contrast between benefits
extended to newly freed blacks versus whites is exemplified in proposals
for the distribution of former plantations and new territories of the
Western frontier. For example, Republicans continued to put forward
homesteading bills to boost the population of the West. Andrew Johnson declined any initiative to grant blacks land, instead pushing forward
the Homestead Act, which literally gave away 160 acres to poor whites
and white European immigrants for free. Under Johnson's program,
blacks were not eligible.

The Free Soil Movement, a desire among poor whites against the
"plantocracy" of slave owners to own their own land and have a stable
means of living from their own labor, had resisted the institution of
slavery and motivated white settlers to migrate westward, enacting their
desire to establish a white utopia of free labor.[40] Consequently, as western territory was being populated and new states were being formed,
white wage earners and white small businessmen intentionally worked
to exclude blacks, fearful that their skills and their willingness to offer
cheap labor in desperation would hurt the economic chances of poor
whites.

Homesteading bills reinforcing notions of white settler colonialism
(see Chapter 2) had long been fought between Northern whites and
Southern slave-owning interests for a simple reason: Southern states
had the hopes of expanding slavery westward, which would further limit
economic opportunities and advancement of propertyless whites, while
homesteading advocates intended to expand opportunities for white
settlers and further secure western borders of the American continent.[41] The egalitarian vision of white settlers assumed neither slaves
nor slave owners. After the radical expansion of territory following the
Mexican-American War, arguments regarding the use of western terri-

tories for entrepreneurial white settlement versus the expansion of slave-owning enterprises eventually resulted in the explosive conflict of the Civil War. With slave-owning interests now gone, homesteading bills went forward, encouraging whites (both Americans and Europeans) to occupy these lands, intentionally promoting the whitening of the American frontier. Homesteading directly benefited these white settlers greatly, and their success contributed to building the Republican Party in the late nineteenth century with the westward expansion of Republican-dominated states and legislators. Immigration policies and the extension of white privileges to new immigrants would further reinforce the presumption of whiteness in America, and restrictions on national origins of immigrants put in place later would further reinforce the expected racial composition of the national identity (see Chapter 4).

With the breaking of slave-holding interests, the Republican government worked to reserve western territories for white independent agricultural producers rather than as sites to further extend the operations of capital-hungry business owners whose profits derived not from their own work but from the exploitation of wage labor. Indeed, the principle of homesteading, rooted in the philosophy of John Locke, asserted the natural right of property ownership based on labor expended to cultivate and improve the land rather than mere purchase of title.[42] Land development was asserted to be the basis for exclusive rights of ownership.

Ownership through land development promoted social equality among whites based on their capacity for labor rather than possession of adequate capital. Opposition to the concentration of capital emerged in the early American republic when the federal government routinely sold land to the highest bidder as a source of government revenue. Over time, property became concentrated among those who already possessed capital, like slaveholders and investment speculators, who owned land only for its potential increase in future value. Auctioning land inhibited actual settlement, preventing poorer, propertyless whites from opportunity for independent economic sustenance. Centered on the assumption of a vast trove of empty and uncultivated land, homesteading allowed renewed opportunity to white settlers who had been deprived of such by slaveholders (and the northern investors who had also made money from that system). Of course, homesteading for whites was itself made possible on the assumption of land dispossession of Native and Mexican Americans. It was also oriented around the new fear of desperate free blacks migrating to new territories, robbing whites of this long-awaited chance for economic advancement. In anticipation of independent land ownership, whites came to see wage labor as a prelude to upward mobility once they gathered enough capital to strike out on their own.

In sum, slavery was eliminated, but a caste system was introduced. Blacks had an inferior citizenship, segregation resulted in obstructed opportunity, and race-based norms required blacks to pay deference to all whites in all circumstances. Any hope of Reconstruction in bettering the plight of blacks or easing their transition from slavery to citizenship was blocked by the generalized intolerance for blacks, both in the North and in the South, and fear of labor opportunities they would take away from poorer whites. Reconstruction was intended to ease the transition from slavery to freedom, but the few programs initiated instead provided new sources for antiblack sentiment. Since propertyless whites had been deprived for so long, why should free blacks suddenly merit free and publicly funded benefits? Indeed, the unwillingness of Southern Democrats to change their attitudes toward blacks and the weakening of Republican resolve meant that both Democrats and Republicans in the post-Reconstruction era reinforced the elevated and protected status of whiteness. Westward expansion further accentuated the presumed whiteness of the American identity, protecting their economic interests, leaving blacks further excluded from future prosperity, and accentuating the wealth gap between whites and blacks with far-reaching consequences.

Chapter 4

A "TRUE AMERICAN" IDENTITY

Immigration and the Restriction of Citizenship

Throughout the nineteenth century, whites formed new social structures (informal and encoded, organized and impulsive) for continuing marginalization, exclusion, and outright oppression of blacks and nonwhite groups thought to be "foreign." In contrast, white immigrants from northern and western Europe were not viewed as degraded or dirty and were actively recruited to take on jobs in emerging industries of the eastern United States and take up newly acquired land forcibly taken from Native Americans in the western United States. That new territory, gains viewed as rightfully obtained from the Louisiana Purchase and the Mexican-American War, resulted in the dramatic expansion of the United States.[1] The Republican Party adopted a proimmigration stance as a strategy for further accentuating white dominance in America, and the Democratic Party, seeing the political implications of Republican policies that favored white settlers, sought to build ties with these new immigrant populations.[2] Both the South and the West welcomed Europeans who "would guarantee white electoral supremacy."[3]

Notions of "whiteness" have been especially important for determining immigration policy. Moving into the twentieth century, the surge of new immigrants from southern and eastern Europe alongside the exclusion of blacks, Mexicans, and Asians complicated questions regarding the future of white American identity, which directly affected access to opportunity and privileges. Catholics and Jews (as well as Hindus and

Muslims) had already experienced the lack of ready acceptance in the American mainstream. And as economic competition increased with the rise in the American population, so did fear and resentment rise among whites toward the growing immigrant populations contributing to it.

Because of an underlying belief shared among many Americans that the United States is a white-settler country founded by Anglo-Saxon and Nordic people, immigration policies reflected deeply held beliefs that the country belongs to them.[4] National laws were introduced to regulate the flow of different groups into the United States. The United States government would soon limit immigration, usually out of fear of unemployment for white Americans as well as the perceived threat of dangerous immigrants that threatened the well-being of native citizens already acculturated into the United States.

Americans entered the twentieth century with a heritage of long-standing debates on who was a proper American. With the new status of the formerly enslaved as free blacks and the increase in European immigration, who had the right to call themselves American? Indeed, who is *truly* American?

ASSUMED BEGINNINGS OF A NEW AMERICAN RACE

In *Letters from an American Farmer* published in 1782, J. Hector St. Jean de Crèvecoeur, a naturalized citizen from France, titled his third letter: "What Is an American?"[5] As one of the earliest immigrants to the United States, Crèvecoeur reflects ideas that swirled around immigration. Crèvecoeur idealized the opportunity available in this newly independent country, framing the new nation as the ground for the emergence of a new man: "Here are no aristocratical families, no courts, no kings, no bishops, no ecclesiastical [church-based] dominion, no invisible power giving to a few [people] a very visible [power]; no great manufacturers employing thousands, no great refinements of luxury." In America, "the poor of Europe have by some means met together. . . . Here they are become men."

What defines this new man? They are certainly Christians, "a strange religious medley that will be neither pure Catholicism nor pure Calvinism." Avoiding the aggressive sectarianism that had led to bloody wars, instead these Christians live in peace alongside each other. The American is also hardworking, contributing to the prosperity of the young nation: "There is room for everybody in America. Has he any particular talent or industry? Is he a merchant? Does he want uncultivated lands?" For Crèvecoeur, people willing to apply themselves will surely achieve the success that had eluded them in their former country: "From nothing to start into being, from a servant to the rank of a master; from being the slave of some despotic prince to become a free man, invested with lands, to which every municipal blessing is annexed! What a change indeed!" Success is assured: "Go thou and work and till [farm]. Thou shalt prosper, provided thou be just, grateful and industrious."

Crèvecoeur himself posed the question: "What then is the American, this new man? [A] strange mixture of blood which you will find in no other country." He continues: "Here individuals of all nations are melted into a new race of men." Most importantly, for Crèvecoeur, the new American is a new race of people, a fusion of the best qualities of all the other nations: "They are a mixture of English, Scotch, Irish, French, Dutch, European peoples in America Germans, and Swedes. From this promiscuous breed, that race now called Americans have arisen." Again, "The Americans were once scattered all over Europe; here they are incorporated into one of the finest systems of population which has ever appeared." Together, they accomplished the impossible: "There never was a people, situated as they are, who with so ungrateful a soil have done more in so short a time." In sum, "The American is a new man."

By the exclusion of blacks and other nonwhite minorities, it is clear that Crèvecoeur understood the new American as an amalgam of people who might differ in national origin but not in race. The new American is essentially white. The assumed whiteness of Americans by Crèvecoeur is further affirmed in the laws passed to regulate immigration to the nation. The influx of foreign-born immigrants from Europe provided the young country an opportunity to establish more firmly the boundaries of belonging.

In 1790, a few years after the publication of Crèvecoeur's letters, the second session of the first Congress approved an initial codification of rules under which persons could become citizens. The Naturalization Act of 1790 allowed citizenship to any immigrant, "being a free white person," who was deemed to possess good moral character and had resided in the United States for two years—an expansive definition that only excluded Native Americans, indentured servants, free blacks and slaves, and, later, Asians.[6] Even when the residency requirement increased to five years (and, for a brief time, fourteen years), citizenship was always racialized and combined with a notion of moral uprightness. Americans were not only *white*, they were *good*.

The abstract right of citizenship in American culture as it progressed in the nineteenth and early twentieth centuries therefore contained profound nativist assumptions of white Protestant culture. The ideal American was a white Anglo Saxon, from Britain, France, or Germany; Protestantism was assumed. Immigrants who considered themselves closer to the myth of Anglo-Saxon "pure white" not only already identified as Protestant but also turned to Protestantism when needed to buttress their authenticity and rootedness. All Irish immigrants until 1830 had been Protestants from Northern Ireland and were easily incorporated into American whiteness.[7] It was only with the crisis of the potato famine in the mid-nineteenth century that poor Catholic Irish were forced in large numbers to America. The Celts, or poor Irish, were seen as "dirty white."[8] They were judged to be racially different from native whites, and poor enough to be paired with blacks. Being Catholic and a minority, they were subject to discrimination, from anti-Catholic legislation to the violence of lynching.[9] This spike in foreign migration motivated the formation of an extreme nativist political party, which successfully elected five US senators, forty-three House members, and seven governors by 1855. Founded as the Order of the Star Spangled Banner, it was officially named the American Party, but came to be popularly labeled "the Know Nothings" (members were asked to keep their membership secret and respond to all questions, "I know nothing").[10] Among their successes was enacting a Massachusetts law denying the vote to anyone who could not read and write in English, even if they were already naturalized citizens.

During the mid-1800s, two major events allowed the Irish to become white. First, barriers to voting based on economic standings were removed.[11] Second, the Civil War encouraged immigrants from various ancestral backgrounds to join, and these became recognized as "white" through serving alongside each other in the military. After the Civil War, the Irish, gaining their new white status, intentionally positioned themselves against the status of free blacks who had been segregated in their service to the military and remained segregated in everyday life.[12]

As immigration continued throughout the nineteenth century, the abolishment of slavery heightened distinctions among ethnoracial groups, dictating social boundaries and eligibility for receiving certain goods and services. With waves of immigrants, stereotypes developed. Italians were too violent, the Jewish were too greedy, and the Irish were alcoholics and prone to insanity.[13] Native-born white Americans who considered themselves *true* Americans pushed back against blacks, not just informally through bullying and other oppressive practices but also formally in policies and laws encoding and further legitimizing restriction and exclusion, which forced distinctions not only between black and white but also between subgroups of new immigrants who sought to position themselves as deserving of opportunity and status that had been denied black Americans. Thus, black codes and Jim Crow laws channeled the direction of white ethnic identity reformation in the United States after slavery, with some groups gaining easier passage into mainstream American culture while others did not.

RESTRICTING "FOREIGN" IMMIGRANTS

The astounding growth of the United States that accelerated into the late nineteenth century is largely explained by the migration of Europeans to America. By the 1850s, immigrants accounted for one-third of population growth, and by the end of the 1890s increased further to about 40 percent of that growth.[14] Mass migration was the key to our national development. Ireland, France, Germany, Norway, the United Kingdom, and Sweden were among the leading source countries, and they were among the people moving westward to lands intended for white settlers, land that was appropriated through the forcible removal of Native Americans and then legitimated through the Louisiana Purchase and the conquest of Mexico.

These voluntary white migrants, sources of cheap labor who could fill the political boundaries of the continent, not only came on their own initiative to grasp opportunities in this new land but also were actively recruited by American business interests aligned with state and federal governments. For example, at one point during the Civil War and in response to labor shortages, President Lincoln pressed Congress to increase immigration, which prompted passage of legislation to encourage immigration in 1864. Together, corporate and government interests sent agents abroad (mostly to England and Scandinavian countries) and drew on an international labor market of white workers to develop agriculture; build new factories; occupy western territories; and expand new industries involving livestock, mining, oil, and timber. Although such labor could have been fulfilled by free blacks and former Mexican nationals in the United States, a pervasive nativist bias resulted in denying blacks and Latinos these opportunities, and even gave preferential treatment to newer white immigrants over native-born blacks. Soon, Asians would also bear the brunt of this racialized exclusion.

As patterns of source countries for migration shifted, congressional legislation crafted immigration policies as a reactionary response to the astounding new flows of people. First, whereas immigration stories typically emphasize Europeans arriving on the East Coast, workers from China and Japan came to the United States on the West Coast. The flow of Chinese alone was significant starting in the early 1800s; Chinese labor helped in mining, agriculture, service work, and the building of the transcontinental railroad.[15] Most settled in California. However, the Chinese were viewed by West Coast whites as a threat to their livelihood. The Chinese became scapegoats for the exploitative labor conditions experienced by poor whites, and white economic fears were projected onto Chinese immigrants under the guise that they were stealing jobs from hard-working Americans. This fear was accentuated when Chinese workers were employed as strikebreakers, hurting protections and progressive reforms sought by white wage earners.[16] The irony of white workers fighting against economic exploitation at the same time that they willingly ignore the oppressions of nonwhite workers has remained a persistent theme throughout all of American history.[17]

Already in the 1850s, local and state laws discriminated against the Chinese by imposing taxes, barring them from public schools, subjecting them to various forms of abuse, and projecting a distinctly unwelcoming ethos to the American mainstream.[18] When more liberal politicians discussed the potential of applying the Fifteenth Amendment to the Chinese, which would extend to them the right to vote, other politicians objected based on both racial difference and religious difference.

In 1871, to counter efforts by Republican Senator Charles Sumner and other legislators, Republican Senator William Morris Stewart from Nevada strenuously argued that the enfranchisement of the Fifteenth Amendment to blacks was justified not only because they were American-born but also because they were Christian. In contrast, allowing Chinese any power in American politics would give our institutions over to "pagans." As with the Catholic Irish, race and religion were intertwined, and both were used to justify exclusion. The initiative failed, and all further attempts to admit Chinese as eligible for naturalization also failed. [19]

Yet these political exclusions were not enough to satisfy white wage earners. White citizens from the West aggressively lobbied politicians in Washington, DC, to protect their interests and leverage the authority of the state to enforce a total ban on Chinese labor. Unique in American history to that point, and after many years of restrictions at the local and state levels, the Chinese Exclusion Act of 1882 explicitly targeted a specific group to prevent Chinese from immigrating to the United States. The Act also dislocated the Chinese from their residences, denied their visas, and deported them back to their home country. Had it not been for this extraordinary legislation, the Chinese would have been a much more populous and far more integrated immigrant group in the United States, likely leading to civil rights challenges against discrimination sooner in our history.

Asians continued to be a target for immigration restriction for decades. For example, the Japanese population had swelled from about 2,000 migrants in the 1890s to 130,000 in the 1900s. Instead of an explicit ban, the U.S. government cleverly entered an agreement with the Japanese government, asking them to not issue visas to citizens wanting to travel to America. This "Gentlemen's Agreement" of 1907 halted the immigration of Japanese laborers (except upper-class Japanese). Japanese workers were turned away because they were believed to be efficient and smart laborers who would deprive white Americans of economic opportunity. The West Coast feared the Japanese because poorer whites felt they could not compete with people who were perceived as possessing a superior work ethic, frugality, and ingenuity. The Japanese were believed to be a racial group over whom whites held no natural advantage. In virtually every endeavor, it was said white Americans were no match for the Japanese. Thus, Japanese immigration was restricted not because of notions of inferiority but out of the conviction that this group would usurp the opportunities that would be otherwise available to unskilled white Americans.

Throughout the nineteenth and into the twentieth century, presidents, Congress, and the Supreme Court committed to a series of decisions that both presumed and advanced notions of racial superiority and inferiority by defining who was legally "white." Although the passage of the Fourteenth Amendment granted birthright citizenship to blacks, even the most recent immigrant understood that a chasm of difference in privilege and opportunity stood between whites and blacks, motivating them to ensure their status as "white." More often than not, this standard of acceptability was associated with skin color. Were Japanese or Mexican immigrants "white"? After a series of Supreme Court decisions, the argument for skin color was substituted for other potential claims to citizenship. Still, the Supreme Court made it clear that the definition of *whiteness* could not be made based on faithful service in the US Army or long-term ancestry from Caucasian regions (*US v. Bhagat Singh Thind*) or the lightness of one's skin or even the extent of a person's long-standing residency in America or demonstrated upright moral characters (*Takao Ozawa v. US*). Eventually, the Court frankly admitted that the definition of *white* was based solely on long-standing custom of which persons were accepted to be white in a popular, common-sense manner. From the latter 1800s through the early 1900s, Hawaiians, Armenians, Burmese, Filipinos, Koreans, Syrians, Turks, and Afghanis were among the groups unable to be legally recognized as white because mainstream social opinion understood them to not be white. In short, race is not a biological category but a legally constructed concept, with profound implications for education, employment, ownership, and residency.

Although the United States has profited from migrant labor—just as it has profited by the expropriated labor of the enslaved—there has been little incentive to protect the well-being of those deemed to be "foreign" while working in the United States. Over time, the United States granted immigrants allowances to enter the country as cheap labor but often denied them basic rights of employment or ownership and treated them poorly. Local, state, and federal mandates often proceeded to exclude and deport them either when they were perceived to be a threat or after they had used up the labor that was needed. In the case of the Chinese, persons of Chinese descent were legally unable to become citizens of the United States until the Chinese Exclusion Act was reversed in 1943. And persons of Japanese descent were not granted rights of citizenship until the McCarran-Walter Act of 1952. In both cases, the quota allowed for immigration from their home countries was miniscule in relation to the total number of residents and children of residents already in the United States.

ENTER EUGENICS, THE SCIENCE OF RACE

The ban on Chinese migration and the threat of the Japanese highlight a persistent issue in American immigration: the supposed *unassimilability* of certain groups. In the midst of political and economic decisions on migration, scientific pronouncements buttressed the emerging prejudices of people, adding a new dimension to the established racism of the United States. The most advanced scientific discussions of the time believed that certain types of people were physiologically superior. The study of *eugenics*—a long-term project among academics and policy makers purporting to accurately measure and catalog racial distinctions—was developed from the later 1800s and well into the mid-1900s. Eugenics was considered to be the most advanced scientific endeavor on the study of human beings and consumed the attention of national governments all over the world. As Robert DeCourcy Ward, a Harvard professor and cofounder of the Immigration Restriction League, wrote in 1913, "The day of the sociologist is passing, and the day of the biologist has come."

Eugenicists sought to carefully, systematically, and scientifically prove a moral hierarchy among races, categorizing them as endowed with favorable or unfavorable traits in arenas of intelligence, temperament, mental illness, propensity toward criminality and other aspects of moral character. As one doctor said, the biologically weak "could not escape the laws of heredity."[20] Teams of eugenicists compared human races to breeds of dogs and horses and, armed with rulers, scales, color pallets, and accounting tables, asserted that certain types of people, bearing genetic stock pinpointed to geographic regions, were physiologically superior. This biological argument culminated in deliberate attempts on the part of politicians at nation building.

A great nation required inclusion of only people representing the strongest race. Those prejudged to be degraded, savage, or "unruly"— less able to be civilized and productively contribute to the commonweal—were stigmatized as perpetually foreign and unassimilable. For eugenicists, biology was destiny, and their biological argument influenced powerful political leaders of the day and convinced them that building a great nation required the inclusion of only people representing the strongest race and the purposeful exclusion of all others. *Mongrelization*, a term that became synonymous with nonwhite immigration and subsequent interbreeding with the majority race, posed a threat to the nation's very existence. African Americans, Chinese, Japanese, Mexicans, and darker-colored migrants from the Mediterranean and southern Europe were targets of a crusade to purify and keep the blood of America pure. Predictably, the federal government established immigration policies based on the belief that whole groups should be excluded because they were deemed to be less than suitable for full membership as Americans.[21]

At the turn of the twentieth century, sociologist Edward A. Ross presented the concept of "race suicide" as a pseudoscientific term, simply defined as the inevitable disappearance of a racial group when its birth rate drops below its death rate.[22] A racial group unable to replace itself through fertility would be overcome by the migration of other racial groups and ultimately lead to the dying out of that "race." Although it seemed to be a neutral term, *race suicide* was dictated as a warning to "old stock Americans" who were believed to be in the process of being replaced by more fertile immigrant "races."[23] Today, such pseudoscientific notions are associated with Nazi Germany and their program of racial cleansing; however, it is well established that these policies were first developed in the United States, and that such beliefs of biological superiority were largely supported by conservative Christians and affected their attitudes toward sex, marriage, and contraception.[24]

WHO BELONGS IN AMERICA

White immigrants from northwestern Europe were seen as more easily assimilated than southern and eastern Europeans, Hispanics, and Asian groups. Consequently, these latter groups experienced far more resistance to immigration. Katherine Benton-Cohen's *Inventing the Immigration Problem* explores the influence of the 1907 Dillingham Commission and their reports that compared "old" immigrants with "new" immigrants to assess who should become eligible for citizenship.[25] In deriving their representations of different groups, members of the commission sought scientific reports and ethnographic insights on new waves of immigrants, and especially focused on assessing immigrants' contribution to the economic stability of the United States, such as whether they were physically capable of keeping a job.

To be clear, members of the Dillingham Commission were focused not on getting rid of *illegal* immigrants within the United States but rather on restricting immigrants deemed unfit for the growing country. Already by 1896, arguments were offered in the Senate to impose a literacy test on all immigrants, buttressed by racial arguments gaining ascendency in Western Europe and the United States. Echoing Crèvecoeur's "new man," Senator Henry Cabot Lodge asserted that British, Dutch, French, Irish, and Swedish descendants had "welded together" into a more excellent "new race" known as the American people.[26] The Dillingham Commission sought to evaluate such assessments and combined forty-two reports that explored social Darwinism, eugenics, and pseudoscientific theory as to who was the superior race in the United States and who is a "true" American.

The attributes of a "true" American included being physically fit, non–foreign born, and white passing. True Americans were also disciplined, industrious, and hard-working laborers who avoided becoming a drain on public resources, whether through criminality, mental illness, or unemployment. In its entirety, and consistent with the prevailing assumptions of intellectual and political elites at the time, the work of the Commission provided a xenophobic picture of the most recent southern and eastern Europeans to justify a restrictive policy already being demanded. One such demand came from Prescott Hall, cofounder of the Immigration Restriction League, who produced a widely distributed pamphlet in 1908 stating that immigration regulations were imperative because "wars and pestilences no longer eliminate the unfit as formerly."[27]

Buttressed by studies like that produced by the Dillingham Commission, a series of restrictive immigration acts in 1917, 1918, 1921, and

1924 drastically reduced the number of immigrants entering the United States.[28] As President Calvin Coolidge—who signed the Immigration Act of 1924 into law—stated in his first State of the Union address, "America must be kept American." Quotas were established to limit the percentage of further migrants based on the number of foreign-born *already* in the country. Annual quotas for each nationality were set at 2 percent of the number of persons of that nationality in the United States. But to avoid the surge of unwanted immigrants around the turn of the century, legislators cleverly ignored the 1920, 1910, and 1900 censuses, deciding instead to base quotas on figures from 1890—which is both *after* the Chinese Exclusion Act and *before* the abrupt rise of southern and eastern European immigration.

This decision of which census to use as a basis for immigration quotas was especially consequential for determining the future racial composition of the United States. For example, because of the Chinese Exclusion Act of 1882, the number of Chinese in the United States was very low; the 2 percent quota restriction meant that further migration of Chinese would forever be limited to a several dozen Chinese at most. In addition, the ancestry designation of applicants for legal migration was based not on their current citizenship but on their ancestral origin such that, for example, an African or Chinese or Jewish person (designated as *Hebrew*) who was a citizen of France was counted against the *African* or *Chinese* or *Hebrew* quota limits, not the limits on France.[29] As Daniel Tichenor, a leading scholar of immigration, concludes, "the primary intent and effect of their national origins quota system was manifestly racist."[30]

Guided by notions of racial inferiority, these restrictive immigration acts consisted of alternative ways to exclude people now legally considered to be unfit based on national, sometimes political, grounds. By preserving an ideal of homogeneity, entire categories of people were excluded from migrating to the United States. Most of the restricted groups were from Asian and southeastern European nations based on the belief that they possessed undesirable traits. When immigration was abruptly reduced, it separated families who were now unable to unite in a new land. The 1917 Asiatic Barred Zone Act, created by legislators who were alert to the dangers of "the Yellow Peril" and the uncontested belief that such people groups could not assimilate, prevented immigration from a vast number of countries from the Asian-Pacific region.

Legislation in 1921, the Emergency Quota Act, effectively blocked the large influx of groups like Jews and Italians and specifically set down an immigration quota such that only 3 percent of the total population of any ethnic group already in the country in 1910 could be admitted. Anticommunist sentiments were a factor, and Jews and Italians were seen as potentially communists, anarchists, or sympathizers; Senator Thomas J. Heflin called it "a wall against bolshevism, which is seeking to aid a world movement by spreading its poison here." A clause that invoked a literacy prerequisite for prospective adult immigrants further added to the capriciousness of who might be admitted. This Act, the first to be passed in response to the Dillingham Commission, immediately cut immigration from Poland by 70 percent, Yugoslavia by 74 percent, and Italy by 82 percent.

The 1924 Immigration Act (also known as the Johnson-Reed Act) proved most consequential. The Act pushed the previously passed 1921 law to limit southern and eastern Europeans much further by making the implicit explicit, dropping the quota from 3 percent to 2 percent and moving the quota baseline from the 1910 census to the 1890 census, which favored whites over nonwhites and guaranteed that only 16 percent of all immigrants were from southern and eastern Europe. The details intentionally targeted years when northern and western European immigration was still strong, and the less desirable nationalities had not yet migrated in larger volume. Although congressional members expressed opposition to this new bill, believing that using the 1890 census was "deliberately discriminatory," Senator David Reed, coauthor of the bill, said, "I think most of us are reconciled to the idea of discrimination." He added, "I think the American people want us to discriminate."[31] Representative Robert E. Lee Allen of West Virginia said, "The primary reason for the restriction of the alien stream is the necessity for purifying and keeping pure the blood of America."[32] The 1924 Act also established the US Border Patrol to enforce restrictions against Asians, prostitutes, anarchists, and many others who had been categorically prohibited from entering the United States.[33] It passed 308 to 62 in the House and 69 to 9 in the Senate.

With the passage of these legislative acts, immigration slowed to a trickle. Before 1924 quotas, between 1901 and 1920, around 475,000 people immigrated from southern and eastern Europe compared with 145,000 from northern and western Europe. In the thirty-year period after quotas, from 1921 until 1950, the numbers were much lower, with just 67,000 from northern and western Europe and only 47,000 from southern and eastern Europe, a move that effectively separated family members who had delayed migration. Together, these Acts reduced US immigration by 85 percent.[34]

With the enactment of these decisions, the new Americans envisioned by J. Hector St. Jean de Crèvecoeur became even more established. Those groups who had immigrated first, coming from England, Germany, and Scandinavia, were embraced as more fundamentally American than newer immigrants, like Greeks, Italians, Jews, and Poles, who were seen as weaker European stock. The Irish were often discriminated against based on prejudices held by earlier American immigrants prior to large-scale Irish migration; yet, as their numbers grew and as the line between white and nonwhite was solidified, the Irish were accepted as white by the early part of the twentieth century.[35] In the coming years, especially during World War II, white Europeans' descendants began to mix together (e.g., through occupational groupings, public schooling, and service in the armed forces), bringing an end to discrimination against US-born eastern and southern Europeans while keeping foreign restrictions in place.

A redefinition of what counted as "white" solidified thanks to fewer "fresh," newly arrived immigrants; the intermarriage of native-born second- and third-generation immigrants; and the post–World War II baby boom that resulted in millions of children who were further removed from their ancestral heritage, and who thus lost their native languages and were unfamiliar with their pre-American customs. The white-based racial hierarchy embedded in immigration policy remained intact until the Hart-Celler Act of 1965.

THE LUMPS IN AMERICA'S MELTING POT

The decisive factor that determined which ethnoracial groups could immigrate into the United States was based on notions of who would be the most easily assimilated into white American culture. This was the foundation of the "melting pot" theory: that many cultures could come together under one flag, leaving old loyalties and languages behind in favor of Americanization. It was not an embrace of diversity but rather a presumption that certain groups were deemed eligible for this process.

Permitted groups would presumably improve America's racial stock, while a succession of policies weeded out supposedly weaker, inferior, nonwhite groups. As the source countries of migration to America shifted, so did the perceptions of who belonged in America. These policy shifts fueled an ideology of *nativism*—a cluster of beliefs regarding who qualified as more genuine and authentic Americans—which John Higham's classic book *Strangers in the Land* demonstrated as a powerful sentiment leading up to the 1924 Immigration Act.[36]

American notions of immigration were now deeply rooted in common-sense narratives of immigration that discounted past exclusions and were buttressed by ideas of the superiority and inferiority of groups based on "scientific racism," such that northwestern Europeans and their descendants in America, Canada, and Australia were thought to be the races most gifted with intelligence, character, and the capacity for self-government. Eastern and southern Europeans, meanwhile, were depicted as racially inferior and incapable, by means of heredity, of assimilating American values and beliefs. This is reminiscent of early postabolition ideas of amalgamation and the notion that certain groups, like Native Americans, could be groomed to be integrated within the white race, while others, those of African descent, could not be amalgamated and would preferably be colonized elsewhere (see Chapter 2).

So, although many European groups were close in geographic origin, some were considered by American standards to be white while others were not. Southern Europeans (like Greeks and Italians) and eastern Europeans (like Slavs and Hungarians)—those with darker skins—struggled well into the mid-twentieth century to be accepted. Jews fleeing persecution in Poland, Russia, and Romania contributed to the stream of immigrants and suffered as the object of prejudice. The switch of source countries was sudden and dramatic. For example, from 1881 through 1890, the United States received 3.8 million northern and western European migrants compared with 1 million from southern and eastern Europe. In the next decade, from 1891 to 1900, migrants from the north and west of Europe dropped by half to 1.6 million while those from southern and eastern countries nearly doubled to 1.9 million, bringing people from countries like Albania, Greece, Hungary, Serbia, Slovakia, and the Ukraine. And by the decade of 1901 through

1910, migration from northern and eastern Europe remained steady at 1.9 million while migration from the south and east jumped to 6.1 million.[37]

Remember that by this point, the West Coast had already clamped down on Asian migration from China and Japan. Now, the East Coast rallied the government to reconsider the extent of open borders. The tired and poor who arrived, often destitute and malnourished, were considered unsanitary, with lower intelligence and greater propensity toward mental illness and violent crime. Those outside the acceptable boundaries of the definition of "American" clustered in dense communities in poor urban centers, often because of socially and financially enforced segregation. These were the immigrants who threatened the American way of life. Americans feared mongrelization with these miserable people from southern and eastern European countries such that the "melting pot" was seen in an entirely negative light. Those who continued to see biology as destiny were confounded by immigrants who exhibited patriotism and high moral character, causing new forms of marginalization to occur.

President Theodore ("Teddy") Roosevelt, first elected in 1901, aspired for the American government to offer "the promise of economic opportunity and political freedom to all citizens, irrespective of their racial, religious, or cultural background."[38] Yet Roosevelt's stated ideals were at odds with both his personal convictions and his enacted policies. He deliberately omitted the value of black soldiers from accounts of the victories at Kettle and San Juan Hills and dismissed the successful collaboration of blacks and whites. It was Teddy Roosevelt who implemented in 1907 the policy barring further immigration of Japanese workers, emulating the Chinese Exclusion Act of 1882 and spurred by the fear of successful assimilation of Japanese and the consequent displacement of poor, unskilled whites. Also under his administration, immigrants were asked to meet many requirements to be granted citizenship, including living in the United States five consecutive years, speaking English (despite there being no official language in America), being neither polygamists nor anarchists, having two witnesses vouch for sound moral character, and committing to adherence to the principles of the Constitution.

Roosevelt made explicit the idea that immigrants were expected to Americanize themselves through rejection of their former nationalities and native cultural practices. When reluctant, they were deemed to have "excessive foreignness." The idea of an enemy within had been a rallying point for those desiring to see America as a nation of whiteness. Even those groups who could become American in Roosevelt's eyes were expected to rid themselves of any lingering cultural traditions, celebrations, and political ideologies. Even if "white," if a person refuses to strip his or her native culture upon arriving to the United States, he or she is insufficiently assimilated, too foreign, and un-American. After all, Teddy Roosevelt said in 1907,

> [W]e should insist that if the immigrant who comes here in good faith becomes an American and assimilates himself to us, he shall be treated on an exact equality with everyone else, for it is an outrage to discriminate against any such man because of creed, or birthplace, or origin. But this is predicated upon the person's becoming in every facet an American, and nothing but an American.

Later, in 1916, the former president repeatedly asserted that the immigrant who does not become an American in good faith "is out of place." Complete assimilation was expected of immigrants, and ideas emerged that some groups could be assimilated into American culture more easily than others. Although exclusionary attitudes and restrictive policies were defended as a protection of American ideology—especially protection against anarchists and communists—the correlation between immigration acceptance and skin color is undeniable. Furthermore, once accepted, the immigrant must devote the utmost loyalty to the United States, shedding any former culture, moving toward a popular understanding of American identity. The supposed uniqueness and superiority of American culture, its language, religion, and even skin complexion, were not to be tainted.

Roosevelt believed his plans for the extension of an American empire overseas could provide a means of forging a united American public through war against foreign nations. Teddy Roosevelt hoped that war would unite Americans around a sense of civic nationalism. He had seen empirical evidence of such unity among the Rough Riders during the Spanish-American War and was determined that another grand, generation-defining war could bring his countrymen together, both on the battlefield and on the home front. Roosevelt claimed the soldiers had "ample opportunity to prove their mettle and strengthen their nation through heroic combat against a savage foe." He once wrote, "The military tent where they all sleep side by side will rank next to the public schools among the great agents of democraticatization."[39] Uniting against a common enemy would lead to the assimilation of immigrants into American society: soldiers would fight side by side, trusting the man next to them, no matter what the race, ethnicity, nationality, or religion.

The multiethnic mixture of soldiers in wars like the Civil War and the World Wars did indeed provide paths of assimilation among those ethnic groups that came to be accepted as white; yet blacks remained segregated, just as Roosevelt had excluded blacks from his own regiment. Segregation was enforced, whereas those deemed to be more assimilable (e.g., Italians, Germans, and Dutch) fought alongside longer-term native American whites. This segregation of the ranks continued for much of the century. The greatness of revealing a racial superiority through battle was limited to Euro-Americans. Throughout American history, the ongoing segregation of black soldiers had consequences for the developing racial hierarchy the black soldiers encountered when they returned home. So, although Roosevelt reminded Americans of ideals such as liberty, democracy, and self-determination, he contradicted those efforts by implying that such privileges were race-based.

Roosevelt's empire-expanding, nation-building project was not shared by Woodrow Wilson. But Wilson did share Roosevelt's racial prejudices. Wilson was unsympathetic to ongoing ethnic or racial oppression during his administration. For example, when Wilson arrived in Washington, DC, he famously ordered federal government agencies to be segregated. Black employees were separated from other workers, affecting offices, restrooms, and cafeterias. Some black employees' jobs were downgraded, while others were simply let go. In spite of this, Wilson held to a romanticized notion of the greatness of America and established the Committee on Public Information (CPI), which distributed news, propaganda, and press releases to build patriotic support for Wilson's war, World War I. In the Great War, immigrants constituted about 18 percent of the army, which was far higher than their percentage in the total American population. Yet these same immigrant groups questioned the idealized America of the CPI propaganda, seeing a disjunction between the America they were fighting for and the America in which they lived. White supremacists also assisted the Bureau of Investigations, which was tasked with monitoring immigrants, particularly Catholics, Jews, and Japanese, as threats. Perceived "un-American" activities were attacked on all fronts; information on "radicals" was collected, as well as information on anyone that may have "excessive foreignness."[40] And it was under Wilson's term in office (1913–1921) that several legislative acts were signed to restrict immigration from southern and eastern Europe, Asia, and Africa.

THE BENEFITS OF WHITENESS

As restrictive laws regulating immigration took hold and the rates of already white-designated ethnic groups took root and intermarried, a common-sense understanding of whiteness and who it excluded was enforced by legal statute and preserved in the demographics of the country. Some groups celebrated the openness and welcome of the country their parents and grandparents adopted, but others found the American "melting pot" to be racially and religiously selective. Immigration policy effectively mainstreamed a panethnic whiteness in America. The high regard for whiteness not only included assumptions regarding the destiny of biology but also the acceptance of certain cultural, economic, and political norms.

For example, for many, switching to Protestantism was a sign of the acculturation and "whitenization" of immigrant groups. Domestic Protestant missionary agencies dedicated funds to aid in this assimilation process, commissioning a steady stream of zealous workers toward evangelization efforts across the country that included educating both indigenous and immigrant communities in English, proper hygiene, and western forms of dress. Urban churches used Sunday Schools and local charity outreach to help with needs and inculcate their Christian moral standards. When they established their own local churches, new migrants were especially eager to find belonging and the benefits of full participation in American culture. Whenever possible, immigrants counted themselves as not being "black"—in other words, not being associated with the stigma of longer-established yet systematically degraded populations of black citizens. Thus the switch from native ancestry in language and customs of food, dress, or religion functioned as a conscientious step toward assimilation into the American political main-stream. In contrast, those of Mexican, Asian, and other ancestries found that being labeled as "not white" carried significant cultural costs.

Nativism restricted access to social welfare programs intended for white Americans only.[41] Therefore, immigration restrictions prompted changes in identity, switching from native ancestry in language and customs of food, dress, or religion toward a conscientious assimilation into the American political mainstream. Of course, such sentiments resulted in immigrants changing their names, some by choice and others by fiat when they were told "this is your name" in English. More than patriotism, nonwhite Americans understood that their failure to achieve whiteness meant they would be systematically denied access to generous economic programs; those prejudged to be more "savage" or less able to be civilized were stigmatized as perpetually foreign and unassimilable. So, although some migrant groups were able to preserve a cultural distinctiveness apart from their white, Protestant counter-parts, it was not easy or welcomed; the children and grandchildren of those groups often faded into the white Christian mainstream to the extent that their phenotypical characteristics allowed.

By the early 1930s, a straightforward racial hierarchy was estab-lished, prizing a Nordic ideal that captured a wide range of white Euro-peans who were legitimized by common sense and by eugenic "science" of their authenticity as members of a supposedly unitary Caucasian race.[42] The restrictions of immigration, buttressed by the segregation of blacks through Jim Crow laws, contributed to race in America as largely binary: white versus nonwhite. For example, Franklin Delano Roose-velt's New Deal policies provided few benefits to black Americans. New Deal programs overlooked people of color even as they embraced the most recently naturalized immigrants. The Social Security Act of 1935 did not appear overtly racist because it appeared to benefit both white and black Americans. However, criteria for inclusion was based not on *individuals* but their *occupations*, and domestics and farm workers were intentionally excluded by the Act; African Americans held the majority of such jobs, which left "blacks twice as likely as whites to be excluded from social insurance."[43]

Another intentional benefit of whiteness concerns how the federal government policy affected the ability of blacks and whites to own a home. The Federal Housing Administration (FHA), established by

Franklin Delano Roosevelt as part of the New Deal, sought to provide the means for home ownership by extending credit with lower down payments and allowing monthly payments to extend for a much longer period. But black citizens were generally not considered viable candidates because they were too "risky." Instead, the FHA decided they would support only whites, believing that black homeownership would decrease property values and that blacks constituted too high a risk. In partnership with financial institutions, their work resulted in residential maps that indicated by color their assessments of risks for sustaining the property values of loans.[44] Zoning by racial composition of neighborhoods was justified on the pretense of preventing race-based conflict. Even when blacks were able to demonstrate their ability to afford down payments and monthly installments, they were denied mortgages. Blacks were explicitly considered to be threats to property values, and areas with even a modest percentage of black households were colored red, a practice known as "redlining." Even when a single black family bought a house in a "good" neighborhood, it would lead to severe price drops, resulting in changing assessments of risks to property values, thereby changing neighborhood color coding from green to yellow to red. So whites kept blacks out through regulations, at times violently, and if black ownership could not be prevented, "white flight" would occur.

Levittown, a famous housing development in New Jersey, was entirely developed based on this race-based system of privilege. Banks refused to provide the credit to build such ambitious suburban housing developments without a guarantee regarding the value of the properties, so they insisted on white-only neighborhoods. Blacks were prohibited from desirable neighborhoods through racially specific restrictive covenants barring owners from selling to minorities. In a segregated, white neighborhood such as Levittown, whites never interacted with people of color. The consequences of these policies not only affected homeownership and the social and economic advantages that accrued to whites, it also shielded whites from exposure to the practical social and economic difficulties experienced by blacks and other minorities in their everyday lives.[45] Even now, whites remain the most socially segregated ethnoracial group in America.[46]

The implications of granting legitimacy to persons as white, and therefore more truly American, has always translated into various programs for employment, ownership of property, eligibility for loans, access to business capital, and other economic opportunities. Although income and education gaps between whites and nonwhites have long been known, there has been little effort to account for them or bridge them through public policy, placing more of the blame for lack of advancement on disadvantaged groups themselves. Such neglect in understanding has been evident in discussions regarding native-born Mexican Americans, Puerto Ricans, multigenerational Chinese and Japanese, and Muslims of all national origins. While whites received "credit," "subsidies" or "relief," people of color received "welfare," a discriminatory wording for economic programs that distinguish deserving versus undeserving benefits on the basis of race.[47]

MEXICAN MIGRANTS AND THE SOUTHERN BOARDER

A critical issue in the growth of the American population revolved around the growth of industries and changing sources of labor, and much of the tension between white and nonwhite groups was the result of economic concerns rooted in a fear of foreigners stealing "American" (meaning "white") jobs.[48] A case in point is the use of Mexican seasonal labor in the southwest. For much of the nineteenth and twentieth centuries after the annexation of Mexico, Mexican migrant workers freely flowed to and from jobs across the American border. The controversy regarding this labor has persisted, with business owners quietly continuing to hire immigrants for needed positions in agriculture, construction, mining, and railroad maintenance, both legally and illegally. Moreover, the racial and social hierarchy placing "true Americans" over Mexicans—including over long-term Mexican-American citizens—remains.

Tension between Mexico and the United States can be traced back to 1848, when the Treaty of Guadalupe Hidalgo ended the Mexican-American War (see Chapter 2). The treaty left Mexico crippled, with a skewed political and economic relationship with the United States that persists today. Concern with controlling immigration at the southern border of the United States was raised during the Great Depression, when economic and racial tensions were especially high. Americans blamed Mexican immigrants for their financial "pressures" and saw deportation as an advisable solution to their problems.[49] In 1931, the first official "repatriation train" brought four hundred undocumented immigrants back to Mexico, and over that decade, schools, local sheriffs, social workers, Mexican consulates, and US federal agents worked together to intimidate Mexican communities, successfully deporting about two-thirds of all Mexican immigrants in America.[50] As with the Chinese in the nineteenth century, immigration control and deportation were reactionary measures taken under the guise of easing economic pressures.

One can better understand the United States's history of immigration control and, eventually, the criminalization of immigrants by focusing on immigration from Mexico. When the federal government became more strict about policing the southern border in the later 1930s by establishing more checkpoints, more federal agents, and more fencing, business owners panicked, appealing to the federal government to secure their workforce. As the porous border was tightened, exceptions for big business owners through the Bracero Program allowed for a continuing steady flow of Mexican labor from 1942 until 1964. Through this period, the Bracero Program allowed an estimated 4.5 million Mexican workers to enter into the United States to work on farms and plantations for low wages on short-term contracts. About 450,000 temporary workers crossed the border annually, with most of the immigrants returning home after the growing season was over. Although the number of Mexican migrants is astounding, their stay was "temporary and circular, and, hence, invisible to citizens."[51]

During the Great Depression, Mexican pay was cut from 35 cents to just 15 cents and their hours were reduced, so Mexican workers organized for better wages, housing, and working conditions. But the Immigration and Naturalization Service (INS) was pressured by business and government leaders to deport the organizers to avoid costly changes for such a cheap labor source—except during crop season, when the INS eased up on all search and deportation processes so as not to threaten the use of workers and avoid damaging valuable crops.[52] Eventually, the Civil Rights movement led the federal government to believe that the program exploited the work of Mexicans. Rather than improve conditions, the Bracero Program was abruptly cut, ignoring efforts to assert worker rights or increase pay. A once mutually beneficial migration of seasonal labor from Mexico to the United States was criminalized by 1964. Although the cycle was "largely invisible" and "innocuous," once politicians recognized the political advantages of "demonizing Latino immigrants and illegal migration," it became a highly visible and feared system, and the program was shut down.[53]

The INS was transferred from the Department of Labor to the Department of Justice after 1940. This meant that issues of citizenship and immigration were now viewed through the lens of criminality rather than labor. Moreover, the locus of criminality was placed on persons crossing the border, not on the business owners who hired them. Therefore, the end of the Bracero Program in 1964 did not stop American business from hiring Mexicans. Instead, the end of this moderately successful guest worker program created a more permanent residence of undocumented immigrants who took the risk of crossing the border, a risk that grew more significant over the years. The desire for cheap labor kept the flow of migration going; it was just made more difficult for Mexicans.[54] Added to border crossings was an increase in the migration of Central and South Americans through Mexico, many of whom were fleeing persecution, dictatorship, economic deprivation, domestic unrests, and civil wars.

In her book, *From Deportation to Prison: The Politics of Immigration Enforcement in Post-Civil Rights America*, Patrisia Macías-Rojas reveals an intriguing connection between mass incarceration and the management of Mexican migration.[55] She highlights how the border state of Arizona grew to be a prominent "pro-business" state in the early twentieth century, one that fostered alliances between conservative state politicians and expanding corporate structures and took advantage of the population boom in the Sun Belt. Although Arizona had been staunchly Democratic in the 1930s and 1940s and New Deal regulations had long protected the rights of workers, the Republican Party successfully fought against "New Deal liberalism" to push for free-market policies of low taxes, antiunionism, cheap land, and nongovernment intervention regarding employment and other processes. With the growth of conservatism, the fight against the New Deal included law-and-order, "tough-on-crime" platforms that pulled away from struggles for civil rights, including protections for short-term Mexican migrants and longer-term Mexican-American citizens. In the southwestern borderlands, Mexicans had long been "viewed as unfit for citizenship, not fully 'American,' despite their historical presence in the United States. Yet in contrast to anti-Black criminalization, they were subject to 'illegalization' that associated Mexicans not with innate criminality but with perpetual foreignness as 'aliens.'"[56]

The 1964 presidential run by Arizona Senator Barry Goldwater became a watershed moment, as he took his conservative, law-and-order, anti–New Deal, and anti–civil rights state policies to the nation. (For example, analysts agree that the Goldwater campaign laid the foundation for Ronald Reagan's win for the presidency.) Indeed, the 1964 Goldwater campaign marked the point at which civil rights concerns and attention to the oppression of blacks in America were entirely dropped from the Republican platform. So although the party of Lincoln had fought to save the Union against the Confederacy and "Radical Republicans" had forcefully advocated for the rights of recently freed blacks, which provided the impetus for the passing of the Thirteenth, Fourteenth, and Fifteenth Amendments, the divisions within the mid-twentieth-century Republican Party caused by sympathy for poor and landless whites as well as the need to gain votes from the constituencies of Southern Democrats meant that Republicans grew tired of advocating for blacks (see Chapter 3).[57] Neither Republicans nor Democrats were sympathetic to the plight of blacks for most of the period from the 1880s to the 1960s. In the 1960s, Democratic President Lyndon B. Johnson, who was not elected but became president after the assassination of President John F. Kennedy, was credited with prominent support for the plight of blacks and minorities, ushering in a new political alignment. White, Southern Democrats, the so-called "Dixiecrats" who opposed civil rights, changed their party affiliation to Republican, and the Democratic Party became the party most attentive to the plight of African Americans.

Following the sentiments of the Goldwater campaign, probusiness policies became aligned with opposition to civil rights, which translated into an emphasis on crime. After all, the agitations, legislation, and "riots" committed by civil rights advocates were seen as disruptive to business interests, pushing all aspects of corporate life to reorganize their hiring, promotion, and service to avoid demonstrably racist actions. With the focus on crime, federal monies flowed toward criminal enforcement, resulting in more broad-based support for fighting crime than for fighting racism and oppression.

In 1965, Mexican migration was further affected by the Immigration and Nationality Act (dubbed the "Hart-Celler Act" to distinguish it from a long line of similarly titled legislation). This Act attempted to formalize equality and nondiscrimination by imposing the same numerical quotas of 20,000 immigrants for every country. Before 1965, aliens with ten years' continuous residence in Mexico and other countries from the Western Hemisphere were exempt from American quotas. Under the new limit, all available visas for Mexico were quickly exhausted because Mexico had been using about 45,000 visas annually— the only nation to use substantially more than the limit imposed.[58] Overnight, the regular flow of Mexicans across the border became mostly unauthorized migrants. The 1965 Act completely ignored the unique contexts of work, family, seasonal labor, and entanglements of business with Mexican migrants. The change in immigration resulted in an increase in what the federal government termed *surreptitious entry* in violation of federal laws. New legislation and abruptly enforced restrictive quotas gave rise to "illegal immigrants" who could not suddenly press pause on their source of income. Thus, the Mexican-sourced and American business–funded "migratory flow did not disappear but simply continued without authorization or documents."[59]

In the 1970s, the weakness of Mexico's own economy motivated the country to encourage its citizens to find work across the border. And businesses in the United States continued to depend on Mexican labor. Although jobs were insecure and low level, with no opportunity for advancement or citizenship, migrants found that low-wage work in the United States was better than no-wage work in Mexico, especially when their own government encouraged it. However, tensions increased because these undocumented workers threatened many union jobs, resulting in union leaders demanding that the federal government prosecute businesses hiring Mexican citizens. Unions like the American Federation of Labor and Congress of Industrial Organizations sought to discourage illegal hiring and targeted employers, not migrant workers. Indeed, the desire for business owners to avoid sanctions for their hiring processes in part motivated President Ronald Reagan to sign the Immigration Reform and Control Act in 1986, a sweeping law that allowed long-standing migrants who had been "stuck" in the United States to have legal status. But opposition within the Republican Party insisted that, rather than curb migration, it only encouraged it.

Throughout this period, the tightening of the border meant that Mexicans could not easily move back and forth, and as the consequences of criminal persecution became more severe, the population of undocumented migrants grew. Official figures show the undocumented Mexican population of the United States grew from around 1.5 million to 7 million between 1986 and 2008 (reducing slightly when Barack Obama pursued more aggressive deportation efforts).[60] Fathers and sons stuck in America viewed the United States as less of a financial windfall and more of an economic obligation known as the *la Jaula de Oro*, or "the Gold Cage."[61] The criminalization of illegal immigrants forces them to stay "below the radar," so they often occupy low-status, low-wage jobs.[62] These undocumented workers are more vulnerable to exploitation, cheapening their labor further, and their fear of deportation keeps them subject to oppressive social control.[63]

The criminalization of immigration resulted in a massive increase in the prison population, fueling more government-funded contracts for privately owned prisons. Paid for by generous state legislatures, the boom in prison building meant that criminalizing immigration contributed to healthy profits for an already expanding prison system. In addition, since the early 2000s, the federal government has been motivated to avoid "catch and release" of migrants and instead detain them for prosecution through criminal courts (rather than immigration courts).[64] The end of the "catch and release" policy was empowered by increases in federal funding by Congress for detention bed space. The granting of prison contracts through local and state legislatures to build and expand detention facilities, brokered by elected politicians, resulted in a powerful scheme by which law-and-order politics based on detaining undocumented migrants at the southern border became lucrative for the prison industry, and provided jobs for local (often rural white) communities and compelling talking points for conservative candidates: a win-win-win.

HART-CELLER ACT RADICALLY ALTERS SOURCE COUNTRIES OF IMMIGRATION

If the Naturalization Act of 1790 initiated American immigration policy, and the 1924 National Origins Act fundamentally shaped it, the 1965 Hart-Celler Act was the boldest revision to occur in American history. The Hart-Celler Act passed with bipartisan support. As a response to the Cold War, the Act was intended to demonstrate the openness of America and its political system to the world; it also consciously sought to drain Communist-led countries by accepting those fleeing from those regimes.

The Hart-Celler Act dismantled the national origins 2 percent quotas, established an annual ceiling of 290,000 immigrants, and set out a rank order of categories of preference, giving family reunion the highest priority. (Note that Representative Emmanuel Celler of Brooklyn, cowriter of the Act, stood on the House floor more than forty years prior, in 1924, opposing the Johnson-Reed Act as "the rankest kind of discrimination").[65] The percentages of visas were distributed under three broad classifications: of the annual total, 74 percent would be devoted to family reunification with already established immigrants, 20 percent to applicants based on their potential contribution to the American economy, and 6 percent for granting asylum to refugees for humanitarian reasons.

With this policy, which has remained largely unchanged for more than fifty years, the great majority of immigration decisions are based on bringing immediate families together (spouses and minor children), followed by contributions to the economy. When examining the composition of recent "illegal" immigrants from Mexico living in the United States since 2016 and 2017, those who overstayed their visas (e.g., students or temporary H-1B skill-based workers) account for 62 percent of undocumented migrants, whereas only 38 percent crossed a border illegally; this most recent data on Mexican migrants demonstrates that since the year 2000, visa overstays have consistently and significantly exceeded undocumented border crossings.[66] In short, when looking at the categories for visa allotment, the majority of "illegal" immigrants consist of recently legal immigrants who had been here based on their potential contribution to the American economy but whose visas had expired.

Regrettably, quotas established through the Hart-Celler Act are not attuned to differences in the demand for visas across countries. The system sought greater equity between Eastern and Western Hemispheres, providing 170,000 visas for the east and 120,000 for the west. But no country was allotted more than 20,000 visas (spouses, minor children, and parents of US citizens were exempt from this limit). That meant that China and India, the two largest countries in the world,

received no more visas than much smaller countries like Bhutan or the
Maldives. Mexico is another country whose people are disadvantaged
by these quota restrictions. All other applicants are placed on a waiting
list. This "chain of migration" linking family members by reuniting
them in the United States allowed extraordinary levels of immigration
from Asian and Latin American countries and, all together, compose
three-quarters of legal admissions in the 1970s and 1980s and 80 percent of new arrivals today. Refugees escaping Communist countries or
the Middle East also grew to more than 10,000 migrants, motivating US
presidents over the years to use their parole power to "forgive" those
from certain countries who exceed established quotas, effectively side-
stepping quotas to legally admit Cuban, Vietnamese, and other significant streams of refugee groups.

Whereas the 1924 Immigration Act restricted immigration radically,
the Hart-Celler Act generally spurred migration, especially the proportion of migrants from previously limited sending countries. As soon as
the 1970s, European countries fell to less than 20 percent of legal
admissions. Unfortunately, the flow of Asian and Latin American migration in the 1970s grew at the same time that the economic crisis of
"stagflation" grew, an economic malaise of low growth and high inflation (see Chapter 6). The growth and diversity of nonwhite migrants
occurred at the same time that economic discontent grew among
American workers, a discontent that was projected onto these new migrants. Additional concerns about the global population boom—highly
publicized anxieties regarding the drastic rise of world population in the
face of falling death rates and high birth rates, especially among nonwhites—further added to the unease of nativist whites in America regarding the economic influence of immigrants. The concern for economics would continue to be interwoven unfairly with historic racial
bias against foreigners and nonwhites.

AMERICANISM AND ACCESS TO THE AMERICAN DREAM

Americanism is an elusive idea. Franklin D. Roosevelt discussed the
concept when he stated,

The principle on which this country was founded and by which it has always been governed, is that Americanism is a matter of the mind and heart. Americanism is not, and never was, a matter of race and ancestry. A good American is one who is loyal to this country and to our creed of liberty and democracy.

But our national history indicates an uneven access among different racial and ethnic groups to being accepted as "American." Is Americanism truly attainable by all people regardless of their ancestral background? Or is it restricted to those who qualify as white?

A nation founded on immigrants might, in theory, consist of inhabitants who are empathetic toward new immigrants. However, it became clear through restrictive policies that Americans adopted a less welcoming outlook. Harkening back to a white settler ethos that privileges an assimilated and panethnic group who possess the merit of taking possession of available opportunities to succeed, Americans who have settled have always feared losing jobs to newer immigrants, especially those who were willing to work for less and under worse conditions. Even as the boundaries of the nation expanded, America grew more and more afraid of these outsiders. Fear grew to encompass not only those who were physically different, such as blacks and Chinese "citizens," but also those who were different in ideas and orientations. People became afraid of radicals (the Red Scare) and Jews, and immigrants from southern and eastern Europe were met with hostility from "original" or "old stock" Americans. Yet among immigrants who made it past restrictive immigration policies and established themselves, regardless of nationality, they then began to feel similar hostility toward the next waves of immigrants. Africans, other Europeans, East Asians, Latin Americans, Middle Easterners, and others have all arrived in the United States to face the suspicions of previous generations. Competition for the American Dream generates resentment as people who are supposedly "un-American" are believed to take from the opportunities and wealth that should belong only to legitimate Americans. Nevertheless, the need for new labor remains.

The American Dream is associated with the idea that all who are willing to make the effort can achieve their own desired destiny. Similarly, American history is defined by a religiously grounded racial bond rooted in an idealized past of Pilgrims, Puritans, and other white Christian religious dissenters pursuing the freedom of their convictions. It is a vision tied to the heroic sacrifices of immigrants who came to this land with nothing but their ambition, resourcefulness, and moxie. But this same promise has been largely denied blacks, Mexicans, and Asians throughout our history; working hard, obeying the law, and espousing patriotic sentiment—even through the fighting of our wars—has not guaranteed social advancement and is not consistently rewarded in American society. It is no surprise "that educated and relatively well remunerated blacks have tended to be far more disenchanted with the American dream."[67] The benefits of opportunity were not equally available to all, and the differences in generational transfers of wealth accumulated over many decades give us a better understanding of the ever-widening gap in wealth between ethnoracial groups. The United States crafted policy to allow migration from some nationalities and radically restrict others, leading to an intentional cultivation of a panethnic majoritarian group who would understand themselves as white and be accepted as collectively white.

Chapter 5

BUSINESS-FRIENDLY EVANGELICALISM

Theological Turn of Mid-Twentieth-Century Christianity

Christianity, despite the considerable diversity in liturgical styles found in its churches, has always been the dominant religion of America. Over time, the revivalist strain, with its primitivist notions of immediate connection to first-century Christians, took greater ascendance, altering the religious landscape toward morally charged positions and an insistence that standards of conservative evangelical morality should become encoded into law.[1] When rallying against a host of social ills like communism, drunkenness, and sexual immorality—moral crusades that became wrapped in the American flag—the appeal to morality was primary, and their moralistic message made clear who was on the right side and who was on the wrong side.[2] Leaders appealed to moral fortitude, creating a sense of urgency that their issues needed to be addressed *now*. Here are the roots of what became white Christian nationalism, a push for the restructuring of American society as a mirror of the Kingdom of God on earth. Grasping the outlines of this distinctly modern evangelical orientation allows greater discernment of the frameworks that undergird the political positions white evangelicals took on later.

As white American Protestants faced a drastically changing country, surfacing from two World Wars, they experienced an economic prosperity made accessible to the lower rungs of the social ladder. At the same time, the early twentieth century witnessed the aggressive growth of Marxist-motivated Communism absorbing major countries across the globe, a political orientation deemed to be not only anticapitalist but also anti-God, anti-Christianity, and anti–religious freedom. All hints of collective economic help and sympathies toward the plight of labor were seen as dangerously close to Communism. Conservative white Christians had held the "most paranoid suspicions, the most absurd superstitions, the most bizarre apocalyptic fantasies."[3] This paranoia stemmed from concern about the overreach of government amid the fear of socialism. Christians took on arguments for the merits of capitalism over collectivism, small government over big government, and economic freedom through market forces above all. They came to believe that economic freedom fostered the conditions that allowed for all other freedoms. As the ideal of American freedom conflated capitalism with the pursuit of the American Dream, the State was only justified in protecting the conditions of a free market economy. In this process, Protestants in the United States made a decisive shift, combining their white-dominant identity with an embrace of free-market economic beliefs.

By the mid-twentieth century, conservative economic policy had forged close ties to conservative Christian beliefs. With the rise in affluence among white Americans, more people felt that, with enough initiative, anyone could make a decent living. The theological turn of post–World War II Christianity involved a distinct moving away from the Social Gospel movement, which had been concerned with poverty and the harsh working conditions of the working class. Now a business-friendly evangelicalism ascended, one that catered to the anxieties and ambitions of the growing class of white-collar workers, salesmen, small business owners, and upwardly mobile corporate executives working in the competitive bustle of growing metropolitan cities across the continent.

White Christian pastors mastered a supposedly apolitical pose that endorsed limited government and the beneficence of the free market. With claims against the reach of the federal government and a rejection of political solutions to economic suffering, these pastors refrained from discussing systemic issues or directly challenging unjust political systems. Avoiding a prophetic voice to agitate for public policy social changes, white conservative churches approached social problems in a more relational, individualistic form, a stance that has dominated American evangelicalism.[4] Rather than challenging the structures of socioeconomic inequality, their message assumes limitless opportunity in the present political economy—a Christian Libertarian conviction urging followers to realize their potential, bolstered by an unfettered confidence in the righteousness of the American Dream.

INTRODUCING WHITE CHRISTIAN LIBERTARIANISM

White Christian Libertarianism emerged as a broad-based religious orientation in America that gained significant ground after the First World War.[5] The term *Christian Libertarianism* may be somewhat awkward, especially because Libertarianism and Christianity have most often been understood as different philosophical and intellectual currents. Yet this label represents a synergy of religious conviction alongside an idealized economic perspective, both of which enable and reinforce one another.[6]

On the surface, it is not difficult to find white Christian Libertarianism among contemporary prosperity theology preachers, including those embraced by the Trump administration, like those appointed to his "faith advisory board" and among those celebrated on August 27, 2018, at a special "State-like" dinner at the White House in their honor.[7] In prosperity theology, the individual is assumed to be gifted by God with talent and agency, able to enter into the freedoms guaranteed on the assumptions of a free market, and trusting God who provides opportunities within a political system premised on the promises of liberty and the pursuit of happiness. White Christian Libertarianism believes prosperity is about hard work, independence, and the ability to invest in capital-intensive assets (like real estate, stocks, and bonds)—with little regard for social structures that create an inability to accumulate investment wealth. Churches modeled after a Christian Libertarian ideal reassert individual confidence in members who become economically self-sufficient, stimulating their productive autonomy.[8] Christian Libertarian pastors believe that keeping churches tax exempt and allowing congregations to aggressively engage in social service provision would ultimately save the government more money than if they imposed taxation. Not that churches would simply give money away. The church's function is to lift people into productive participation in the private enterprise system. In prosperity theology, the best goal for the Christian in day-to-day life is to produce wealth, which benefits the individual, the church (through tithes and offerings), and the world (through stimulating the economy, paying workers, and contributing to charity). The ultimate exemplars of virtue are successful entrepreneurs.

Looking back historically, white Christian Libertarianism is a distinctly American sociopolitical framework with roots dating back to the Gilded Age of the United States, an era when the rise of industrialization and the advancement of corporate financial structures generated enormous wealth for a small caste of Protestant elites (e.g., Carnegie, Getty, Rockefeller, Vanderbilt, and similar others).[9] These elites largely accepted that society was composed of autonomous, rational individuals who had the capacity for self-determination. In general, the history of labor in the United States from this point forward overlooks the systemic oppression of blacks and unwanted "foreigners" and always orients around whiteness. Corporate financial structures expanded enormously in the decades after Emancipation during the Reconstruction period, yet the exclusion of blacks is particularly notable. Cheap black labor served corporate interests that systematically barred them from nearly all capital-intensive financial opportunities, a consistent and blatant denial of access to mechanisms for the accumulation of wealth (see Chapter 3).[10] During this era, Chinese migrants were also sources of cheap labor—especially integral to western mining and the completion of the transcontinental railroad—yet they also were systematically excluded from paths for financial wealth and soon were excluded not only from citizenship but also from the opportunity to immigrate (see Chapter 4).[11] Also during the Gilded Age, Mexican Americans and Mexican migrants along the southern border were subjected to outrageous racial violence, depriving them of the fruits of their labor, rights over private property, and residency as neighbors living in their own private dwellings (see Chapter 4).[12]

Because exclusionary practices against blacks, Chinese, and Mexicans in America are so often neglected in reporting American economic development over the course of the nineteenth century, the economic expansion of our country's prosperity is mythologized among Christian Libertarians as a mixture of ingenuity, strategic leveraging of available resources, and trust in divine providence. Local and federal governments were deeply invested in this vision, monitoring who should succeed and which groups adequately fit into the notion of a "good American," willing to extend help to those deemed desirable and deserving. By ignoring the ways in which white Americans (and the immigrants who "pass" for white) have benefited from the expropriated labor of blacks, Mexicans, and Asian groups and the hindrances to their economic advancement, these wealthy elites accepted the current sociopolitical system as good and proper, rewarding the talents of hard-working people with opportunity and prosperity.[13] If problems occur and obstacles are encountered, Christian clergy, politicians, businessmen, and citizens all assumed those problems were only individual problems and individual obstacles.[14]

Christian Libertarianism is embedded in the perpetuation of this systemic and institutionalized racism, whether it was officially encoded into law or not. For example, the cultural strain of white Christian Libertarianism worked to actively counter the influence of the Social Gospel movement, a form of Christianity widely taught by clergy and theologians like Walter Rauschenbusch. The Social Gospel movement biblically interrogated corporate greed and argued for the needs of workers. But Christian businessmen viewed Social Gospel teachings as much too close to the threat of socialism. These businessmen did not just politely disagree. Philanthropically minded business titans forcefully countered Social Gospel influence by funding an alternative theology, offering significant financial support to resonant evangelical ministers who promoted a capitalist-friendly form of faith.

The CEOs of corporations like Chrysler, General Motors, and Eastern Airlines joined eponymous businesses with names like Pew, Hilton, and Kraft, leveraging generous donations to promote biblical teachings that endorsed legitimacy for a "Christian economics" that fully embraced principles of free-market enterprise.[15] These men wanted "to enlist religion explicitly in the defense of laissez-faire" government to "show that market principles were compatible with divine truths."[16] They preached capitalism and anticommunism as part of their Bible-based gospel message. For them, "Jesus appealed to many motives, but at no time did He appeal to disinterested altruism. . . . [I]nstead, He constantly invoked the profit motive."[17] For example, the Foundation for Economic Education was an evangelical organization that spread its message through books, pamphlets, and other media, and Christian

capitalist groups like Business Men's Committees and Spiritual Mobilization drew business men to embrace a capitalist-friendly spiritually.

As corporations grew, their leaders knew their businesses were perceived as avaricious and materialistic. Therefore, they sought to be portrayed in a more favorable light, pushing against the assumptions that
their priorities were based only in self-serving greed. Toward that end,
Christian businessman J. Howard Pew and Los Angeles minister James
Fifield established Spiritual Mobilization. Spiritual Mobilization was an
organization that worked to retrain clergy, providing them theological
justification for free-market policies. It innovated and then disseminat-
ed religious reasons for the promotion of profit-seeking and entrepreneurship. Indeed, Spiritual Mobilization "took as its mission the invention of theological justification for capitalism."[18] It also sought the removal of government social services, all of which were viewed as unnecessary, wasteful, and dangerously expensive for tax payers. The organization argued that "altruism, selflessness, and devotion to helping the
poor" were principles that would lead otherwise good Christians to
advocate government intervention in the economy.

Spiritual Mobilization galvanized clergy, giving them a sense of how
sound religious truths were accessible business principles when the
Bible was interpreted "correctly" and constituted the foundation of the
American way of life. In essence, the creation of Spiritual Mobilization
attempted to establish conservative economic ideals as fundamental to
biblical Christianity. Corporations and businessmen were major donors
to the Spiritual Mobilization organization, seeing it as a means to effectively uphold the notion that hard work within the American market
economy would be rewarded with profit. Economic ills were traced
back to spiritual shortcomings, and liberal policies would only keep
spiritually weak people in bondage.

Not surprisingly, a Christian Libertarian understanding of how the
American economy works had racial consequences. For example, Christian Libertarianism asserted the priority of respecting private property.
Private property owners and their rights, as well as the need to keep
business enterprises strong, created a set of ideals that clashed with
contrary notions. The consequences for attitudes toward race relations
was disastrous to oppressed minorities. We know that the language of
the free market could be used to push against efforts at racial integration.[19]

The crucial step among Christian Libertarians was to move away from defending segregation to advocating for the rights of private property. During the lunch counter sit-in protests in Greensboro, North Carolina, a white Christian spokesperson said protesters should not boycott because disrupting the business of a private property owner should be avoided. Landlords had an inalienable right to do what they wanted with their own private property; imposing social obligations like racial integration promoted "a myth used by the weak to hamper the strong."[20] Senator Jesse Helms did not attack black people or defend segregation, but rather attacked socialist beliefs and the disregard for the property rights of shopkeepers. Helms, like others, did not believe in the interference of government in the private affairs of people, which is how he critiqued the Civil Rights movement, even though it is clear he did not believe in racial equality. Jesse Helms in the late 1950s said, "I cannot attack the Negro as a race, but I can in good conscience attack a socialistic system that lends itself to undue power by any group."[21] Government obligations to honor racial integration violated the conscious objection of white Christian business owners and their customers. A supposed economic focus on private property attempted to hide the resistance to racial initiatives, and further exacerbated racial tensions. Thus, out of a misguided respect for private property, white Christian Libertarians provided justifications for systematically discriminating against blacks and other people of color not just at restaurants, but also in churches, hotels, occupational training, storefronts, tenant housing, and more.

White Christian conservatives did not consider race to be an economic issue because they avoided the racialized effects of economic policy and centered all of their discussion on the defense of general notions of the free market and, ultimately, theological principles that could not be questioned. Defending abstract principles were more important than tackling concrete injustices. Their molding of corporate economic priorities with conservative evangelical values was pioneering, and it significantly shaped the development of mainstream evangelicalism throughout the rest of the twentieth century.

THE RISE OF BUSINESS-FRIENDLY DISPENSATIONALISM

Together, these free-market, Libertarian Christian businessmen argued that Christianity did not have a completely selfless agenda; after all, every Christian's actions are oriented toward achieving an eternal afterlife. They depicted religion as guided by self-interest, making their views of religion consonant with their views on capitalism. Crafting a theological justification for capitalism grew under the specter of communism, an anticapitalist but also anti-Christian and anti–religious freedom political movement that haunted mid-twentieth-century Christian America. In the days when control by atheist Communists was a rampant fear, Christians forged arguments to demonstrate that market principles were consonant with divine truths.[22] As James Fifield preached, "The blessings of Capitalism come from God."[23]

Although Christianity conventionally entails benevolence and altruism, critics believed that this moral code was a real danger to capitalism. In the early twentieth century, Billy Sunday gave sermons that attacked immigrants and progressive reformers, preaching, "If I had my way with these ornery wild-eyed socialists I would stand them up before a firing squad."[24] Sundays' sermons illustrate the amalgamation of the moralistic tone of sermons and the legitimacy of free-market capitalistic structures. The poor damaged the economy when accepting government help because it kept the poor from becoming independent and economically self-sustainable. The initiative to bring together Christianity and capitalism justified free-market ideologies and absolved Christian businessmen and those who supported their ideals from a societal responsibility to take on the never-ending burden of elevating the poor. Support for business-friendly economics were strengthened, believing that honest, dedicated work is rewarded with personal wealth, sanctioning the profitability of corporate leaders and successful entrepreneurs.

Christian Libertarians promoted a view that God established our world to reward responsibility. Christian businessmen are imbued with God-sanctioned virtue because their wealth was earned with integrity. Prosperity is not a product of wishful thinking but a direct result of piety mixed with a solid work ethic. Wealth is a good and expected outcome of a life well lived.[25] Initiative and entrepreneurship are welcomed and highly esteemed. There is a close connection between salvation and success, and poverty is a punishment indicating a moral failing.

The implications of these views is a disdain for government-sponsored social welfare programs and especially for state-sponsored wealth distribution, because these are not consonant with the morals of Christian Libertarianism. Liberal initiatives for programs to assist the needy and impoverished are seen as actually uncaring as they fail to meet the "real" need for character development. The State is viewed as corrupt, and so direction from the State to address social problems is to be avoided; better to place it into principled, private hands of business, supplemented with charity from churchly neighbors. State-sponsored actions against hard work and upholding Christian morality weaken the American people.

According to Kim Phillips-Fein, in her book *Invisible Hands: The Businessmen's Crusade against the New Deal*, the key to understanding this new wave of Christian conservatism lies in the backlash against New Deal economics.[26] Under the New Deal, American's standard of living increased without creating a larger division between the upper class and lower class. However, New Deal legislation brought a backlash. Businessmen felt targeted by the programs and reforms instituted, and they fought back with a religious orientation that claimed there was no government responsibility to care for the neighbor and, therefore, did not cut into their profits. J. Howard Pew and James Fifield resonated with the ideas found in Hayak's *Road to Serfdom*, an economic-political treatise that was written against Nazi totalitarianism but quickly reinterpreted as an argument against any sort of big-government planning (see Chapter 6). Initiatives like Spiritual Mobilization began after Franklin D. Roosevelt passed New Deal legislation. William Rusher, publisher of the *National Review* and another conservative critic of the New Deal, believed these social welfare programs incentivized poverty, allowing a higher proportion of the population to remain lower class and expanding the number of people who fed off the work of others for their survival. What was required was a smaller national government, one that encouraged individual initiative, involved no government interference with the pursuit of wealth, and encouraged the promotion of ever-increasing profits derived from business activity. They believed their economic views were consistent with their Christianity.

The argument to limit social welfare by government, therefore, was not merely an economic position; it stemmed from a cultural orientation based in a tangle of political and religious ideals among white conservative Christian businessmen. The mission of Spiritual Mobilization and the clergy who resonated with its ideals was not to save souls but to save American capitalism. Christian businessmen donating to their cause believed they contributed to improving the "spiritual health" of America by generating "economic growth."[27] Spiritual Mobilization centered on providing certain economic arguments to religious leaders, who would then justify political aims and spread them to their followers. Capitalism was promoted as a common good. Tapping into their religious identities, Christian businessmen fostered significant political support for their economic initiatives. In short, by sowing capitalist-friendly Christian identity, they eventually harvested a movement's political power to shape economic policy.

Ironically, conservative Christians believed they were politically neutral. In actuality, they avoided discussion of the unfair and exclusionary actions toward blacks and other stigmatized groups. Segregation allowed them to remain aloof from racial problems because the geography of their everyday lives kept them distant from the realities of such ongoing oppressions. Ignoring the concrete conditions of the lives of blacks, Mexicans, and Asians in America, they clung to spiritualized principles skillfully harmonized theologically alongside a more modern development of "biblical" world views.

It is crucial to grasp the social and structural consequences of conservative Christian belief. Evangelicals preach and teach that their social bond is actually a spiritual connection made through personal conversion and salvation by faith made personally accessible through Jesus Christ, followed by a lifetime of commitment to a local church. Yet the history of conservative Christian belief shows these bonds do not remain merely "spiritual" but are incarnated through changing political and economic attitudes. Members of the evangelical right constitute a politically relevant interest group that has opposed a long list of other social groups, including Communists, Jews, homosexuals, liberals, feminists, progressives, transgender persons, unwed mothers, and others who do not fit a traditional Christian mold. These are types of people who act contrary to evangelical notions of the Kingdom of God and contribute to the turning of America away from God. They remove the favor of God from our nation. Even when evangelicals appear to shy away from outright political positions, their involvement in their churches and the trajectory of the mobilization of groups who share their faith makes clear the parameters of their political participation.[28] The accretion of capitalist sympathy added a distinctive economic ideology into their political identity.

This ascendant, business-friendly evangelicalism merged into a burgeoning new theological orientation that stressed adherence to the "fundamentals" of the faith. More literal readings of the Bible accompanied an implicitly political lens for interpreting it. The rise of dispensationalism and "the Fundamentals" in the South and Midwest, and in Southern California via migration,[29] were associated with an anticommunist and antisocialist, procapitalist and promarket Christianity, fusing patriotism with an aggressively redefined pietism. A "true" capitalism, one that soon became intertwined with Christian values, would undo labor unions (seen as socialistic and communistic), social welfare (which failed to reward hard work and helped women raise children without husbands), and government deregulation (to increase freedom of business to manage their workers and their profits as they wished). Demonizing the "liberal" party generated support for conservatism and Christianity. All in all, policies labeled "liberal" were believed to reject the Christian faith.

With the help of notes in the *Scofield Study Bible* and popular preachers like J. Vernon McGee, conservative white evangelicals committed themselves to a theological schema that bracketed out periods of history, stressed we were living in the "end times," anticipated further decline in the general society, and emphasized that neither the government nor the church could halt the God-intended and biblically prophesied demise of the culture. True believers would be "caught up" or raptured, taken right out of their daily lives in an instant, saved from the wickedness of the world, leaving the unsaved to face the apocalyptic nightmare of the Antichrist and the host of disasters accompanying him. Conservative evangelicals rejected the possibility of social interventions for creation of a better world, political and economic initiatives that moved toward socialism (including programs created under Franklin Delano Roosevelt's New Deal), and other movements urging collective solutions or sympathies toward the plight of labor, which were deemed to be, as prominent preacher J. Veron McGee said, "a halfway house to Communism."[30]

Dispensationalism informed a white Christian Libertarian faith. Evangelical theology did not remove financial difficulties, it only reinterpreted them. Churches struggled financially, and the entry of a business-friendly theology provided means for clergy to align closely with people who had ties to the economic prosperity of the country. What better way to grow one's ministry than by gaining support from wealthy, conservative businessmen? Moreover, these businessmen had powerful incentives for altering the economic climate, and the power of crafting religious identities that could be successful in the marketplace and faithful as spiritually empowered leaders in society was formidable. By addressing non–working class businessmen as victims of the New Deal, these conservative businessmen invested their money in churches and used their power to work toward what they believed was good for themselves and good for the moral imperatives of their congregations.

Fundamentalists were seen most often in the early twentieth century fighting against evolution being taught in schools; in the 1950s through the 1980s, they focused on abortion, communism, pornography, homosexuality, and other social issues. They also sought to promote a conservative economic plan, mainly centered on lower taxes and less government intervention. Although preachers like Carl McIntire and Billy James Hargis believed there was a split between God-fearing and godless people, in reality, the various imperatives were fractured among such a large religious group. The fundamentalist movement decentralized, with multiple groups forcefully asserting their own distinctive arrangement of nonnegotiable truths, making it difficult to focus on broader political issues in a comprehensive manner. One thing that did continue to unite them was that they did not support government involvement in the redistribution of wealth, which became the default economic position of white evangelicals.

Accompanying the rejection of perceived moves toward communism was a radical affirmation of individual freedom, especially the ability for the ego-oriented individual of character to pursue his or her religious convictions. The concern for workers, the underprivileged, and the racially oppressed accentuated in the Social Gospel movement was lost; instead, evangelicals stressed individual faith in God and the need to dedicate oneself to ambition and hard work. The rise of more individualistic, ego-affirming theology was encapsulated in one of the best-selling books of all time, *The Power of Positive Thinking* by Norman Vincent Peale, the pastor of Marble Collegiate Church in New York, where Donald Trump's family attended. (In a National Public Radio interview, Trump called Peale "my pastor," adding, "He was so great.").[31] Peale and like-minded pastors like Robert H. Schuller in Southern California stressed the need for the ego-oriented individual to dedicate oneself to ambition and hard work.[32] In this decisive shift, the concern for workers, the underprivileged, and the racially oppressed was reoriented into a set of imperatives that assumes every person is able to deliver themselves out of their difficulties by following biblical principles in the conduct of their lives.[33]

The notion of a self-sufficient, hard-working, white Christian patriot blossomed into white Christian nationalism, a push for the restructuring of American society as a mirror of the Kingdom of God on earth. The more Christian business entrepreneurs succeeded in gaining profits, the more they accentuated the independence of their faith with the freedom of their religious convictions, culminating in the 1950s in a political movement to insert "Under God" in the pledge of allegiance and to place "In God We Trust" on US currency. Revivalist and primitivist notions took greater ascendance by the middle of the twentieth century, altering the religious landscape toward morally charged positions and an insistence that standards of conservative evangelical morality should become encoded into law. The expansion of Christian Reconstruction or Dominion Theology, which asserts the need to remake secular society into an interlocking set of God-honoring institutions, is consistent with these developments.[34]

The ministry of Billy Graham is certainly one of the greatest examples of the intertwining of business, political power, and an individualistically oriented Christianity. Graham received significant funding from wealthy Christian businessmen, and such corporate funding allowed the multifaceted religious empire consisting of Graham's books, movies, and international crusades to take off. Graham famously became America's minister to our nation's presidents, building close relationships regardless of the questionable morals and at times outrageously oppressive policies promoted by their administrations.[35] Graham's biography is, in itself, a bridge on which white Christianity moved away from the Social Gospel to an embrace of the principles of Christian Libertarianism.[36]

BIRTHING OF A MODERN CHRISTIAN RIGHT

Conservative evangelicals in America, deemed the "new Christian Right," have now demonstrated immense political and cultural prowess during the last century. Although not explicitly aligned with the Republican Party, the intense loyalty these followers demonstrate to the GOP's often morality-based conservative policies makes them an ideal ally for the right wing, and the relationship has grown closer over recent decades.[37] This loyalty stems from the combination of spirituality with public policy, evoking a passion for activism and conversion that is central to the core of the religious conservative's identity. The devotedness of these individuals to their religious communities makes these groups a breeding ground for echo chambers within their own networks to amplify conservative ideals. Issues are presented in emotional, zealous terms, and they raise anxieties and call out commitment from large groups, often in the messages given in churches or through mass-media channels. The pressure to conform to their Christian community's standards is deeply rooted in the culture of these institutions, making sacred spaces the place to organize for or against political causes.

Among the most important political imperatives for this impassioned Christian Libertarian group is the preservation of free-market capitalism, which they believe is sanctioned by God and is the only correct way to orient economic policy in the United States. This support for an unregulated capitalism has been evident in the movement from the New Deal to Ronald Reagan's presidency (see Chapter 6). During the 1930s, there was an attempt to show that free-market principles were compatible with Christian ethics, extrapolating connections between theology and economics. By the 1940s, coalitions of Christian church leaders and businessmen formed, especially across the economically expanding Sun Belt states, with increasing assertiveness against what they viewed as excessive taxation and federal intervention. Thus, politically, even when evangelicals claim to separate themselves from politics and unite around a sense of political alienation and social persecution, their faith continues to have relevance for their political action as, for example, when they claim that the freedom of their beliefs is compromised in our "secular" society. Support for gays, for example, is experienced "as an unprovoked, unilateral assault on Christians" and provokes sentiment and voting patterns that enact those sentiments.[38]

White evangelical goals, therefore, are not only to transform souls but also to transform society. For many, their religious sentiments are expressed as a desire to go back to what America was founded on, to bring back the moral integrity of their most Christian founders, and to actualize their dreams of godliness and prosperity—notions on the origins of America that are contested by contemporary scholarship.[39] The most compelling aspect of the new Christian Right is their firm belief that what they are advocating is sanctioned by God, a belief that fuels the zeal behind their movement. Imperatives are presented in moralistic terms, with emotionality, arousing anxieties and calling out commitments. America, a nation that was chosen and blessed by God, must be protected.

Their motivation for a stronger activist orientation that combines their faith with their vote is fueled by uncompromising stances on highly emotional issues centered around traditional morality. After all, specific policies can be debated, but it is hard to oppose morals. In earlier times, Christian revival campaigns focused on a person's individual sins. Now, sins are defined in terms of their effect on society as a whole, and the public effect of sins has moved toward a consideration of politics. Their motions and actions have characteristic fervor that are similar in the way they gather support: through emotional testimonies that arouse anxieties common to many white Americans. More conservative Christians made family matters the focus of public policy, centering their arguments around issues like abortion, homosexuality, sex education in schools, and the role of women (see Chapter 9). The conservative ideal family structure centers around a patriarchy emphasizing the innate strength of the husband, a wife who serves, and children who obey. Independence among housewives and children is frowned upon and women are encouraged not to join the workforce if they have young children living at home. The call to protect "family values" has generated intense devotion and highly emotional activism, dedicated to protecting communities form sin and devilish influences. Communities must be protected. They seek to establish a standard of morality among citizens and integrate faith into public policy, elevating American exceptionalism to a heightened status and moving America toward a type of theocracy.

Religious groups that make up the new Christian Right consist of mostly evangelical or otherwise "born-again" Protestant Christians who find common ground not in their religious beliefs per se but rather in a unifying fear of modern progressivism and liberalism, which they view as a threat to Christian thought. Rallying around controversial moral issues rather than on biblical doctrine or public policy proved to be a strategic route for entering politics, enabling conservative Southern Baptists to advocate alongside Seventh-Day Adventists alongside Word of Faith prosperity preachers—religious bodies that would otherwise hold each other in disdain, each preaching against the shortcoming of the other. By binding themselves together around the desire for a public role for a conservative God and religiously tinged policies, their coalition amplifies their collective outrage and strategizes on how to infiltrate the political ranks, gaining access to powerful politicians and bending policy in their favor.

Despite their belief in their own marginality, these mostly white Christians (about three-quarters of evangelical or "born again" Protestants are white)[40] have not faced the same kind of discrimination, disenfranchisement, or lack of funds that other grassroots political movements faced. Money was available, networks were extensive, and organizational structures of churches and media outlets were effectively mobilized around similar and consistent themes. Voter suppression laws did not affect them, and they did not face discriminatory legislation based on their religion. Wealthy conservative businessmen were willing to fund initiatives, like the World's Christian Fundamentals Association (WCFA).[41] The new Christian Right found support from the business elite and built on whatever political experience already gained. So although conservative Christians persist in narratives of religious persecution even to this day, the actualities of their power and mobility are immediately evident. Their difficulty is solely that in an increasingly pluralistic society, one that includes many people who *were* conservative Christian and have left it behind, they can no longer assume that every person in their work, school, grocery stores, and even their own families will abide by their distinctive moral demands.

The conservative Christian right is also biased toward more traditional notions of strong, white masculinity. Masculinity is important among the Christian Right, and it is part of asserting a binary notion of gender. Men are reserved patriarchs (Promise Keepers) and women are submissive mothers (Concerned Women of America). Men are better suited for positions of power, especially in business and politics. Although conservative women have made significant contributions to conservative causes,[42] there is a broader pattern of publicly welcoming and supporting strong and charismatic male leaders who leverage fundraising sophistication, mass media, and networks of organizational structures to exert political influence. Their faith forms a backdrop to the cultivation of positions and policies in support of particular politicians and policy maneuvers. The strong advocacy for capitalism merges into the proscription of men who are providers, who leave the home to aggressively contend with a competitive marketplace and, with their integrity and God's help, sustain a stable family lifestyle with their wife and children, together embodying the image of a true Christian home. Overall, the spiritual health and economic prosperity of American society is associated with work toward adhering to traditional gender roles as manifestations of Christian virtue.

An especially intriguing and influential group of conservative white Christians forcefully advocating to impose their religious standards on civic society are Dominionists or Christian Reconstructionists.[43] Reconstructionism is a traditionalist movement formed in the 1960s that gained momentum during the Reagan era. It differs from mainstream Christianity because of its insistence on practicality and modern applicability of the laws found in the Bible. Adherents do not generally use the *Reconstructionist* label among themselves, and many conservative Christians would not recognize the term. Nevertheless, Reconstructionists are those who support the need to rebuild American social and political society in line with their own particularistic definition of Christian beliefs. Their intent is to make the United States true to its origins as a Christian nation, and reinstate moral authority in an American society believed to have moved toward lawlessness and spiritual chaos. According to Reconstructionists, America was founded on Christian values and should be guided by more fundamentalist Christian ideals; it is God's country and He has favored the United States above all other countries in the world. Personal religious freedom is prized, but it should be accompanied by rulers guided by their understanding of godly righteousness, using their political power to enforce moral standards.

The radical political ideals of Reconstructionism are pitched at the national level. They not only work to establish laws and policies consistent with their moral imperatives but also seek to appoint and elect judges, politicians, and other public office holders to interpret and implement decisions consistent with their desires. Doing so would affect not only churches but also schools, workplaces, and courts of law at the local, state, and federal level. It is a grand strategic effort, one that is often unseen by the general public, especially as the mobilization to elect and promote such people is most aggressively done among their own social networks. Although Reconstructionism is not mainstream, the sentiments are prevalent, although often unnamed, among the Christian Right.

CAPITALISM AND CONSERVATIVE CHRISTIANITY

New Deal economics and the primarily Democratic control over the government in the early twentieth century promoted the belief that government should exercise significant control over the economy to reduce income inequality. Some may have publicly supported this on the principle of national prosperity, but there was constant pressure among conservative Christians against adopting this liberal economic policy. By the 1950s, close ties were forged between free-market capitalism and Christianity—especially over and against the evils of an atheistic communism.

With the promotion of capitalism came the acceptance of the observed inequality in the attainment of wealth inherent to capitalism. Rather than applying biblical principles of justice to focus on long-term consequences of racialized policies that resulted in differences in economic affluence and opportunity among different racial groups in America, white Christian Libertarians believed that capitalist principles did not contradict Christian ethics. As political scientist Daniel Schlozman writes, "political entrepreneurs from outside evangelicalism made white evangelicals into an organized movement with priorities compatible with most elements in American conservatism, above all through embrace of low taxes." Religious leaders spread the message that large, intrusive government threatened the traditional morals of evangelicals and their right to certain freedoms. The rhetoric resonated with the white working class, but it clearly benefited the business elite. Then the progressive movements of the 1960s advocating for various civil and social rights provoked conservatives to push back. The conservative Christian Libertarian ideology helped to transform government regulation of business practices and policies affecting the wealthy elite, like the tax code, which contributed to the longer-term development of neoliberalism. The decisive, probusiness turn of white evangelicalism paved the way for even more significant developments, with racialized economic consequences no one could readily foresee.

Chapter 6

THE ESTABLISHMENT OF FREE-MARKET CONSERVATISM

Religious Imperatives of Reagan-Era Economics

The period of Ronald Reagan's presidency, 1981 through 1989, coincided with the sharp rise of individuals labeling themselves as "born-again" Christians. Reagan successfully communicated a deep sincerity regarding his own religious faith, assuring conservative Christian voters that his faith was rooted in an unwavering evangelicalism. For example, on January 30, 1984, he gave a compelling speech in his "Remarks at the Annual Convention of the National Religious Broadcasters,"[1] where he spoke of Pat Boone and Pat Robertson; the successes of Christian broadcasters like CBN, PTL, and Trinity; and the "booming industry" in Christian book sales. He said that "God is the center of our lives" and that the "family stands at the center of society," thereby affirming not only revivalist understanding of the faith but the notion of "family values" and the related implications against pornography, sex outside of marriage, divorce, and homosexuality. He spoke for prayer in school and advocated private religious schools. He spoke against abortion, "the taking of some 4,000 unborn children's lives every day." He spoke of the Bible, saying, "Within the covers of that single Book are all the answers to all the problems that face us today if we'd only read and believe."

Reagan boldly brought the social values of Christian conservatives into the Republican Party, which translated into immense political support for prolife causes and opposition to gay marriage. He argued directly against abortion, homosexuality, and pornography. Although Reagan signed a bill to legalize abortion in California, opposed a ban on gay teachers in public schools, and had been divorced, he made profound connections to leading evangelicals, stating his intent to embrace their causes in his political agenda. His platform incorporated growing concern regarding the Supreme Court's 1973 decision in *Roe v. Wade*, leftist advocacy of the Equal Rights Amendment, greater visibility from the gay community, and the Internal Revenue Service (IRS) threat to remove tax-exemptions from private schools that racially discriminated.[2] This was appealing to groups like the Moral Majority, an organization originally founded by the Reverend Jerry Falwell Sr. to further a conservative "traditional values" agenda, which effectively politicized frustrated fundamentalist evangelicals and fused them into a political voting bloc.[3] Reagan was a standard bearer for this group. The Moral Majority encouraged pastors to motivate their people to engage the political arena. Thick packets of biblical passages showed their connections to contemporary politics. Reagan himself crafted religiously charged political speeches. Buttons were given out with the word "VOTE" in which the "T" was turned into a cross. There were slogans like "Christians Are Citizens Too" and plans for "Christian Voters Sundays." Voter guides with lists of approved candidates were widely circulated in church services. Not voting was declared to be a sin against God. Voting became a means to promote a moral revival of the country.

Drawing from the Bible, Reagan quoted John 3:16, perhaps the most famous and fundamental Bible verse shared among all evangelicals: "For God so loved the world that He gave His only begotten Son, that whosoever believeth in Him should not perish but have everlasting life." In this, President Reagan was interpreted as unashamedly sharing the gospel to the entire world. Actions like this appealed to the anxieties of white evangelicals. In his book *American Evangelicalism: Embattled and Thriving*, Christian Smith argues that the resolute strength of American evangelicalism derives from its self-perception as being weak. Evangelicals are united by the adversity they face, and the ongoing confrontation with diversity and pluralism energizes them. As Smith says, American evangelicalism "perceives itself to be embattled with forces that seem to oppose or threaten it. Indeed, evangelicalism . . . thrives on distinction, engagement, tension, conflict, and threat."[4] The embattled stance connects evangelicals and Libertarians. Indeed, evangelicals and neoliberals are similar in their belief that they face great opposition from mainstream society and are under constant threat.

Yet another scripture was even more telling: "If the Lord is our light, our strength, and our salvation, whom shall we fear? Of whom shall we be afraid?" (Psalm 27:1). The president who stood up to Communist Russia emboldened Christian conservatives to forcefully advocate their own political positions on social issues—as long as they could be justified as being under the direction of God's initiatives. His antiabortion, profamily stance and ability to mimic the rhetoric of white evangelicalism was decisive in winning over this block of voters. Reagan not only preached the gospel to the heathen, he also called out cultural warriors—like those associated with the Moral Majority—to war for the soul of America. In part bolstered by President Reagan's welcoming of their religion's sentiments, a white Christian sociopolitical identity crystalized. To be a white, Republican, capitalist-friendly "Christian" came to be an all-encompassing personal identity that was not only widely affirmed but also sacredly charged as good, right, and true.

Equally important, and yet more often unrecognized, is the legitimation of Reagan's economic policies as consistent with a capitalistic-affirming Christianity. The actor-turned-politician and clever Cold War warrior attracted many politically moderate Americans to the GOP and successfully merged Christian conservatism with a novel fiscal conservatism developed out of his opposition to unions and sympathy toward corporate management.[5] Christians have generally been seen as taking part in politics by electing politicians they believe support their ideals. As an anticommunist who strongly supported free-market capitalism, Reagan showed antipathy to welfare programs and supported a strong Christian work ethic. Reagan supporters who were businessmen and evangelical wanted the government to take a more laissez-faire approach to business and the economy. Reagan also appealed to people concerned with protecting their families and their communities from the danger of radicalism—*radicalism* often being a code word for government programs on behalf of blacks. The push to establish private schools to avoid desegregation made race relations a private matter for conservatives, not a public issue for all Americans to address. Centering on such issues, Reagan forged connections between white evangelicals and an emergent libertarianism, especially in bending the legal mechanisms of the State toward neoliberal economic ideology.

For Reagan, economic policy had a profound moral component. Reagan and business owners believed that the free market had the ability to create economic abundance and moral order at the same time, as an invisible hand that would punish the lackadaisical and reward disciplined entrepreneurs. Company presidents were recruited to tell their workers that they should elect a president who understood the basic economic system that made America great. Reagan's tax cut, the largest in US history to that point, eventually made him a reverse Robin Hood, taking from the poor to give to the rich, shifting economic power increasingly back toward the upper class, creating greater social inequality. He appointed antigovernment businesspeople to his cabinet, all of whom weakened the power of their respective offices. Neoliberalism shifted wealth away from an aristocratic tradition of old money to new money of generous CEO salaries and investment bankers, buttressed by healthy stock options and expanded investments. The financial sector was freed of many of the restrictions by which it had been regulated previously, and the upper class in the United States and United Kingdom were granted enormous behind-the-scenes political power.

Under Reagan's "trickle down" economics, productivity rose, but wages fell. Under his administration, taxes on corporations and the wealthy were aggressively cut, welfare and other direct payments to the poor and underemployed were attacked, and military expenditures on protecting the country from foreign invasion were expanded. Labor unions were deliberately undermined. Minimum wage hikes were resisted. And, generally, the results of his economic policies resulted in increased polarization between the rich and the poor and a broadening of America's underclass of chronically sick, homeless, disabled, and long-term unemployed—those at the bottom being disproportionally black and other minorities. Handouts were discouraged; the American belief in merit and equality of opportunity was stressed such that hard work was the solution to poverty. A neoliberal economic agenda was implemented, sanctioned with the patina of Christian piety.

ORIGINS OF NEOLIBERALISM: FRIEDRICH VON HAYEK AND ECONOMIC LIBERTY

Under the New Deal, conservatives in America were afraid of the direction of capitalism in a society that supported welfare. They saw the rise of totalitarian regimes and were especially apprehensive about Communist sympathizers and their potential to thwart the current capitalist economic system in place. Many of these conservative thinkers were bolstered by the polemics of economist and philosopher Friedrich von Hayek, a Viennese intellectual who argued that government intervention in free markets was a form of tyranny.

Friedrich von Hayek is certainly one of the most important thinkers influencing today's conservative economic ideologies. As a founding member of the Mont Pelerin Society, a think tank with a mission to champion "freedom-loving" theories of neoliberalism (membership included Ludwig von Mises, Karl Popper, and Martin Friedman), Hayak fiercely advocated reduction of government spending and elimination of government management of the economy to enable an idealized free-market system. For Hayek, individual liberty was inextricably linked to economic liberty. He viewed federal government as a "leviathan" (a reference to Thomas Hobbes's best-known work) and described government regulation as a European import to America and Britain.

In his most influential book, *The Road to Serfdom*, Hayak drew from his experience of Hitler's Germany, arguing that Nazism was a fierce reaction to socialist trends imposed on a formerly democratic society. The threat of tyranny and Nazism is a useful rallying point, made up of emotional rhetoric that provides common, negative connotations to the public. Americans saw the devastation caused by World War II, and they recalled the rebellion of the American colonies from King George III. Later, Libertarians like James Buchanan argued that government is filled with politicians who pursue their own self-interests, and the temptation to spend other people's money—especially money belonging to the rich—is too great in the face of demands from the mass of their constituents. Riffing on Hayak's ideas, Buchanan argued that decisions by democratic systems could easily lead to socialism and, eventually, totalitarianism. The financial discretion of the wealthy elite needs to be preserved.

Hayek championed individual economic freedoms as the highest good. For him, government intervention in free markets was equivalent to tyranny. His ideal state had very little influence over the economy, and the rule of law by government would serve to "guarantee the conditions of free competition." Economic freedom was interconnected with political and civic freedom. As David Kotz writes in *The Rise and Fall of Neoliberal Capitalism*, "Individual freedom of choice is seen as the fundamental basis of human welfare, with market relations understood as the institution that allows individual choice to drive the economy. The state, by contrast, is seen as the enemy of individual liberty, a threat to private property, and a parasite living off the hard work of individuals."[6] Modern society was composed of rational, self-determining individuals, and their autonomy in making decisions for themselves was conceived as a fundamental right. At the same time, the political freedom of individuals was fused into the assertion of the economic freedom for individuals to pursue and protect their private property, overseen by the protection of the State. In Hayak's framework, there can be no real freedom without economic freedom.

Hayak's ideas also buttressed an orientation prioritizing individual rather than collective interest. Ayn Rand, another innovative sociopolitical thinker, was significantly influenced by *The Road to Serfdom* and wrote her own works of fiction and nonfiction proclaiming that no morality existed that was higher than one's own self-interest.[7] For Rand, as for Hayak, collectivism was a danger to capitalism. Private property is seen as sacred, and democracy is a threat to the "wealthy minority."

Hayek asserted that "everyone had equal access to the market" and that "social mobility was possible." Hayek and other neoliberals demanded that the individual was paramount, and this would have critical implications for blacks and other minorities because Hayak's neoliberalism asserted that inequality was unavoidable. He acknowledged that the economic consequences of neoliberalism would inevitably have profound social and political effects as well, again further perpetuating racial inequality. Thus, neoliberal beliefs, although economically rooted and focused, have racial implications that contribute to the growing racial inequality. Given that racial inequality was already prominent at this time, it is unreasonable to believe that blacks and minorities had equal access to the market or the ability to change their social rank in a system driven by individuals. A free market focused on the individual

incorporated into a society where racial groups are already clearly unequal results in a society in which that inequality is magnified.[8] Not only
was it a challenge to access opportunities but blacks and minorities
continued to be disadvantaged and ill-equipped in education, training,
and relational networks because of the racial injustice that had pigeon-
holed blacks for so long, leaving them unable to compete at an equal
level. Economic ideals as developed and emphasized by people like
Friedrich von Hayek are representative of the neoliberal movement in
the United States that perpetuated the inequities that had accrued over
the country's racial history, and of course, largely disregarded issues of
race.

Although Hayek never turned away from asserting the value of individual freedom for the rest of his life, the political context of his time
was against the totalitarian regimes of the Soviet Union and Nazi Germany. The excesses of power seen in these countries, and the belief that
any form of socialism invariably leads to the control of the fortunes of its
citizens against their will, was absorbed into modern libertarianism and
used as a weapon against progressive policies that redirected tax dollars
toward government protections of neglected citizens and larger initiatives that work for the common good like public education, health care,
and environmental protection. His argument in *The Road to Serfdom*,
while speaking of a different time and appealing to different circumstances, was reinterpreted in America as a screed against the overstep-
ping of government that limits the rights of free, wealthy citizens.

ARGUING FOR NEOLIBERALISM: JAMES BUCHANAN AND PROTECTION OF WEALTHY MINORITY

The Road to Serfdom was a favorite text of Libertarian Noble Prize
winner James Buchanan during his studies at the University of Chicago
and helped form his convictions that centered around avoiding government assistance and instead promoting self-reliance. Like Hayak, Buchanan was also a member of the Mount Pelerin Society. Economic
liberty was a basic, most essential liberty, such that all other liberties are
derived from economic liberty. Ironically, for Buchanan and others inspired by Hayek, the promotion of "liberty" does not carry the meaning
it seems to imply. For Buchanan and wealthy elites influenced by

Hayak, self-determination centered on the freedom of individuals to determine where their monies should go, inherently resisting the broad power of taxation later introduced into the United States (federal taxation was an initiative that was introduced by Republicans under the Lincoln administration in 1861 and further expanded in the coming years to fund a variety of national objectives). The notion of "liberty" among the wealthy moved them to resist taxation and expenditures whenever they disagreed with the uses of government funds (having the "liberty" to do with their money as they please), and they were prepared to fight to maintain discretion over their own wealth in the face of historical forces propelling the use of tax dollars for the common good.

In the carefully researched book *Democracy in Chains: The Deep History of the Radical Right's Stealth Plan for America*, Nancy MacLean investigates how neoliberal intellectuals like James Buchanan set up an elaborate ideological justification for a political system that would most benefit the wealthy elite. Neoliberal apologists like Buchanan and his supporters (including Charles Koch) target the workings of democracy because they felt themselves under threat, fearing that decisions stemming from a democratic system will interfere with the necessary workings of the free market. Their feeling that the government is not there to protect their wishes means that America is no longer a safe place for them. Buchanan stated that representative government would "destroy capitalism by fleecing the propertied class—unless constitutional reform ensured economic liberty, no matter what most voters wanted."[9] To ensure protection of the market (i.e., the free use of property by the elite) from the interference of more popular initiatives desired by the democratic majority, the highly propertied class works to limit democracy, knowing that the majority would not willingly choose the policies that most benefit the already wealthy.

MacLean warns of an emerging oligarchy, a group that wants to return to an American economy closer to that of the Gilded Age in which disenfranchisement and poor treatment of labor unions allowed a powerful few to control government, and thus the economy.[10] The enemy is democracy, because a collective vote would not produce what this group desires, so therefore it must be upended. MacLean summarizes Buchanan's argument:

[T]he cause must figure out how to put legal—indeed, constitution-al—shackles on public officials, shackles so powerful that no matter how sympathetic these officials might be in the will of majorities, no matter how concerned they were with their own re-elections, they would no longer have the ability to respond to those who used their numbers to get government to do their bidding.[11]

It may seem counterintuitive, but in neoliberal politics, the wealthiest 1 percent present themselves as an "oppressed" minority in America. The feeling of being threatened can be traced back to twentieth-century New Deal legislation, further back in the nineteenth century to the postemancipation period and Southern white property holders who resisted Reconstruction, and even further back to the pre–Civil War period when Southern slave holders fiercely opposed tariffs and taxation. Although the political will of the nation can be expressed by the majority in America—because elected officials are intended to represent the majority of constituents—the wealthiest Americans do not believe their voices are adequately heard. With the advancement of liberal economic policies from the New Deal forward, the wealthy elite have lost their faith that the political system protects their own propertied interests. Associating their own interests with a particular vision for American society, they insist that democracy should be associated with a pure and unregulated economic freedom. Ultimately, the goal is to decrease taxes on investments and capital, which benefit the wealthy who have substantive investments, and to increase taxes on wages and salaries, which would most affect the bottom 90 percent of Americans.

The use of the terms *majority* and *minority* is important to note because, among neoliberal thinkers, those terms do not operate as they are typically defined. The early nineteenth-century leader Senator John C. Calhoun, from South Carolina, was a fiery political strategist whose ideology inverted these founding notions of democracy. Calhoun expressed disdain for the federal government regarding its legislation in favor of the rights of blacks against the rights of propertied Southern whites. Calhoun cleverly argued that states' rights, enshrined in the Tenth Amendment of the Constitution (that state governments have the right to refuse to abide by federal laws they find distasteful), were being violated. And he strongly advocated that the state-defined rights on behalf of a "minority" of wealthy white slaveholders were sacred and inviolable, far more than the attempt to provide the protection of equal rights to blacks who were deemed to be inferior.

Calhoun's principles centered on the desire to have the will of one particular minority, plantation owners, overrule the desires of all other classes. His goal was to create a government that this class could manipulate toward its own ends. Wealthy slave owners did not lack the material resources, but they needed political favor to legitimate their desires and preserve their wealth. Calhoun and slave-holding sympathizers embraced an intriguing irony, accepting the legitimacy of government interference if it was beneficial to their cause but rejecting it when it was not. As Calhoun's class diverged from those of their (mostly poor) fellow citizens, a greater fear of government intervention took hold. Calhoun believed he was morally right in his conviction. Of course, he viewed himself as a true Christian and believed that slavery was condoned in the Bible, which justified wealthy slave-owner interests and enforcement of slavery by the State: "Slavery is an institution ordained by Providence, honored by time, sanctioned by the Gospel, and especially favorable to personal and national liberty." [12]

Similar to Calhoun, neoliberal apologists like James Buchanan leverage usual understandings of the term *minority* to assert that white, wealthy elites are also a minority because they are subject to decisions made by the majority in a democratic government. He asserted that the majority rule now "intended to violate the liberty of the minority, because it yoked some citizens unwillingly to others' goals." [13] Trained as an economist, he took from his University of Chicago training that socialism in any form, any tampering with the freedom of the marketplace, was sentimental and dangerous. During his tenure as the chair of economics at the University of Virginia, Buchanan sought to construct a strong ideological argument, promoting particular economic and political notions with the backing of a university affiliation. Libertarian in principle, Buchanan's economic beliefs center around laissez-faire fiscal policies and social order. Sternly against collectivist ideology or collectivist solutions, he emphasized self-reliance and individual liberty. [14] At the same time, Buchanan did not believe in a completely unregulated government; the idea was to remove all constraints on the mechanisms of current and future privilege wealth, while instituting new mechanisms to protect wealth already achieved.

Buchanan's social ideas and fiscal policies did not bode well for the working class, especially African Americans. For Buchanan, the failure of Reconstruction and the fact that blacks were hindered from economic success after emancipation was not the result of systemic obstacles but merely showed that "the thirst for freedom, responsibility, is perhaps not nearly so universal as so many post-Enlightenment philosophers have assumed."[15] Blacks themselves were to blame.

As the Civil Rights era brought some successes in securing rights to black citizens, the white elite grew concerned about their own "liberty," given that government control was now viewed as infringing on their "freedom." Until then, whites had largely had the privilege of ignoring the racism and discrimination toward people of color in America. Segregation was so intertwined with the workings of American social institutions that business leaders held to a rigid view of maintaining that social order, assuming their own persistence and security was based on holding that racialized order in place.

In light of the Civil Rights movement, we can more clearly see the significance of the polemic use of *minority* as a political term by Buchanan (and Calhoun before him). *Minorities* are typically defined as those who are oppressed and who must struggle for access, opportunity, and equal rights in a system. However, through the Civil Rights movement in the 1950s and 1960s, now whites were subject to the protests of blacks—often nonviolent involving access to bus seats, lunch counters, and waiting rooms—and the federal government began to pass legislation making race-based discrimination illegal. Because they no longer had the power to keep private and public spaces segregated and saw integration happen against their will, white elites began to feel like a minority. The government appeared to be changing spaces that had been racially ordered according to the wishes of a white-defined hierarchy, such that whites felt that the America they had known was being taken away from them. These white Americans increased their level of distrust and criticism of the federal government.

The word *liberty* was also now redefined to a far narrower conception of the discretion to exercise one's own prejudices, to mean the free exercise of a group's desire to serve their own interests, regardless of the consequences to others. Their standard for democracy was not about the majority determining what might be best for the general will but rather was seen as working against the historic privileges that had

been exercised among whites since the beginning of the American republic. So, although their stated value for liberty would seem to imply
that they would support other Americans who also sought freedom and
liberty, in actuality the white elite had systematically ignored the social
problem of black inequality (in educational, political, and economic
realms).

When faced with the considerable power of the federal government
toward their own narrow interests, they came to believe that any
government control would lead to total government control. For them,
government now possessed too much control over the rights of citizens.
These are people who feared progressive social movements and the
collective power of the majority in asserting the rights of neglected
citizens. Because their numbers alone could not hold sway in voting,
they generated tactics to influence public opinion, often through clear
misrepresentation and disenfranchisement of voters. Any move by the
federal government perceived to hinder attempts to foster their own
economic success was viewed as negatively affecting their liberty.

The protection of property rights was especially important to the
white elite. MacLean writes, "What was happening was that the majority, without the consent of the elite white minority, was taking something they considered intrinsic to the promise of America—the protection of property rights."[16] They viewed their property, which included
land and investment capital, as in circulation of the economy of America, and therefore they believed they made a significant contribution to
the country. Moreover, their tax dollars were larger in absolute numbers than all other groups. Elite taxpayers were taxed at higher rates
than those who receive lower income, which infuriated them, perceiv-
ing that their "hard-earned" cash was used to assist those who could not
make enough to sustain themselves (although, among the wealthy, the
majority of their wealth came from investments rather than wage income from their own labor).

By advocating for "freedom," Buchanan and others concealed the
issue of race through abstraction, using notions wedded to sacred ideas
held within our American ideals. He and others were masterful in dis-
guising the underlying racism in proposing legislation. He coated his
argument in economic terminology and logic. He attacked politicians
for pandering to constituencies in exchange for votes, and thus made an
argument against the representative power of the federal government.

Buchanan even believed that the wealthy of America conceded their interests too quickly and were too charitable and "compassionate for [their] own well-being or for that of an orderly and productive free society."[17]

NEOLIBERALISM AS A MORAL GOOD

The interests of the wealthy were further served with the expansion of neoliberalism. The neoliberal form of capitalism has been prominent since about 1980, its form coalescing in response to the economic conundrums of the previous decade. Nevertheless, defining "neoliberalism" is a challenge because it is an expansive concept with many interpretations.[18] It consists of a set of ideals like *individualism, laissez-faire government*, and *free choice*, but it also takes on power as a political project authorized and endorsed through state and national governments. Historian Lawrence Glickman writes, "Like most invented traditions, free enterprise discourse worked not only through its links to the American past but by defining itself in opposition to the dominant political regime at the time of its initial emergence."[19] That political regime was Keynesian-influenced economics, one that endorsed the involvement of the federal government to ensure both economic vitality and assistance to the economically distressed. But the precise administration of regulation and taxation were perennial issues, subject to controversy. Core to the birthing of neoliberalism is the accentuation of open-market exchange—market mechanisms over state management—fostered by reducing regulations imposed by states, corporate bureaucracy, unions, or professional associations. Sometimes called "free-market capitalism," neoliberalism was forged in the economic downturn of the 1970s, and it owes much of its worldwide proliferation to the changes in the United States's domestic and foreign policy at that time.

Until then, the principles of the economist John Maynard Keynes had reigned, encouraging national governments to consciously manipulate aggregate demand through the rise and fall of interest rates to control rates of inflation, thereby expanding or contracting the availability of capital for private spending and business investment in a society. Tax cuts offered further incentives to stimulate the economy. Keynesian economics further advocated the use of government funds to hire workers and expand private investment; moreover, the government had the ability to borrow to finance increased spending and run a deficit when needed. Essentially, the State actively intervened in the economy to fill the lag in demand until "natural" processes of the private sector resumed as expected.[20] Before Nixon's election in 1968, the Democratic Party dominated the White House and American politics, and people generally supported the Keynesian economic framework, believing that government assistance should be given to the impoverished to boost the economy and bridge their capacity to operate independent of government help, culminating in Lyndon B. Johnson's "Great Society" programs.

But for the first time since World War II and the creation of the New Deal, the American economy became stagnant in the 1970s. Inflation was rampant and the unemployment rate was high, which created an unforeseen combination of daunting dynamics coined *stagflation*. Unemployment and inflation were major problems, and wealth declined. Neither Nixon, Ford, or Carter could curtail the ensuing economic unease and their approval ratings demonstrated the frustrations of many Americans, as they were historically low for the time.[21] In response to the economic situation, the federal government loosened credit, freeing the flow of capital by deregulating the markets. The origins of neoliberalism are tied to attempts to fix the political and economic rut of the 1970s. There was also great motivation to phase out taxation on income and on investments and capital gains. The protection of wealth was key, and because wealth at the highest ends are invested in assets, keeping wealth actually results in the expansion of wealth—especially because growth of investments always outpaces growth of wage income (see Chapter 8). Amid these changes, white evangelicalism was on the rise, creating a union between evangelical imperatives and neoliberal policies.

The ideological ties forged between white evangelicalism and neoliberalism were facilitated by their shared belief in the value of affective associations (family, neighbors, church) that would ground individuals in bonds of affiliation and mutual care. Although the State mediates interests, it does so via market mechanisms governed by an instrumental (rather than affectual) rationality. Faith is private, whereas fairness is made public. Presumably neutral bureaucratic rules of exchange would be enforced to ensure fairness. In short, attacks on the welfare state dovetailed with calls from white evangelicals to restore "family values."[22]

Neoliberal ideas took shape in the wake of expanding American infrastructure, increasing education and literacy, and hope among whites for continued social mobility. One of the most influential political philosophers resourced by neoliberals is John Rawls. Combining bold assumptions regarding the nature of humanity and a societal vision that would build on what he most admired about American democracy, he once wrote that societal rules should result from "discussion" by "reasonable men" who were thought to be "average, rational, and right-thinking and fair men, irrespective of wealth, social stratification, nationality, race, creed, or religion."[23] The equalitarianism implied seems appealing. However, by avoiding inconvenient sociological realities regarding power and privilege, Rawls (and those who followed his lead) proffered a theory of justice on the basis of rational consensus—a utopian society overcoming both interests and ideology.

Rawls's ideal liberal society presumed that neither class nor wealth would affect the deliberations establishing legal and political guidelines and that sensible actors would exempt themselves from the distortions of prejudice and discrimination. Political problems became legal ones, and individuals served as the locus of activity, not social structures.[24] Through the right application of laws thereby instituted, individuals would be free to pursue their economic fortunes, having the liberty to live out the convictions and desires of their own private lives. Rawls's thought reflects a post–World War II optimism for the potential for liberalism, but he failed to approach his theorizing in a manner that would adequately account for the Jim Crow disparities, working-class oppressions, and other pervasive repressions plainly evident around him. And although Rawls acknowledged that social inequality could not be avoided, he naïvely believed that "these inequalities work as incentives to draw out better efforts."[25]

David Harvey, in his book *A Brief History of Neoliberalism*, offers an overview of the movement and its consequences from a historical and sociological perspective. Harvey defines *neoliberalism* as a theory of political economy that "proposed human well-being can best be advanced by liberating individual entrepreneurial freedoms and skills within an institutional framework characterized by strong private property rights, free markets, and free trade."[26] The main drive of neoliberalism is to liberate aspects of the economy (business and financial institutions) into the hands of the citizens themselves, although, in practice, these are citizens who already control these entities and desire to do so without government interference. So neoliberalism sounds like it has something to do with freedom because it has the word *liberal* right in the middle. Neoliberals see themselves as fighters for freedom, especially individual freedom. Theoretical neoliberalism demands that the state "favor strong individual private property rights, the rule of law, and the institutions of freely functioning markets and free trade."[27] These initiatives do not at first seem a mismatch with our American understanding of freedom. Indeed, such notions seem consonant with the Bill of Rights and general views of American liberty.

However, in practice, neoliberals define freedom in a darker, less democratic sense. For those holding to neoliberal ideals, the neoliberal state "favor[s] governance by experts and elites" and "democracy is viewed as a luxury."[28] The practical outcome of neoliberalism warps the traditional definition of *freedom* to the point of making it unrecognizable. As seen in Hayak, Buchanan, and Calhoun, this freedom is not so simply understood as it does not align with its typical use. Neoliberalism's main focus is ensuring that collective security does not override the principle of individual liberty.

Similar to the arguments of James Buchanan, neoliberalism champions individual liberty, the free market, free trade, and reduced government intrusion. Neoliberals believed that economic regulation enables the exploitation of the wealthy, which encourages a narrative of white victimization, one that had been characteristic of government attempts to curb the abuses of the wealthy and overcome the oppressions of the lower strata of society since the first days of Reconstruction (see Chapter 3). By forcibly taking wealth from the upper class to the undeserving poor, the government engaged in "a violation of the liberty of individual taxpayers."[29] By fostering a system in which the burden was placed on the individual, the blame was also squarely placed on the individual. Individuals should suffer from the consequences of their own actions. Neoliberalism is therefore a radical form of individualism. The failure to succeed in such a society, it was supposed, had nothing to do with systemic issues but rather an inherent laziness of people, especially those from certain racial and economic backgrounds.

Neoliberalism touts that the best way to support human dignity and individual freedom is to free the market from regulation and to deregulate trade. Although neoliberalism touts sentiments of equality, in practice, its policies propel more elite citizens toward money and luxury, while the working class continues to struggle. As an ahistorical framework, neoliberalism neglects to account for the origins of inequality or the structures that perpetuate it. It flows from an attitude among the already wealthy that by creating conditions that supposedly level the playing field, anyone can succeed by hard work, smarts, and inventive entrepreneurialism. The problem is that neoliberals want to remove regulations and protections that were created to correct historic abuses. The belief that market exchange guides action is a substitute for ethics.[30]

Indeed, the assumption that removing regulations and supports that protect the vulnerable; that provide support for common projects like air, water, and power; and that work to sustain help for older and disabled Americans through Medicaid and Social Security would provide the conditions for individual liberty does not hold up. Rather, the removal of government programs is more adequately explained by acknowledging that the wealthy do not wish for their tax dollars to go toward things that do not directly benefit them. Neoliberals believe that such services should be born by those who use them, and therefore taxation on the wealthy is seen as a type of robbery or gangsterism.

Neoliberal ideologies have consequences for government spending. In an important book titled *Welfare for the Wealthy: Parties, Social Spending, and Inequality in the United States*, Christopher Faricy uses rigorous quantitative analysis to examine the legislative spending passed by Congress over a long span of history.[31] Faricy finds that whenever the Republican Party achieves majority, it uses its legislative power to grant tax cuts, an intentional reduction of federal revenue that economists agree is a type of government expenditure. Essentially, failure to collect available revenue is the same as expanding the cost of government. Tax cuts are overwhelmingly passed by Republican majorities, consistent with their neoliberal ethos, allowing the wealthy to grow more wealthy at the expense of programs that help the much larger majority of Americans who have no significant wealth. In enacting special provisions of the tax code such as exclusions, deductions, deferrals, and credits, Faricy's analysis shows that the main goal of these changes in policy are to direct the wealth of middle-class taxpayers to those above them. The shift moves spending away from public programs and toward private benefits and services. As Faricy states, "Republican administrations have enacted fiscal polies that focus on lowering inflation and decreasing taxes, especially for wealthier individuals, and the cumulative effects of these policies are to distribute money up the income ladder."[32] In short, Republicans favor tax policies that result in a massive upward transfer of wealth.

Both Republicans and Democrats make claims on the public demand for federal social welfare spending, yet both respond differently regarding how to distribute government benefits to their constituencies. Republicans replace initiatives put in place by Democrats, shifting spending away from programs that assist the poor in favor of subsidizing businesses and wealthier citizens, which constitutes a sort of private welfare. As the clever title of Faricy's book states, whereas the modern Democratic Party favors direct payments to supplement the needy (like retirees or those in need of health insurance), the modern Republican Party favors credits and tax breaks, a withdrawal of collecting funds, which constitutes a *welfare for the wealthy.* Moreover, when Faricy compares the expenditures based on the direct payments of Democrats compared with the intentional loss of revenue based on favorable tax and credit toward the already wealthy by Republicans, he finds that Republicans far outspend Democrats. Despite claims of reducing the cost of government, Faricy reveals that the cost of Republican programs is far greater than the direct payment subsidies preferred by Democrats.

Consistent with Faricy's analysis, neoliberalism seems as it if would be beneficial for everyone, given that it advocates individual rights, but the benefits accrue to private business owners and the ultrawealthy occupying the top 1 percent. By obtaining big tax breaks for business, wealth is not invested in a collective institution but rather in the further consolidation of private wealth. Although such wealth could be distributed through charity, philanthropic giving does not equal the broad-based, systemic, and equally accessible help needed by so many of the dispossessed in American society. Charitable wealth can be directed to certain people and certain causes, yet those acts are not intended to address larger, systemic social problems involved with health, income, job opportunity, educational access, or environmental protection. Charitable help is often given in piecemeal fashion, to individuals or particular organizations, rather than directed toward structural arrangements. Indeed, some of the help that would most benefit the poor and marginalized may actually threaten bases of elite wealth. As long as neoliberal sentiments guide economic policy, the poorest Americans will continue to depend on doses of private charity because of the inability or unwillingness to restructure the system as a whole.

Neoliberal restructuring of the economy through deregulation, lower taxes, and privileging asset protection and expansion were intended to increase business investment and encourage the wealthy to save and invest. But lower taxes for business and the rich actually propelled a surge in corporate profits and incomes from investments of the already rich. The "lean" business structures unencumbered by worker protections could now bring in more temporary, contract "gig" workers, leaving workers less stable in longer-term jobs. Privatization removed pensions, making saving for the future a responsibility of individuals—who required payment for service to financial professionals to open accounts, consult on strategies, and manage funds over time. The search for gains from investment vehicles resulted in speculative bubbles and excessive borrowing on assets that were assumed to grow (as long as the future price was greater than the cost of borrowing, a "rational" incentive to borrow further remained).

Neoliberalism therefore relocates power from the collective political realm (government) to private economic sectors (business and finance), transforming the strength of the State to the strength of the market. Neoliberal policies do not produce economic freedom but rather expand the divide of wealth between lower and upper economic strata. It serves to push for reduced regulation and increased privatization, expanding plutocratic structures. And instead of acknowledging the historical barriers that have prevented African Americans, Mexicans, Asians, and other ethnic and religious minorities from thriving, conservative neoliberals see a free and fair labor market. They fail to acknowledge that individuals do not start from the same places. At the same time, neoliberal principles are celebrated among the most "successful" of Americans, as the widening wealth gap further accentuates those exceptional persons who interpret their success as solely the result of "hard work."

In the end, neoliberalism is an economic orientation that carries consequences for addressing issues of racial inequality. Those advocating for neoliberal principles view inequality as inherent to a neoliberal society, and the existence of inequality can be viewed as itself fostering a moral good. Those who achieve do so on the basis of pure merit—so it is believed—and collectivism thwarts the laws of nature. Leveling the playing field or helping the less fortunate is immoral. Ending racial discrimination on the basis of manipulating economic realities is equated with socialism and communism and would compromise the "liberty" that is essential to American ways of life. Taking away from the achievements of others to reward the indolence and immoral lives that result in poverty is also decidedly un-Christian. Instead, neoliberals and their conservative Christian allies argue that Americans should eschew group measures by race and only emphasize the achievement of individuals, and everyone should be responsible for themselves and their families.

LIBERTARIANS AND THE ELITE I PERCENT OF AMERICANS

Libertarianism is closely related to neoliberalism as an ideology that promotes the success of those already at the top. Nancy MacLean explains, "Those who subscribe to the libertarian philosophy believe that the only legitimate role of government is to ensure the rule of law, guarantee social order, and provide for the national defense."[33] Libertarians oppose Medicare, Medicaid, and Obamacare as forms of "socialized medicine." They would rather move Social Security into private savings accounts; defund public education in favor of vouchers and private schools; and seek to deregulate water, food, drug, and power sources. Even recently, former Speaker of the House Paul Ryan stated that "public provision for popular needs not only violates the liberty of the taxpayers whose earnings are transferred to others, but also violates the recipients' spiritual need to earn their own sustenance. He told one audience that the nation's school lunch program left poor children with 'a full stomach—and an empty soul.'"[34]

Following a consistent theme found in neoliberal arguments, Libertarians take on an identity, believing that the power of the majority does not represent liberty or democracy, calling it "coercion" and "oppression" of the propertied minority. Historian Quinn Slobiodian writes, "Democracy meant successive waves of clamoring demanding masses, always threatening to push the functioning market economy off its tracks."[35] Framing their "concerns" under the notion of property rights, they interpret their profits as private property, and they view private property as sacrosanct, believing that only property owners should have discretion over the use of their property. Intervention by the government negates that achievement, such that any intervention from the government is a form of stealing. Therefore, tax dollars being used for purposes they do not want or do not agree with is equivalent to the government "stealing" their property. Governance is seen as a threat to individual rights when governance involves decisions by regulators and lawmakers and the rights involve the use of tax dollars obtained from the wealthy. What the general principle conceals is that propertied whites already exercise considerable economic and political power, and they desire to protest and veto what they see as "unjust" laws.

Neoliberalism involves a cluster of beliefs and Libertarians tend to be associated with the allegiance of highly wealthy people. Here again the fear of "the majority" is because the interests of the wealthy elite (the 1 percent) are so different form the interests of the rest of the country. That taxation for purposes beyond the perceived benefit of the wealthy is viewed by the wealthy as stealing helps us understand the anger and zeal directed toward changing policies of taxation on the wealthy. As James M. Buchanan and his co-author George Tullock discuss in their book, *The Calculus of Consent*, majority rule could force a minority to pay for programs in the public sector through "discriminatory taxation" that they consider to be unfair. Arguments like this ignore the historical unfairness to other groups.

Yes, the wealthy are a minority given the gross inequities in the distribution of wealth in the United States. Yet their ideals concerning economic freedom through their vision of a properly framed laissez-faire economy actually provide greater freedom for wealthy individuals and wealthy corporations to gain even more wealth, without needing to be concerned with the true sources of inequality, assuming "the market" is a neutral arbiter of talent and access to opportunity. Ultimately, Libertarians are individualistic and antigovernment, advocating that we give up all government programs that pay for public services like welfare or social security, programs that obviously depend on tax funding.

While criticizing the supposed self-interest of others, they actively put their own interests forward, claiming the inviolability of private property in doing so. Ironically, although not willing to use their wealth to contribute to the country that made that wealth possible for the common good, the most wealthy are willing to spend a considerable amount of their wealth funding political campaigns and mobilizing against taxation (see Chapter 8).

PRIVATIZATION AND RACIAL PREJUDICE

Among Libertarians, individual liberty is a higher good than racial equality. This is because private property, market competition, and the means to secure the free movement of capital and investment of private property is the highest good. Political philosopher Michael Sandel argues that promotion of personal freedom and the myth of a neutral State arbiter emerged when long-standing white-settler colonial visions of joint rule became unfeasible (see Chapter 2); with growing immigration from other nations, the changing racial and ethnic composition of the United States, and the market power of consumers, the idea of a communal, self-governing republic founded on a shared democratic vision of citizenship was lost.[36] Now, the American population is made up of "makers" and "takers," with the wealthiest citizens paying the most money into public services, suffering the most under the oppressive hand of the selfish majority. They argue that "makers" pay more in taxes, so they should be entitled to a greater share of the vote on the use of tax dollars and the selection of public services being offered. Simply put, the wealthy should be in control.

Remember, Libertarian economic ideas center around the idea that people are best supported through economic freedom and the privatization of every industry possible, a privatization that "frees" the economy from government interference. Where markets do not already exist, neoliberal ideology mandates that they be created. In recent years, this has allowed industries in fields such as health care, the prison system, and even national defense to be privatized. The rise of school vouchers also moves in this direction. The State is not to be trusted on the assumption that the State lacks the necessary information to understand what the market would "naturally" figure out on its own. Correspondingly, neoliberalism also carries with it an inherent mistrust in those who hold office and influence government decisions. The primary means of securing neoliberal desires is to privatize as many industries as possible. In doing so, wealthy elites would have the opportunity to control the greatest part of society.

Although the beliefs of this "fiscal right" are not the same as that of the "religious right," both promote a cynicism toward federal government initiatives, and both call for a curtailing of the activities and expenditures of government programs concerning ideals they do not support. For example, Buchanan advocated for the privatization of public education, claiming that because public schools had the "monopoly" on education, they had no competition and no incentive to improve. Conservative Christians also advocated for private education to have the freedom to teach their own curriculum without the controversial subjects they shunned (like evolution and sex education) as well as the ability to resist forced racial integration. Although both claimed their stance would be beneficial for the nation, there was a persistent underlying racial component. Their proposals created greater barriers of entry for low-income people and especially racial minorities in America.

In Virginia after *Brown v. Board of Education*, both Libertarians and conservative Christians hoped that tax-subsidized vouchers would allow them to avoid desegregation, implying that the neoliberal movement was not entirely focused on the economic freedoms of individual liberties but also intended to reserve the South's tradition of racially charged policies. Some recognized that advocating for private education was racially coded. As Oliver Hill, an attorney for the National Association for the Advancement of Colored People, stated, "No one in a democratic society has a right to have his private prejudices financed at public expense."[37] The controversy over tax-exempt status for private Christian schools, and the fact that President Jimmy Carter had backed plans to revoke tax dollars from segregated academies, roused conservative Christians, which led to solidifying a political identity that set aside concerns over racial discrimination and rallied against what they viewed as federal overreach into their private religious convictions, decisively contributing to a particularistic emphasis on religious liberty over a more generalized advocacy for racial equality.[38]

THE REAGAN REVOLUTION:
AN ECONOMY BACKED BY GOD

Ronald Reagan was a fierce advocate for neoliberal policies, serving as an "Apostle of Free Enterprise,"[39] believing government should be small, with limited power, leaving individual Americans to make their own choices. As professor of government and social studies Katrina Forrester writes, under the Reagan administration "markets were introduced into new areas of public and private life, and weaponized as the alternative to the State in attacks on its welfare and democratic functions." It was at this time that "various forms of neoliberalism gained ground in liberal and conservative intellectual circles: antibureaucratic public choice theory, Austrian-inspired libertarianism, rational expectations theory, and supply-side economics."[40] This convergence of economic orientations into the 1980s and following Reagan's election dramatically shifted the American economy, making neoliberal economic policy mainstream. Reagan's economic policies greatly expanded the workings of neoliberalism under a veil of Christian virtue, much to the delight of wealthy Americans.

As discussed previously, in response to the economic stagflation of the 1970s, deregulation and the loosening of financial regulations led to an explosion of credit. The United States had a new dependency on foreign capital, and changing US monetary policy affected the allocation of federal funds to prop up capitalism.[41] In 1979, the Volcker shock—a dramatic rise in the federal interest rate to halt inflation—raised US federal funds to the highest they have ever been in an attempt to curtail inflation that was getting as high as 13.5 percent annually in 1980, the year Reagan took office. The last major economic event before the Reagan administration took over was the deregulation of interest rates. This had a major effect on credit as funding was now able to go "to the highest bidder" and could be easily passed along with higher rates to another party.[42] Loans were no longer held for decades, but for days, reflecting the cost of money at the moment rather than a return for investors over many years. The abrupt shifts in interest rates would have devastating effects on the middle class when paired with economic policy about to be made in the next decade.

Reagan's administration took steps to lower taxes as well as inflation and deregulate the economy.[43] Thus, "Reaganomics" was born. Reagan aggressively cut taxes on corporations and the wealthy and attacked welfare and other direct payments to the poor and underemployed. The highest marginal tax rate in 1988 was 50 percent, and this was abruptly lowered to only 28 percent in only two years; taxes were lowered for corporations as well.[44] Paired with the continuing trend of manufacturing jobs being sent overseas, this allowed greater flexibility for companies to place and extract funds in search of profits based on financial calculations of the current global market conditions rather than on long-term strategic initiatives. This exaggerated further the stratification of wealth in America as those in the middle and working class had trouble finding jobs outside of service industries and their wages stagnated for the first time in a generation; however, large corporations saw their wealth skyrocket with the financialization of the economy (see Chapter 8).

Reagan's administration took steps to lower taxes as well as inflation and deregulate the economy.[45] Thus, "Reaganomics" was born. Reagan aggressively cut taxes on corporations and the wealthy and attacked welfare and other direct payments to the poor and underemployed. The highest marginal tax rate in 1988 was 50 percent, and this was abruptly lowered to only 28 percent in only two years; taxes were lowered for corporations as well.[46] Paired with the continuing trend of manufacturing jobs being sent overseas, this allowed greater flexibility for companies to place and extract funds in search of profits based on financial calculations of the current global market conditions rather than on long-term strategic initiatives. This exaggerated further the stratification of wealth in America as those in the middle and working class had trouble finding jobs outside of service industries and their wages stagnated for the first time in a generation; however, large corporations saw their wealth skyrocket with the financialization of the economy (see Chapter 8).

The Reagan administration not only made the rich richer but created disastrous effects on middle- and working-class Americans as well. Inflation in the 1970s was not met with an increase in wages, and as corporations globalized, more and more jobs were sent overseas. Minimum wage hikes were resisted. Computerization raised worker productivity but further contracted middle-management and administrative-support jobs. In addition, labor unions were greatly weakened. Reagan famously took on eleven thousand striking air traffic controllers, firing all of them after they failed to report to work in a forty-eight-hour period. Federal judges ruled that the union would be fined $1 million for every twenty-four-hour period that the strike lasted.[47] After the strike, it was clear that unions could no longer protect workers from the government and that striking, in general, was no longer a viable option for those seeking economic reparation.

The Reagan administration hyped neoliberal truisms, stressing equal opportunity and promoting hard work as the solution to poverty. But with payment for tax cuts and military spending coming from government borrowing, the federal deficit bloated under Reagan to unprecedented levels, which was justified by the imagined prosperity of "trickle-down economics." Instead, Reagan's economic policies resulted in a wider gap between the rich and the poor and a broadening of America's underclass, which was disproportionately black and other minority.

Evangelical sentiments toward the economy mattered during the Reagan presidency, and they became more important as the proportion of evangelicals in the American population grew. Crawford Gribben describes the 1960s through the 1980s as the Third Great Awakening in America, a spiritual revival signified by the astounding growth of "born-again" Christians.[48] These fervent Christians argued moral issues and cultural conflicts amid patriotism and free-market economic agendas. For example, on the fiftieth anniversary of the 1939 stock market crash that led to the Great Depression, in October 1979, Pat Robertson sent out a special report to Christian leaders titled, "A Christian Action Plan to Heal Our Land in the 1980s."[49] He believed that liberal government policies plagued the American economy. Pat Robertson believed Christians should elect politicians who "pledged to reduce the size of government, eliminate federal deficits, free our productive capacity, [and] ensure sound currency."[50] He called for a "profound moral revival" to combat economic weakness, and he said Christians should elect officials who would reduce the size of government and eliminate the federal deficit. White Christian businessmen moved toward freedom and individuality; at the same time, they moved against labor unions and government social programs.

The fight over IRS rules in the 1970s pertaining to Christian private schools was especially important during this time, setting the stage for Reagan's alliance with the ascending Christian Right. Although not directly related to asset wealth, the issue concerned federal intervention in areas seen as involving religious conviction, crystalizing an economic sentiment toward taxation that merged attached itself to a specific focus on government policies in relation to the exercise of religious freedom. The government had attempted to force compliance of the 1964 Civil Rights Act among private schools (labeled "seg academies") established using church buildings across the South following the *Brown v. Board* decision—schools that intentionally shirked requirements for racial integration—by threatening to remove their tax-exempt status.[51] Indeed, the IRS did revoke tax exemption from Bob Jones University. Sharp reactions ensued, and, as a result, any legitimate concerns regarding racial discrimination were subdued to accentuate religious liberty. Conservative Christian narratives merged with the tax revolt taking place in California and affirmative action conflicts over racial quotas in college admissions.

The State's power to tax and enforce regulations also became tied to notions of secularization, making a host of "liberal" government actions inherently anti-Christian. The State's confrontation with conservative Christian organizations galvanized conservative Christians to reject political isolation as sufficient for protecting their interests; they would need to organize themselves to fight against growing political pressures. In a real sense, this resulted in a nationalization of Southern politics. As a result, churches were cast as victims, displacing the plight of African Americans and other minorities (including gays and women) as unimportant when placed in relation to the sacredness of Christian conviction.[52]

With claims against the reach of the federal government and a rejection of political solutions to the problems of economic suffering and poverty, groups like the Moral Majority argued that the Bible could be linked with economic concerns. Jerry Falwell, who with Paul Weyrich formed the Moral Majority, ran a segregated academy through his Baptist church (Lynchburg Christian Academy) and saw threats to other entities under his leadership, including Liberty Bible College (which became Liberty University, whose current president, Jerry Falwell Jr., became a prominent supporter of future president Donald Trump).[53] Many leaders of the Moral Majority were Baptist ministers whose churches had private schools.

So although concerns regarding morality were important, an economic attitude against government social reforms took root among a broad and highly influential swath of Christian leaders. Pastors like California's megachurch and *Hour of Power* televangelist Robert H. Schuller of the Crystal Cathedral preached "possibility thinking"; his sermons and best-selling books boasted titles like *You Can Become the Person You Want To*; *If It's Going to Be, It's Up To Me*; and *Tough Times Never Last, but Tough People Do!* Ignoring broader systemic issues, Schuller and others refrained from looking toward collective solutions for the alleviation of social problems.[54] Instead, promoting Christian Libertarian principles (see Chapter 5), pastors sought to encourage the rising suburban white middle class with messages that they were gifted by God with talent and agency, inspiring them to enact the freedoms that were guaranteed them, waving the American flag, and assuring them of core neoliberal, free-market assumptions: opportunities for achievement are available to those who apply themselves to grasping them.

In contrast to support for government initiatives for moderating the effects of discrimination, blacks and other minorities were given the same Christian Libertarian message—the only thing required to lift them toward wealth was to exercise their own will; to move forward, confidently stepping into those opportunities; to not be discouraged; and to place their trust in the God who provides options. Conservative evangelicals and their macroeconomic assumptions and political stances stigmatized the poor and chronically unemployed, further legitimated the concentration of elite wealth, and asserted the difference as the result of the disciplined individual rather than the stark bias toward asset accumulation, the weakening of unions, and the sharp decline of government assistance. The primary obstacle was an individual's own initiative. Individuals must overcome their own selves. Having done so, nothing could hinder their successful entry into the system of rewards assured by God and available for all.

Thus the Reagan presidency was a time when neoliberal principles were wedded with the moralistic language of the Religious Right. Evangelicals were encouraged to resist the power of the State, combating initiatives like the IRS revocation of tax exemption from Christian schools still participating in racial discrimination. As had been seen with Fredrick von Hayak and James Buchanan, racial issues were entrenched alongside Libertarian approaches to wealth and power. Indeed, given that evangelicals believe that their personal connection to

God lets them hear what God tells them to do, the sense of freedom from regulation aligned with their Christian Libertarian ethos.

CAPITALISM: MORE THAN JUST THE FREE MARKET

Influential people like J. Howard Pew endorsed the neoliberal principles of the free market as "compatible with divine truths."[55] And capitalism, meaning free enterprise and the promotion of business to achieve material prosperity, is presented as the backbone of the American economy. However, this does not adequately account for the striking and ever-increasing concentration of wealth by a small number of highly wealthy elite. It also ignores that multinational corporations have a considerable amount of control not only over their workers but also over local, state, and federal governments, in which they can dictate the terms of their operations, garnering generous tax breaks from localities competing for their revenue, and paradoxically weakening the areas they purport to be strengthening through job creation and local expenditures. When the wealthy elite fear the power of democracy, the wealthy leverage their money to influence democratic structures in favor of their own interests.

The connection to restricting government programs and decreasing taxes for evangelicals became even stronger when, according to prominent conservative activist Paul Weyrich, the fight against the IRS "galvanized evangelical Christians and made them enter politics—not the Equal Rights Amendment, not abortion, but the fight against the tax man."[56] By 1993, when asked about messaging for conservative candidates, political strategist Ralph Reed said, "[S]tart with taxes. Working families with children feel over-taxed and under-appreciated by the government."[57] Taxes had been viewed as a means for the State to regulate Christian organizations, like private Christian schools, and a burden to traditional families committed to raising children through those private schools, so fighting against taxation further spurred the alliance between Libertarians and conservative Christians. Conservative white evangelicals may not have agreed with the progay, proabortion, and proimmigration policies of Libertarians, but they were able to join in as part of the Republican base with its shared attitude against meddling by the federal government and a desire to reduce the power and scope of its activity, fostering support for an unregulated market.

Evangelicals have not grasped that capitalism is not solely defined by the participation of people in an open market. Rather, capitalism involves the possession and management of assets (both tangible and intangible) that increase and decrease in value. The value of one's assets is generally established on the basis of their value to others through trade. Assets are often thought of as tangible (like an automobile) but they are most often intangible (like a trademark or rights of ownership); increasingly, assets are acknowledged to be defined as such only because of their legal protection.

What *capitalism* truly means and how it operates remains largely unexamined among evangelicals. For many, the term *capitalism* is simply the opposite of *socialism*, contrasting a supposed freedom of individuals buying and selling in an open market against a menacing picture of despotic government bureaucracies exercising autocratic control over consumer freedom and the distribution of goods. Socialism was believed to be a system that took away the earned rewards of honorable producers and gave them to undeserving consumers, a contrast between "makers" and "takers."

By ignoring the broader structural characteristics of the split between owners and laborers or the entanglements of property ownership and political power, conservative white evangelicals reduce capitalism to the idea that individuals are free to participate in the market; therefore, success in the market depends on how an individual mobilizes his or her personal freedom. Among evangelicals, should difficulty ensue, individuals should seek God and the support of family and friends until, by the providence of God, new paths are opened. The openness of the market to faithfully disciplined individuals is a rousing claim, one that had moved evangelicals away from the Social Gospel and then directly contributed to the shrinking of the welfare state.[58]

An understanding of assets is crucial because to understand capital today is to understand how legal mechanisms encode through policy certain things as capital—such as when a deceased celebrity can have rights over his or her own image because even humans who are no longer alive can be coded to be capitalized as a corporate entity.[59] More than sheer discipline or self-initiative, legal codes can change the status of what is capital and what is not through legislation; for example, at one time slaves were a legal asset, and then they were not, which resulted in slave owners losing the entirety of their slaves' value not due to the loss of the asset but because of the change in the legality of slavery. Indeed, the federal government recognized this, and efforts were made to compensate former slave owners for the capital loss of their slaves, reimbursing as much as $300 per slave. It is the power of law enforced by the State that gives any asset (like dollar bills) an assigned value eligible for trade. Slave owners gained wealth not by their labor but by the legal recognition of their ability to invest, manage, and trade on the profitability of slave bodies—to the extent of even being able to borrow money against their bodies. The concept of capital as dependent on legal enforcement is reminiscent of Max Weber's understanding of the State described in *Economy and Society*, in which he explained that the power of law is due to the monopoly of the State to legitimately coerce compliance to a law that has been transgressed.[60] As long as slaves were legally recognized as property, even those who objected to slavery were bound to respect their value.

As Katharina Pistor writes in *The Code of Capital*, recognizing the legal basis of capital "contradicts the standard argument that capitalist economies are defined by free markets that allocate scare resources efficiently and that prices reflect the fundamental value of assets." Instead, "legal coding accounts for the value of assets, and thus for the creation of wealth and its distribution." Every nation requires State mechanisms to preserve order, and a strong military is consistent with the protection of capital and its mobility. The State provides a framework for the operation of capitalist activity.[61] In short, because the State is central to the coding of capital, capitalism cannot exist without the coercive power of the State.[62]

This contemporary, and more accurate, approach to capital helps diffuse the dominant discussions among Libertarians and their Christian sympathizers on the nature of capital as well as the misunderstanding of how the "freedom" of capital requires that its "freedom" be guaranteed from the State, a point aggressively argued in the past by Hayak and Buchanan and adopted by Christian Libertarians. The fundamental antagonism often pitted between capital and the State leads to profound confusion regarding the circulation of wealth and the means by which wealth is encouraged or stifled, placing far too much emphasis on individual initiative and not enough on the manner in which wealth can shrink or grow through the political decisions made regarding assets themselves. Indeed, the power of taxation, how the State raises funds by taxing income or assets, is one of the most important mechanisms for the legal revealing or obscuring of assets that has nothing to do with individual initiative, resourcefulness, or discipline.

The legal understanding of capital productively moves us away from market-transaction images of capital, lifting us away from a moralistic approach to capitalism, and allowing us to grasp the increased saliency of financialization (see Chapter 8). The legal construction of new instruments for the bearing and trading of capital directly led to the financial crisis of 2007. Of course, lawyers and those who are able to hire legal experts become enormously powerful in their ability to shift and reclassify assets, as long as they fall within legal guidelines. As Pistor writes, "After all, law is the predominant means by which democracies govern themselves; yet the law they furnish is used by private parties, the holders of capital assets and their lawyers, to advance their private interests." Moreover, as financial industries develop new instruments for investment, they essentially create new forms of capital—entities that become more intangible, more obscure, and more open to manipulation and misunderstanding.

In the end, the modern structures of capitalism reveal that capital is not just made by the result of hard work but rather through legal mechanisms guided by preferential policies that are enforced by the coercive structures of the State. When the State decides to promote the interests of asset-based wealth more than the interests of wage earners, legal coding of capital leads to dramatic boosts in private wealth among those already possessing such assets, leading to their further expansion and thereby magnifying the "gap" between those with few or no assets and those who have much. In short, wealth is determined more so by policies of the State than by the "gumption" of individual work.

Chapter 7

REACTIONARY POLITICS OF THE TEA PARTY

Barack Obama and His Critics

President Barack Obama generated as much antipathy from white evangelicals as President Ronald Reagan generated enthusiasm. Although Obama generated tremendous excitement as a candidate, he received majority support from nonmajority populations. White Americans were far less likely to vote for Obama than any other racial or ethnic group. In 2008, about 43 percent of whites voted for Obama; in 2012, the vote shrank further, with 39 percent of whites casting a vote in his favor. Furthermore, the white "born-again," evangelical vote was even lower. Only 26 percent voted for Obama in 2008, and even fewer, 20 percent, in 2012 (the lowest among all white religious groups). Although white evangelicals made up less than a quarter of the electorate, they were strongly against the Obama presidency. Obama not only lacked support from white evangelicals, he also was opposed by Libertarians who advocated for the reduction of taxes and the expansion of corporate-favoring free trade.

A new group also opposed Obama. Promoting Democratic policies and furthering the move toward universal health care, the Obama administration provoked a reactionary backlash in the Tea Party movement: a loose affiliation of politicians, activists, and wealthy sympathizers who claimed principles of small government, the free market, and reduced federal budgets were more effective than social programs to "fix" pervasive social problems. In reaction to the Obama presidency, they believed they were working toward a correction of a political system that was broken. Given what we know about the development of white evangelical political sentiments to this point (see previous chapters), it should not surprise us that a majority of the Tea Party were white evangelicals. With a broader coalition building a more energetic, conservative base, white evangelicals, Libertarians, and Tea Party supporters worked together and paved the way for the rise of Donald Trump.

INTRODUCING THE TEA PARTY

In their book, *Change They Can't Believe In: The Tea Party and Reactionary Politics in America*, political scientists Christopher Parker and Matt Barreto analyze the Tea Party in great depth, specifically its supporters, the underlying reasons for their support, and the group's influence. Perhaps the most troubling discussion found in the book relates to their reaction to Barack Obama as a person. Obama's race as an African American itself was a cause for deep concern. Tea Party supporters were troubled by President Obama as the first black president.

Parker and Barreto review the long-term racist history of America; for example, racism permitted early Americans to view Native Americans as savages and therefore justified driving them from the land. Africans were permanently branded as inferior. The Naturalization Act of 1790 restricted citizenship ("naturalization") to "free whites of good moral character." Racism provided the rationale to appropriate half of Mexico's territory in 1848. Racism barred people of Asian descent from immigrating to the United States; and even when they were able to naturalize, racism asserts Asians as perpetual foreigners in the United States. Of course, these policies predated the Tea Party, and Tea Party members deny racism or even outright hostility against blacks and other nonwhites. Yet Parker and Barreto maintain that support for the Tea Party is tied to this heritage of oppression.

Because the American presidency is a political symbol, Tea Party members, activists, and supporters reacted to Obama because his presence as the face of their country undermines their own sense of who truly belongs. They saw Obama as degrading the status and prestige of

America.[1] A racialized antipathy toward Obama emerged frequently throughout his tenure, beginning with controversy involving his black pastor, the Reverend Jeremiah Wright, who once preached from his pulpit at Trinity United Church of Christ in Chicago that blacks should not sing "God bless America" but "God damn America."[2] Soon, criticism of Obama's membership in a church rooted in black liberation and deliverance grew to denying that he was a Christian at all. Belief that Obama was a Muslim surged. In 2015, Public Policy Polling found that 54 percent of Republicans believed Obama to be Muslim (the same organization found that among Trump supporters it rises to 66 percent).[3] Indeed, Donald Trump was among the most aggressive advocates challenging Obama's birth in the United States, asserting he was born in a foreign country and therefore disqualified to be president. Those who supported the "birther movement" constitute the strongest supporters of Trump today.

There are numerous sects of political ideologies, and these ideologies can differ widely. There are important differences among conservatives. What distinguishes the Tea Party orientation is not simply economic conservatism but also a deeply rooted claim of who is a "real American." Tea Party supporters have a limited view on who can claim this title; specifically, they believe the label applies only to white Americans who are English-speaking, native-born, and Christian. Tea Party members believe that Obama and his policies threaten to take away the America they see as rightfully theirs. It's no surprise, then, that Tea Party sociodemographics are majority white and "born-again" evangelicals who exhibit great negativity toward blacks and undocumented immigrants (including recipients of the Development, Relief, and Education for Alien Minors [DREAM] Act—undocumented children of immigrants with long-term residency in the United States known as *DREAMers*). Some in the Tea Party advocate a repeal of Section 1 of the Fourteenth Amendment, which provides automatic citizenship to those born in the United States.

The Tea Party claims to be more committed to conservative principles than mainstream conservatives. At least in theory, they stand for many of the same principles as the majority of conservatives. They preach a state's rights approach to government and a desire to limit federal power and spending.[4] They also fight for traditional values when it comes to gender roles, heterosexual marriage, and maintenance of a racial hierarchy.[5] They champion small government, lower taxes, the free market, and government fiscal responsibility. However, there is also a persistent message of intolerance that attracts highly loyal supporters to the Tea Party. Members feel that their heterosexual, middle class, Christian, mostly male- and white-dominant country is being displaced, and therefore they want to elect officials and enact policies that will return America to a country they recognize, filled with people who look and talk "American." They outline what they want America to be, but the implication is that they know what America should be and feel entitled to define it through political policies. They are threatened by a changing America, which largely means a *white, conservative*, and *Christian* America is threatened. The country is being taken away from "real" Americans. This reflects a fear of subversion, a threat they perceive from outsiders.

THE "BIRTHER" CONTROVERSY AND OTHER ANXIETIES

The New Deal was just the beginning of actions that conservative Christians found unsettling. Many conservatives felt that the "modern list of sins grows longer with each night's news."[6] According to conservative Christians, America is dominated by heterosexual, Christian, middle-class, white males.[7] As minority groups gained rights through progressive policies, conservative Christians felt their sense of what is normal, good, and true to be threatened. For example, traditional Christianity teaches that men are to be leaders of the household, and that they are the true "managers of God's creation," pushing them to take on leadership of churches, communities, governments, and corporations.[8] But women's rights in America brought more women out into the workforce and made them more central to decision making and policy setting. Rights granted to lesbian, gay, bisexual, transgender, and queer (LGBTQ) people and the legal recognition of same-sex marriage further threatened the assumptions of marriage and heterosexuality. These "moral" threats were familiar anxieties drawn out from the "Family Values" platform proposed by the politics of the Moral Majority that had supported President Reagan (see Chapter 6).

The reactionary core of the Tea Party is evidenced by their full-throated support for outrageous rumors that accompanied Obama's rise to popularity. The Tea Party sought to delegitimize Obama's presidency through the "birther movement," a fictional conspiracy claiming that President Obama's birth certificate is false and that his "true" religious affiliation is Muslim. Tea Party supporters raised questions about his true nationality, and claimed to believe that Obama was not actually born in the United States. For example, a Tea Party–sponsored book "claimed that the president wasn't born in the United States, insisted on his allegiance to Kenya, and stressed his upbringing in a Muslim environment in Indonesia."[9] They not only questioned his birth citizenship but also questioned his Christian faith, believing that he was a "crypto-Muslim" who secretly followed Islam while publicly professing Christianity. Even after Hawaii released an official birth certificate, Tea Party adherents still viewed him as un-American. Barack Obama as the "other" would disqualify him as the leader of this country. This strategy is reminiscent of right-wing movements of the past like the Ku Klux Klan and the John Birch Society. The shared central tenets of their ideology include dedication to preserving an America in which the superior role of white, Christian men, already established in the American social hierarchy, would be secured and reflected in government.

Obama's foreign-sounding last name, a distinctively Muslim and Middle Eastern middle name (Hussein), his father's African ancestry, his Indonesian stepfather's connections to Islam, and his childhood spent partly outside America gave footing to the rumor. Although never a majority of people, analysis shows that Conservatives, Republicans, and those with negative views of Muslims and other out-groups were more likely to accept this rumor as true.[10] For them, the president was immoral, lived as a secret Muslim, and expressed religious bias, discriminating against faithful Christians. The birther movement extended to the fear that Obama wanted to radically change the core values of America. Although it is abundantly clear that Obama was both a Christian and born in the United States, Tea Party supporters believed otherwise. They hoped his policies would fail and sought to further discredit him.

In building their political platform, the Tea Party successfully garnered support from the religious right. Indeed, the Tea Party became more conservative not only on economic issues but also on social issues, despite a Libertarian desire to keep the movement agnostic.[11] Looking at their attitudes, 64 percent of Tea Party members opposed same-sex marriage, 59 percent think abortion should be illegal in all or most cases, 51 percent want better border security, and 78 percent believe that protecting gun rights is more important than controlling gun ownership.[12] White evangelical support for the Tea Party is considerable; although almost half of white evangelicals had no opinion of the movement, had never heard of it, or refused to answer the poll, a remaining 44 percent of white evangelicals agreed with the Tea Party movement, in comparison with only 8 percent who disagreed. That translates into white evangelicals being about five times more likely to agree with the movement than disagree.[13]

The religious and economic alliance represented in the Tea Party remains misunderstood and out of the public eye.[14] The Tea Party movement was formed primarily as an antitax movement, aimed at limiting government spending and reducing taxes, drawing on the symbols of the Boston Tea Party.[15] As important as these initial catalysts were, the power for the movement came from its adoption of white evangelical conservatives. For example, although the Tea Party Movement attracted a relatively high proportion of secular members, the majority of its members believe America is a Christian nation, including a disproportionately high number of nonreligious members. As sociologists Ruth Braunstein and Malaena Taylor report in their analysis of the movement, "in light of Tea Partiers' shared concerns about rising immigration, and especially about Muslim immigrants, it is probable their appeals to a Christian America served as a subtle means of marginalizing members of religious traditions, like Islam, that they viewed as threats to the American way of life."[16]

According to historian Darren Dochuk, Tea Party observers have radically underestimated the white evangelical support that buttressed the movement. By 2011, white evangelicals had come to be "driven by a theology of small government, free enterprise, family values, and Christian patriotism, and backed by a phalanx of politically charged churches, corporations, and action committees."[17] As Dochuk writes, this "late Tea Partyism has come into focus as principally a revitalized evangelical conservatism."[18] Among white evangelicals, the Tea Party did not constitute extremist positions but rather elevated the values they saw as neglected yet sorely needed today. Similarly, David Campbell and Robert Putnam also find religion to be central to the Tea Party; alongside their Republicanism, they "want to see religion play a prominent role in politics."[19]

The alignment between white evangelicalism and the Tea Party political orientation exists because "evangelicalism was nurtured in a belief system that, among other things, celebrated states' rights, white supremacy, and small central government. Moreover, evangelical Protestantism tends to adopt a Manichean approach to conflict in which differences are reduced to a battle of good and evil." Members of and sympathizers with the Tea Party believe that "anything that fits into their way of life is perceived as good. Anything that doesn't is generally considered evil."[20] Working from this conceptual schema, they are unable to accept loss and see any concession as a defeat. Sociologically, the Tea Party manifests a general principle: among those who have become accustomed to privilege, a little exertion of equality by excluded groups is falsely experienced as a form of oppression. Moreover, by ignoring broader issues of racial justice and democracy, the Tea Party is less patriotic than nationalistic, advocating for an ethnoracial presumption regarding who deserves benefits and belongs in America. Generally speaking, the Tea Party is a group that appears afraid and is suffering from the anxiety of a threatening "presence" they do not recognize. To protect themselves from losing their rights or from a "black" or other "colored" supremacy, they affirm each other with any resource or idea they can.

The America that Tea Party supporters want to protect is one within which they identify, that is, white with an ingrained conservative and capitalist-affirming Christian mindset. Fox News provided a supportive community for Tea Party loyalists to root for anti-Obama sentiments. They increased exposure to Tea Party ideals to attract like-minded conservatives with similar values. They led some Americans to adopt certain arguments and rationale that resonated with their notions, even when not explicitly stated. Moreover, Fox provided these groups a place to idealize a unified American identity apart from Obama and the Democratic Party. In one interview on Fox News radio, a Tea Party supporter said, "I do not believe Barack Obama loves the same America that I do, the one that the Founders put together. I do not believe that. I think he wants that changed." Conservative Christians increasingly gravitated toward Fox News, making the network also more closely associated with the language and sentiments of white evangelicals, spurring a new political label: "Fox Evangelicals."[21]

Of course, the intertwining of evangelical and Tea Party values has been forming for quite a while. Remember that in the wake of the New Deal, white evangelical preachers and business viewed Roosevelt's welfare programs as counter to sound Christian economics (see Chapter 5). Their work against Roosevelt's policies, Keynesian interference in government, and prolabor advocacy was fueled by a theologically couched ideology of free enterprise. A vast array of Christian executives and sales people (who joined auxiliary associations to support their business networks like the Rotary Club) networked throughout the mid-twentieth century, articulating and persuading good Christian men to mobilize against regulation of industry and pushing against the power of Union bargaining, seeing these as antithetical to a Christian capitalist orientation. The mobility of white evangelicals to Sunbelt regions in the South and Southwest resulted in an unanticipated economic power for what Dochuk calls *Sunbelt evangelicalism*—"an assertive pro-business politics that sanctifies tax inducements, lower wage scales, deregulation, and anti-unionism."[22]

The vast institutional reach of contemporary white evangelicalism allows Tea Party principles to spread through a broad network of Christian channels, including Christian schools and colleges and an array of homeschool curricular materials. As Dochuk writes, "[T]he gospel of Christian free enterprise is not simply preached from above; it is also propagated below in the pews, and the Tea Party has seized on this momentum."[23] With Obama as president, Christians who had taken on this ideology now saw in Obama a focal point to galvanize their fight against the excessive reach of big government.

That Obama operated as a focal point for coalescing a cluster of concerns is evident in how quickly opposition to his presidency formed. Just three months into Obama's term, the Tea Party had already shown irritation with his job performance, a stark contrast to the 70 percent general approval rating that Obama held at the time. A whopping 78 percent of Tea Party conservatives wanted Obama's policies to fail (compared with 36 percent of non–Tea Party conservatives). Many found fault in Obama as an inexperienced leader who lacked knowledge about the mechanisms of government. Mainstream conservatives have been forced to work with the Tea Party to effect their own change against the power of Obama's initiatives since Tea Party supporters proved themselves to be among the most involved interest group in all of political life. Tea Party members show up and get things done politically.

No matter his birthplace, citizenship, or religious identity, a closer look at Tea Party attitudes reveals that just having a black man like Obama in the White House was unacceptable. Tea Party members frequently described Obama as both Kenyan and Muslim, which contributed to perceptions of his blackness and his foreignness, an especially potent attack in the wake of the September 11, 2001, terror attacks. Parker and Barreto reveal an astounding statistic: 71 percent of Tea Party conservatives believed that Obama would destroy the country.[24] Under Obama, there was now a black president, a female speaker of the house, and a Latino on the Supreme Court. All of this contributed to the sentiment of a real feeling of change felt by the Christian Right. The world was slipping into madness, motivating them to take political action to elect and reform a white Christian America.

Sentiments persisted among Tea Party constituents that the Obama administration sought to bring socialism to America and to trash American values. Fear of immigrants and the perceived threat to national identity dominated. Despite the general shift of the country toward a more progressive and equal society, fear and paranoia remained.[25] They countered what they saw as conflicting ideals of what makes up the fundamental substance of the United States, particularly as immigrants from Central and South America and the enactment of certain "liberal" recognitions of groups like LGBTQ persons challenged their notions of the idealized American landscape. The Tea Party's distrust went beyond political motivation. Confident that Obama intended to devastate the country, they stressed political participation. Anxiety mixed with anger fueled their zeal.

A CHANGING AMERICA AND POLITICAL MOBILIZATION

Initially, it appears that Tea Party sympathies were motivated by economic ideals: limitation of the role of government in society, defense of free-market capitalism, and personal and fiscal responsibility in the marketplace. The Tea Party believes that America is rooted in individual autonomy, hard work, and meritorious achievement, and thus deems social welfare policies un-American.[26] But economic issues—although important to the identity of conservative Christians—were not the central predictive factor for the 2016 election. Although small-government reforms and calls for fiscal responsibility were promoted—especially during the Obama administration—in reality, fears of immigrants and a disappearing "American" identity were the most salient issues for Trump supporters. Although the Tea Party presents itself as a movement for small-government, fiscally responsible conservatives, its sentiments run much deeper, incorporating authoritarianism, racism, and existential anxiety.

The sentiments defining the Tea Party have deep roots, not only with respect to racial attitudes but also the political mobilization that exploits the discomforts and resentments of social change among whites following the gains from the Civil Rights movement. Simply said, even the smallest advances experienced by African Americans (who were seen as undeserving) were deemed to result in excessive losses directly affecting whites, which developed into a white-resistance countermovement.[27]

An impressive book-length study by political scientists Angie Maxwell and Todd Shields titled *The Long Southern Strategy: How Chasing White Voters in the South Changed American Politics* demonstrates how the GOP capitalized on white racial angst, making a series of decisions to court Southern voters by orienting their politics around not only their racial prejudices but also their concerns regarding societal shifts in gender ideology and religious assumptions. Their tactics became known as "the Southern strategy."[28] As Southerners felt abandoned by the Democratic Party's new commitment to civil rights legislation, especially in reaction to Lyndon B. Johnson's signing of the 1964 Civil Rights Act, Southern politicians, like South Carolina Senator Strom Thurmond, switched their party affiliation from Democrat to Republican, and Southerners (and other whites across the country) similarly defected to the GOP. The enlarged Republican base believed that federal initiatives to undo the long-term effects of Jim Crow (like affirmative-action policies) were unnecessary and, in fact, unfair to whites. In describing this racialized sentiment, Maxwell and Shields write, "[E]quality feels like an attack when privilege is all one knows."[29] Even in more recent times, those who believe that blacks in America have "gotten enough" are likely to be Republican.[30] These racial attitudes translate into economic issues that distinguish between "makers" and "takers," or more pointedly "tax payers" from "tax recipients." The racism that centers the Long Southern Strategy is reinforced by patriarchy and religious fundamentalism, and allows conservatives to leverage claims of higher morality to their political advantage by playing off conventional notions of a "normal" and "good" society. In this way, seemingly positive advocacy for wholesome virtues like "family values" and opposition to the abuses of "big government" became code for expressing the desire for a racialized and religiously sanctioned social order.

One of the most consequential racialized attitudes among Tea Party members is their stance on immigration. Clearly, Tea Party members believe that immigrants are an economic and political burden; they do not want to see their country escape their grasp by allowing immigrants to overwhelm the demographics of our nation, especially if it would allow minorities to take power in local, state, and national governments. The distinct distaste for the "other" stems from anger and anxiety that reflected how much the country has changed since the 1950s. The United States has shifted demographically, especially after the 1965 change in immigration laws, which began the process of expanding foreign-born populations as more Asian and Latin American immigrants obtained legal status in the country (see Chapter 4).[31] The Civil Rights movement in the 1960s also threatened a significant portion of white conservatives who believed that decisions like *Brown v. Board of Education* were a communist plot. As Barreto and Parker write, "[T]he colored man looms large in the Communist plan to take over America."[32] By conflating Communism, the most un-American form of government, with people of color, the far right made it clear that anyone who was not white was not American and therefore against all that the Constitution represented.

As at the turn of the twentieth century (see Chapter 4), immigration is again viewed as a dire threat today, a threat that motivates conservatives to continually resist immigrants coming to America. Although the strongest antagonism is voiced for undocumented immigration from the Southern border, opposition extends to legal migration for work, family reunification, and refugees escaping the horrors of violence and war in their home countries. Their resistance to all immigration means that the

Tea Party is often seen as hostile to minority groups. Their attitudes toward immigrants, combined with their sentiments about the racial make up of "true Americans," reinforce a hostility toward groups that do not conform to the Tea Party's broad American stereotype.[33] For Tea Party members, the United States should keep to the social and political norms as they understand them, notions that have been intentionally crafted through United States policy for over a century (see Chapter 4).

Although Obama deported many Latinos near the Mexican-US border, the percentage of foreign-born people living in the United States went up during the Obama presidency, edging toward 15 percent of the total population.[34] That immigration spike and the perceived momentum created a surge of panic. Larger demographic changes saw the proportion of the white population decline compared with nonwhites, which raised "cultural anxiety" among those who did not recognize these newcomers as Americans. Even though border patrol and enforcement continued to tighten throughout the Obama administration, many white Americans felt that the United States was losing control of its borders, which really meant that the United States was losing control over the composition of its people. Essentially, anyone who did not fit the mold of the traditional white Protestant American became a source of discomfort and paranoia. Consequently, the majority of Tea Party sympathizers want to repeal naturalization citizenship and the DREAM Act, believing that immigrants are too powerful and contribute to increasing crime. To the Tea Party, America had begun to feel less and less American. America once belonged to these white-assimilated groups, but after Obama's election, they increasingly felt themselves to be strangers in their own land.[35]

President Obama's election to the White House affirmed for the Tea Party that the threat they perceived to the social, economic, and political hegemony of white, free-market, conservative-Christian ideology was legitimate. Obama and his policies are interpreted as subverting the social prestige that white, middle-class evangelicals had come to enjoy. *Authoritarianism*, defined as a desire for social conformity that means that "any threat to upset the social order is worthy of punishment," played into their initiatives; for example, conservatives supported limiting the rights of the gay and lesbian community and eschewing racial tolerance such that they saw no problem with widely recognized social inequality.[36] Such groups were marginalized because, for these conservatives, they simply should not be accepted into mainstream American society.

The Obama presidency therefore greatly contributed to a racialized sorting of the demographic composition of political parties. Research by Michael Tesler, professor of political science at the University of California–Irvine, found that, with Obama's election, blacks felt themselves to be more strongly associated with the Democratic Party, and Latinos even more so; both groups viewed the Republican Party as the party for "white people."[37] As affiliations for people of color became more partisan, whites increasingly sensed that nonwhites were united against whites as a group, fostering feelings of racial antipathy and a narrative of racial threat. The Obama presidency elevated racially sensitive attitudes not because he forcefully advocated on racial issues (progressive activists felt he sorely neglected such issues) but rather because as a black man he was perceived to be allied with people of color. With these shifts, terms like "white backlash" notably emerged, which aimed to explain the manner in which whites saw themselves as their own distinct ethnic group that was being neglected and whose interests were threatened—especially in recent times around the issue of Latino immigration.[38]

In short, the ideological background of the Tea Party (whose members and sympathizers became supporters for Donald Trump) stems from demographic changes within the United States that acted as an impetus for political mobilization around preserving an ideal America. Sympathizers are important because they may not belong to a political organization or actively work to advance certain sentiments, but their support carries the vote for Tea Party Republican candidates. The rhetoric of "my America" and "you are taking away my America" is voiced by Tea Party sympathizers. For Tea Party members and sympathizers, the concern is not for "the other," minorities who are not "catching up" to what they merit as citizens, but rather that the growing presence of minorities takes away opportunities from "deserving" Americans.

THE TEA PARTY AS A REACTIONARY
CONSERVATIVE MOVEMENT

Barack Obama's election as president of the United States was the
worst-case scenario for the Tea Party. For many, Obama was the epito-
me of an anti-American president. Republicans lost both the Congress
and the White House, and they believed Obama would seize control
over the country with policies and initiatives that went against their
values. Parker and Barreto write, "President Obama, by virtue of his
position as president, and the fact that he's the first nonwhite person to
hold the office of president, represents to some an assault upon a specific ethnocultural conception of American identity and everything for
which it stands."[39] In short, Tea Party supporters stem from mainstream conservative values and the deep anxiety and fear over the
changing demographic landscape of America.

In laying out the motivation and sentiments of Tea Party supporters,
Parker and Barreto's analysis reveals that the Tea Party is not simply a
fringe movement of the far right but a logically and historically rooted
form of reactionary conservatism.[40] They are "reactionary conservatives:
people who fear change of any kind—especially if it threatens to undermine their way of life."[41] The Tea Party first emerged in December
2008 when the Libertarian Party of Illinois gathered in Chicago to
promote conservative ideals immediately following John McCain's defeat in the 2008 presidential race. But the movement exploded in April
2009 when the vague cloud of conservatives who supported low taxes
and limited government formalized an organization. Lobbyists brought
together a single movement out of six separate Tea Party factions from
around the country. Media further elevated their visibility, reporting
their outspoken negative reaction to the Affordable Care Act in March
2010. They criticized all of Obama's actions, soon calling his religious
identity and his citizenship status into question.

For many observers, the Tea Party seems a radicalized version of
conservatism because they hold so many of the same values but are
more willing to act upon what they believe is wrong with the country.
Members of the Tea Party are exceedingly outspoken about what they
believe and strongly advocate for the preservation of what they perceive
as traditional (and thereby "correct") American ideals. Whereas conventional conservatives express anxiety and hope to return the country to a

conservative sense of normalcy, reactionary conservatives reject change more absolutely and work to return America to a time in which the country reflected their values, believing the clock can be turned back to an ideal moment which would then never change again. Reluctance to change is integral to understanding much of the Tea Party's social stances. For example, the Tea Party differs fundamentally from the Republican Party in one crucial aspect: "Tea Party sympathizers don't appear interested in ensuring that everyone is treated equally."[42] They proclaim this doctrine more openly than their mainstream conservative counterparts.

Whereas most conservatives preach limited government, law and order, and state's rights, all within the limits of the Constitution, the Tea Party seems undeterred by Constitutional restrictions and openly advocates for the deportation of immigrants, making no distinction between legal and illegal status. The Tea Party has advocated repealing parts of the Fourteenth Amendment, specifically the birthright citizenship clause that grants citizenship to those born on US soil, which they see as an incentive for illegal (and legal) immigrants to come to America in the first place.[43] Although Tea Party members support freedom of speech in accordance with their commitment to liberty, they react negatively to outside groups exercising this right. *Multiculturalism* is a bad word; *pluralism* is even worse.

In many ways, the Tea Party sets out to remake America into its own image. The birth of the Tea Party in 2008 and its subsequent growth owes its existence to reactionary conservatism defined by a fear of the loss of a perceived American national identity, which is deeply intertwined with xenophobia. Research shows that Tea Partiers are more hostile toward outgroups than mainstream conservatives. The Tea Party identifies with similarities from other right-wing organizations such as the John Birch Society or the Ku Klux Klan of the 1920s. The foundational concept of wanting to preserve certain principles regarding traditional ideals of patriotic American citizens is tied to the characteristics of white supremacy paired with middle-class, Christian working men who represent their families. Any group belonging to an outside minority group is subject to attack.

Indeed, Parker and Barreto see consistent patterns between Tea Party core beliefs and that of other far right movements such as the Ku Klux Klan and the anticommunist John Birch Society. Careful to avoid claims of exaggeration, the authors reveal multiple ways Tea Party sentiments aligned ideologically with these organizations. They report about 450,000 official Tea Party members in the United States, with about forty-five million Americans being sympathizers, effectively giving tremendous political sway to an otherwise fringe political movement.

The distrust the Tea Party felt for government was a call to arms as it aimed to retain the power structure that had historically favored their members who were predominantly white and middle- and upper-class Protestants. Freedom is seen as the lack of restraint by government, and patriotism is putting the interests of the country or community (as they understand it) before oneself, both insisting that their own venerated notions be enacted despite offense or resistance by groups who do not share or fit their particularistic ideals.[44] If patriotism is defined as putting the interests of the country or community before the self, and if racial injustice is only defined as an interpersonal problem, then the advocacy for racial problems will be seen as selfish. When conservatism is an "ordered liberty,"[45] then loopholes and ambiguities emerge that are said to enforce patriotic archetypes while allowing abandonment of civil liberties, such as free speech or equal access to opportunities, as a means of getting there.[46]

So conservatism alone does not explain the Tea Party. Indeed, the Tea Party is not a classically conservative group; it has redefined the basis of conservatism in ways that are different than the historical trajectory of "conservative thought." So, although 73 percent of Tea Party affiliates identify as conservative, 42 percent say the Tea Party is a new and much needed voice in politics.[47] Shared concerns involve advocating for small government, individualism, and conservative Christian morals, with white Protestant males acting as the standard bearers. Indeed, in reaction to various social changes, both the Tea Party and traditional conservatives are reacting to the decentering of the white, Christian, male-dominated, heterosexual, and native-born American.[48] They oppose LGBTQ rights, are hostile to "illegal" immigrants, and seek to reimpose an order they believed was not only a past default position but the very foundation of US society.

In sum, the Tea Party itself is a historically significant reactionary backlash that combines a cluster of attitudes regarding race, religion, and economics. What some view as social progress the Tea Party views with distrust. Most significantly, many members and sympathizers of the Tea Party believe that America is "slipping away" from their grasp. The United States has seen exponential population growth in the past forty years, with the white non-Hispanic population now forming only 63 percent of the population; in 1970, the same group made up 83 percent of the population. As immigration increases, Tea Party sympathizers have become more concerned with the increase of crime in the United States; a slight majority (55 percent) believe that increased immigration leads to increased crime. Whereas mainstream conservatives are more concerned with "law and order," Tea Party conservatives believe that "immigrants are taking over their country."[49] Tea Party conservatives are angry that immigrants are altering the demographic profile of the United States, while mainstream conservatives fear a country that is dangerous for their children and themselves. Although both of these groups assume that immigrants bring crime, there is a clear distinction in their disdain for immigrants. Tea Party anger focuses on significant outgroups in the United States. Core to their opposition is an understanding of the American identity. Maintaining and upholding a particular picture of American identity is of the utmost importance.

VOTING FOR A RESTORED AMERICA

Behind the anxieties resulting from Obama's election to the presidency was the urgency some whites felt to establish their rightful place at the top of the racial hierarchy, a notion buttressed by the history of slavery, Jim Crow laws, restrictive immigration policies, and ongoing controversies against integration of the foreign "other." As historian Gary Gerstle summarizes, the Obama presidency "became the occasion for remobilizing the racial nationalist sentiment on an epic scale, much of it centering on a powerful conviction held by millions of whites: namely, that no black man, even one who was half white, had the right to sit in the White House."[50] These anxieties instigated mobilization for what became the Tea Party.

The Tea Party is important because its successes led to a dramatic increase in polarization, as the right-shifting Tea Partiers pulled mainstream conservatives and Republicans further right. The Tea Party relies on *affective polarization*, the process by which a group isolates and defines itself more by anger and distrust with the opposite side than by its own belief systems.[51] Affective polarization not only contributed to voting behavior in the 2016 election that offered up the sentiments of Donald Trump but also correlated with the decreasing likelihood of bipartisan compromise.

Ultimately, the Tea Party is composed of reactionary conservatives who feel that their country is being overcome with minorities. They feel a loss of control. This leads some observers to say that the Tea Party upholds the American tradition of whiteness. Those who simply do not align with their definition of a true American, such as racial minorities, become a scapegoat. Immigration is a threat to American culture and to Americans, which instills fear into the public, normalizing racial profiling and dehumanizing rhetoric. Fear and distrust of immigrants are associated with fear and distrust of the government. Trump's campaign rhetoric played into these sentiments, using outright racialized insults and ugly stereotypes that were contested in the media but broadly affirmed among white voters.

Given the theme of loss and the slipping away of American identity, it is easier to see how election sentiments after Obama's two terms as president had the character of restoration, of bringing back, setting aright, tipping the scales, and placing things back on course. The Obama presidency mobilized white, evangelical opposition, affirming the concerns of the Tea Party movement.[52] Indeed, fears about cultural displacement and support for deportation of undocumented immigrants, free-market economics, and partisanship predicted Trump support. Preserving the whiteness of America and the fear of immigrants were more important than economic issues when voting for Trump, more so than party loyalty, such that whites who feared cultural displacement were 3.5 times more likely to vote for Trump.[53] Racial resentment became a key factor among Trump's base. Sensing racial coalitions forming at the expense of the interests of white people, alongside their perception of a slip in their prominence in American society, white voters accentuated insecurities and placed their political hope in Trump's promises to return to an America they recognized as good, right, and proper. These sentiments of threat to their well-being received broad-based support. As a result of these attitudes, people who ultimately became Trump supporters wanted to see a change—really a correction—in American politics. They no longer trusted "career politicians" and were ready for someone from the periphery to shake things up and to "Make America Great Again."

The irony is that despite the feeling of threat, as a consequence of America's long history of favoring whiteness, whites *still* retain status and privileges over people of color. Even with the historic gains from the Civil Rights movement, white people still understand their inherited social status in society. This is illustrated in a viral video featuring educator Jane Elliot, a former school teacher and innovator of the "blue eyes/brown eyes" eye color exercise, speaking with a room full of white Americans.[54] She looked out at the group and asked, "If you, as a white person, would be happy to receive the same treatment that our black citizens do in this society, please stand." The room was utterly quiet, and no one moved. After clarifying the question, and there was still no movement, she said, "Nobody's standing here. That says very plainly that you know what's happening, you know you don't want it for you." As the African-American comedian Chris Rock once joked to a live audience, "There ain't a white man in this room that would change places with me. None of you. None of you would change places with me, and I'm *rich*!" The line prompted huge laughter. In America, white people as a group still receive better loans; are not subject to implicit racism; have lower unemployment; are more likely to graduate from high school, enroll in college, and complete a college degree; have the freedom to live where they wish; and generally are more likely than blacks, Latinos, and most Asian groups to generate wealth over generations. It is the feeling of threat that moves so many to react so strongly toward an aggressive correction they believe is required to maintain the comfort of those presumptions.

Chapter 8

INCREASED CONCENTRATION OF ELITE WEALTH THROUGH ASSET GROWTH

The 2007 Market Collapse and the Rule of Finance

During Obama's tenure, the dominant economic philosophy of conservative Christians further dovetailed with the economic desires of neoliberal libertarianism, a political movement that cared little for conservative agendas and instead focused solely on the reduction of government and the protection of accumulated wealth (see Chapter 6).[1] Neoliberals lack sympathy for the difficulties faced by nonwhites in achieving social mobility. In addition, despite egregious fraud, misrepresentation, and greed manifested in corporations as well as the long-term stagnation of income and the further concentration of elite wealth, conservative Christians do not show signs of turning away from neoliberal, free-market ideologies. During the Obama administration, a religious grounding was established to justify the expansion of an American *plutocracy*—government ruled by and intended for the wealthiest of society. When so many racial and ethnic groups cannot take advantage of the opportunities afforded as part of the American Dream, it puts into question whether they are truly American.

By the time Obama became president, modern economic structures had shifted dramatically. Obama inherited the economic problems of the 2007 economic crisis occurring late in the presidency of George W. Bush, which led major investment banks into failure or to the brink of failure. The causes of the crisis are becoming clearer. A core contributor to the crisis is how much neoliberal capitalism relies on growth based on the expansion of debt and a rise in the price of assets.[2] These were intended to result in both wage and productivity growth, but globalization of the flow of capital and changes in the nature of competition for profits added additional pressures.[3] Financial deregulation allowed for an expansion of credit and a slew of new financial instruments built on redefined risks and new approaches to speculation. The resulting bubbles of value burst in the 2007 decline in the stock market, which continued through 2009, and excessive debt, which either defaulted further or sank available income and capital, delayed expansion of continued growth.

The 2007 financial crisis is widely assessed as not merely an emergency but rather a critical failure of the neoliberal form of capitalism.[4] Obama did not inherit a short-term crisis; instead, the entire economic system threatened to implode. The capitalist economic system of the United States was under threat, prompting extreme measures to save it. The problem also resulted in new speculation, from credit extended to undeserving borrowers to careless oversight of the financial industry by government watchdogs. Ultimately, these and other measures were superficial, dependent on happenstance understandings of the new complexities of our contemporary financial structures rather than careful and rigorous analysis. More careful considerations of our financial system was required.

Thomas Piketty's thick and ambitious volume, *Capital in the Twenty-First Century*, brought attention to a host of distinctive financial developments, including the growth and significance of central banks, the expansion of household debt, the creation of new financial instruments for trade, the leveraging of investment instruments based less on property or material production, and risk profiles with propensities toward default.[5] He demonstrated that the workings of modern capitalism depend on a novel mixture of fiscal policies and inventions by private firms—especially since the 1970s—that coalesced into a steady stream of profit-enhancing practices, all legitimated under an overarching ideology of neoliberalism that idealized the free market while eroding the bases of what a truly free, open, and transparent market would be.

A SURPRISE BESTSELLER

It is rare for an economic textbook to become a best seller, especially one filled with charts and graphs and dense discussion of government policies over the past hundred years. But Piketty became an academic star as his *Capital in the Twenty-First Century* achieved broad readership and reoriented economic discussion not only among academics but also among policy makers, nonprofit executives, and business leaders seeking to understand the long-term direction of wealth and inequality across the world.[6] The fruit of more than a decade of research, based on an original data set from twenty countries, and ranging as far back as the eighteenth century, Piketty's seven hundred–plus page book caused a sensation.

Piketty's remarkable achievement was the culmination of nearly a decade of increased focus on wealth and inequality among economists, many of whom moved away from mere quantitative assessments of interest, unemployment, and gross domestic product to more historically nuanced assessments of the mechanisms of modern finance. New attention was given to the growth and significance of central banks, the expansion of household debt, the creation of new financial instruments for trade, the leveraging of investment instruments based less on property or material production and more on risk profiles and propensities toward default. And while the structure of modern economic structures had shifted dramatically, few outside of Wall Street understood the workings of these instruments or the implications of their expansion. In fact, the stock market collapse of 2007–2009 revealed that few Wall Street *insiders* even understood the workings and repercussions of these new, core profit mechanisms that had become foundational for their industry.

When the dangers of newly crafted investment vehicles and overextension of loans to risky borrowers were realized, the market collapse abruptly initiated in 2007 revealed that wealth and inequality were caused not by abstract economic conditions but rather by human-constructed financial strategies that trace their origins back to corporate strategies from the 1950s and political interventions in the 1970s.[7] Exposing the ironic relationship between market collapse and corporate profits, Piketty shows that, although political and economic leaders broadly tout the value of competition and public ownership of shareholders, in actuality, much has been done to buffer *already* successful, *already* wealthy firms. Aggressive moves to continually raise profit for shareholders resulted in the aggressive management by corporate executives to sustain their capitalistic fiefdoms and further raise their executive bonuses. The majority of incomes among the top 1 percent of earners in America go to executives in finance and Americans possessing the largest share of capital investment (wealth) also have the highest annual salaries (income). Yet, adjusted for inflation, wages for the bottom 60 percent of American men have fallen since 1979; those who cite recent statistics refer to the increase in total income of American families, but this is primarily due to the increase of dual-earner households and the increase in the number of hours parents are working: the equivalent of seven additional weeks of full-time work per family.[8]

Federal political structures under Republican leadership resist providing practical economic help to the lower rungs of society, favoring tax cuts benefiting the already wealthy and granting even greater freedom to corporations to supervise themselves in their pursuit of higher profits (see Chapter 6). This is not an opinion but a demonstrated fact, as seen in careful and systematic analysis like Piketty's.[9] The 2007 market collapse was devastating to many families in America and it disproportionately hurt blacks and other minorities. Because minority populations have historically been and continue to be disenfranchised, our economic system is much less likely to find African Americans or Latinos belonging to the top 10 percent of wealth, let alone the top 1 percent. These trends are the result not of personal character deficiencies but of institutional barriers. It is simply inaccurate to assume that every individual has the freedom of choice to get out there and gain wealth.

Even more, when discerning where there is a lack of sympathy for the financially struggling or impoverished in America, evidence shows that this most certainly is because the white-dominant, conservative economic elite and political leadership of the United States has been largely unaffected. The economic divide is also a racial divide. Blacks and Latinos reside at the bottom of the economic ladder. Rich, primarily white elites have become better off, yet stagnant mobility prevents blacks and others from making significant financial improvements. The inequality along racial lines is stark. The Forbes 400 lists the richest Americans, and the wealth of these billionaires is greater than the wealth of all African-American households plus one-third of Latino households. Even the typical white household has a net worth twelve times that of the typical black household.[10] Thus the wealthy minority is composed almost entirely of whites, a group for which the American economic system has historically worked in favor; it continues to do so.

Piketty's rigorous quantitative work shows that even as wages of all Americans declined and unemployment expanded, *corporate profits continue to increase.* And more federal political structures in both Republican and Democratic governments, adopting a more neoliberal economic stance, resisted practical economic help to the lower levels of society, instead favoring tax cuts most benefiting the already wealthy, and giving even greater freedom on the part of corporations to manage themselves in pursuit of higher profits. Even more, despite the naming of specific individuals who had intentionally abused laws to further economic gains during the market collapse of 2007–2009, the increase in the circulation of elites between political, economic, and legal realms resulted in nearly all lawsuits against those named to be dropped or settled for miniscule fines.[11] The average American family's net worth declined, and the wealth of black and Hispanic households fell by more than double that of white households.[12] Yet the white-dominant, conservative economic and political leadership were largely unmoved, and their companies and investments actually increased. In the years after the 2008 market crash, while the bottom 90 percent of America declined in value, the top 1 percent grew by 11 percent.[13]

Piketty's work addressed issues of wealth inequality head on. His analysis demonstrates that countries like the United States are approaching levels of disparity not seen since the Gilded Age of the late nineteenth and early twentieth centuries. During that time, the top 1 percent simply lived on their inherited wealth, which provided two and one-half times the standard of living achieved by the top 1 percent of wage earners. In other words, asset-based wealth has always been a greater economic force than income derived from wage labor—even among the most highly paid workers in our society. Americans possessing the largest share of capital investment (wealth) also have the highest annual salaries (income). Not only did Piketty show that income and wealth inequality has been worsening since the 1970s, he also explained the continuation of that expansion as long as the wealthy are able to continually reinvest their huge surpluses (inconsumable profits) back into the market, further expanding their capital wealth; gains from income alone (and the associated miniscule investment of any available surplus) are left further behind.

The elegance of Piketty's analysis comes through in clarifying sources of wealth in America. Piketty attributes contemporary wealth accumulation to social and political developments rather than some sort of "natural" economic deus ex machina. Piketty demonstrates that the role of public policy has shifted and these changes have had significant influence, sending western nations like the United States in a "drift toward oligarchy." Economic inequality in America and parts of Europe has increased greatly since the 1970s, and that widening of the wealth gap is due in great part to the effective efforts by the very wealthy to protect their own interests in keeping and building their wealth. Furthermore, because public policy has led us to the current levels of wealth, Piketty is confident that further, progressive changes in public policy can lead us to halt and even reverse this trend—if there is political will to do so.

So, although wealth inequality itself is not a recent phenomenon, the enormous extent of the gap between rich and poor certainly is. In 2015, the United States had the largest wealth inequality of any industrialized country, characterized by a very small proportion of Americans owning the great majority of the wealth. As lower- and middle-class Americans struggle to survive financially in a time of extreme economic inequality, elite Americans use their political influence to maintain a grip on their large share of the national wealth. The unequal distribution of capital plays an enormous role in ensuring that everyday Americans are hindered in their ability to achieve a healthier financial profile. And it is a concern because the extent of this gap is attributable to government policies that have consistently favored the rich, especially since the 1970s, and is therefore something that can be changed.

How might accumulated inequalities in wealth be decisively addressed? Piketty recommends a "tax on wealth," suggesting that the wealthy would be taxed more based on the amount of wealth and assets they have accumulated than on their annual income.[14] This would more directly create a greater economic balance and allow funding of programs to assist those without the means to care for children and elderly, to receive superior medical attention, to choose private education and tutoring as required, to receive job training and continued adult education, and to care for other practical family needs. Of course, as has been evident throughout the history presented in this book so far, the wealthy resist taxation because they believe they should not have to pay for services to support others who have failed to support themselves. The "Buffet Rule" (named after the famed investor, Warren Buffet) was introduced in Congress under Obama to shame Republicans into increasing taxes on the rich. The proposed 30 percent tax rate on those making more than $1 million ultimately forced Republicans to justify their policies; still, wealthy Americans continue to see exponential gains in income and returns on capital that greatly outpace the vast majority of Americans today.

Thus Piketty sees the role of the federal government in terms opposite those of neoliberal Libertarians like James Buchanan and his contemporaries (see Chapter 6). Buchanan sought to cut the majority voice out of democracy and give power to the wealthy economic minority to affect change in government officials. Buchanan claimed to give everyone an equal voice in democratic government by giving each individual voter a veto, claiming that should a single voter disagree with the majority vote, it should not pass; however, the cry for equality among Libertarians like Buchanan is shown to be a play for the dominance of the wealthy. Buchanan and the economic class for which he argued may be *under*represented among voters, but they are *over*represented in economic power. They believe that their wealth should be accorded an equivalence of political power. In contrast, Piketty saw that "it is morally reprehensible in a democracy for citizens not to have equal voice and influence," and asserts that "the skewed nature of control over economic resources may be poisoning the promise of equal representation."[15]

Piketty also recognized the extent of political advantage granted to those with significant economic means. Voters with money have the ability to affect change in politics substantially more than the average voter. On this aspect, Buchanan and Piketty agree. Both see politicians as self-serving, only following the political beliefs, ideals, and commitments that will get them reelected. Recent research affirms their views, showing that "the behavior of senators as measured by congressional roll call votes aligns more closely with the preferences of the rich than the poor."[16] This is due to the economic elite's ability to donate campaign funds and bankroll fundraisers to keep politicians in office. In campaign rhetoric, these are the "supporters" often referenced by politicians, as in "my supporters want" or "those who put me in office tell me." In short, Piketty offers counterarguments to Buchanan's Libertarian views regarding the relationship between government and the economy. Piketty argues for a government of equal representation, whereas Buchannan and neoliberal Libertarians like him want to suppress the majority voice.

ELITE CONCENTRATION OF WEALTH

Piketty's analysis comes to a single, devastating conclusion: society's wealthiest 1 percent not only control an enormous portion of available wealth, but that proportion will inevitably expand even further—unless governments implement policy changes to alleviate the vast extent of this inequality. Piketty's research found that the rate of return on investments generally outpace the growth of the economy, and those returns concentrate advantage among very few. The wealthiest 1 percent of Americans hold 40 percent of the nation's wealth, and the wealthiest 20 percent hold more than 80 percent of the nation's wealth. These percentages continue to grow because of the inability of the middle and working classes to gain significant wealth.

In a chapter published in *After Piketty: The Agenda for Economics and Inequality*, Elizabeth Jacobs summarizes Piketty's work, saying that "capitalism automatically generates . . . inequalities that radically undermine the meritocratic values on which democratic societies are built."[17] Merit and hard work do not readily lead to wealth. Instead, those who already possess assets, those who already have wealth, are the most able and most likely to accumulate significant additional wealth. The difference between wealth and income distinguishes the top 10 percent, even more so the top 1 percent, from the rest. In the same edited volume, a chapter by Robert M. Solow similarly explains the difference between wealth and income, describing inheritance as a key factor within wealth and further reinforcing the dynamics of income derived from labor versus income derived from accumulated wealth. So although most may still believe wealth is the result of education, hard work, and a bit of talent and luck, the arithmetic shows that the concentration of wealth and its ability to grow favors inheritance more than skill or talent. Indeed, the majority of wealth in America is not earned but passed on through inheritance. Solow writes, "A great bulk of wealth, around 90%, was inherited rather than saved from earned income."[18]

To understand economic inequality in the United States, it is important to distinguish between income and wealth. Wealth is not only the amount of money received but includes all of a person's assets, including property, savings, and investments, minus the amount of debt owed like mortgages or credit cards. Income does not represent ownership but the stream of money received, generally characterized as the annual amount of money earned through wages and investments. To be clear, *wealth* includes all assets, most of which is inherited, minus *liabilities* (like debt); in contrast, *income* consists of earnings, which, if invested in assets, can contribute to wealth.[19] That is, income can be invested toward wealth, and wealth, either through dividends, rent, or outright sale of assets, generates income.

Income from wealth accumulates differently than income from labor because income from wealth has a greater rate of return than wealth through wages. If someone's entire income comes from accumulated wealth and "they earn *r* percent a year . . . they are likely to consume only a small fraction of their income. The rest is saved and accumulated."[20] Inherited wealth fares well in the current system (and proposals put forth under the Republican-dominated Trump administration would reduce taxation further on estate taxes). The tax burden has fallen greatly since the 1970s, and this has largely benefited stockholders and corporations. The changes in taxation contribute to the fact that, throughout the past twenty-five years, only America's most affluent families have accumulated more wealth, an excess of wealth that is jaw dropping. The capital accumulated by the ultrawealthy comes from returns on investments, not labor. Investments compose a bigger percentage of wealth among the elite compared with labor income, and those investments are also minimally taxed.

The top 10 percent averages more than nine times more *income* than the bottom 90 percent, and the top 1 percent averages more than 40 times more.[21] The top 1 percent of household average income is about $1.7 million and the bottom 40 percent is about $15,000. The top 1 percent of wage earners receive 21 percent of all wages, such that, although they make up a small portion of the population, they hold a large portion of both income and wealth in the country. In the United States, the top 1 percent of the population controls 42 percent of the capital, and nearly half of the wealth invested in stocks and mutual funds.[22] In contrast, the bottom 50 percent of Americans own 0.5 percent of stocks, bonds, and mutual funds, which means that working-class individuals without enough capital to invest in the stock market are left out of the most profitable sector of the American economy.[23]

It's a "rich get richer" scenario in which the increase in wealth among the ultrawealthy is so high that inherited wealth will become an increasingly important dynamic of the highest class, reducing the role of merit-based or talent-based fortunes to those who simply accept it as part of an intergenerational transfer of wealth. Piketty observed that the wealth of the top members of society has had a consistently higher growth rate than that of the general economy. Wealth is highly concentrated at the top, and its ability to grow faster than incomes means that wealth is being accumulated based on nothing more than the fortune of birth.

Recognizing the drain of household debt is necessary to grasp the financial dilemmas of most Americans. When the amount of liabilities owed in debts is greater than the amount owned outright in assets, one's net worth is negative (less than zero). Wealth is a calculation based on the difference between assets and liabilities. A person may own a $500,000 home, but with a $400,000 mortgage on the house, combined with $50,000 in auto loans and another $50,000 in student loan debt, that person's assets and liabilities cancel each other out. The net worth of this individual comes to $0. Because the discretion on the spending of funds can be limited as a result of the need to pay for debt and meet ongoing obligations (like food, clothing, electricity, and gasoline), a single health crisis can immediately send a person into a financial hole, leaving that person with $20,000 or more in hospital bills and no way to pay it. Now the person who had $0 net worth has gone negative.

The pressure of debt obligations is easily increased with the rise of everyday "needs" of Americans and the immense expansion of consumer items available for purchase pushed on Americans over time. In 1980, household debt made up about 60 percent of a person's disposable income, but by the mid-2000s, that percentage more than doubled to 125 percent. This massive growth in consumer debt solved the problem of demand in the macro economy, which had been caused by the stagnation of wages beginning in the 1970s. In addition, the safety features of cars make automobiles more expensive, internet connections constitute a monthly fee, and computers to use the internet can be financed, as can smartphones required to stay in touch with work and family. Houses are the most widely owned asset among Americans, and rising home prices inflate the available equity, which can be borrowed against. However, banks have made it much easier to borrow against a home (essentially a rolling second mortgage), making checking accounts available to homeowners to purchase other seeming necessities and pay for repairs, so Americans obtained about 10 percent of their disposable income in 2001 through 2006 through lines of home equity.[24] Consumer spending rose significantly from the 1970s through the 2000s, but, remember, so did consumer debt, and the share of income from consumer debt went mostly to the highest percentile families.[25]

Because American income inequality is the highest in the advanced industrial world, it is naïve to believe that Americans have the social mobility to move up the ladder with persistence and hard work. Inequality has become "more rapid and extreme in the United States in the last three to four decades than in its peer countries."[26] Americans spend more time working because their incomes have remained stagnant, and they can no longer sustain themselves comfortably. From 1979 to 2014, the average middle-class family works nearly 280 hours more per year—or about seven extra weeks of work. Costs of living (like meals, housing, and transportation) are quickly eaten up in the average income, and unexpected expenses (resulting from accidents, illness, or unforeseen disasters) quickly result in an increase in debt merely to survive. Even more, the divide between lower and upper classes has increased, and opportunities to move into the higher class has been hindered. Social mobility has not risen in the same way and inequality has skyrocketed. Income growth has been about 20 percent since 1979, yet among the top 1 percent it has grown over 200 percent. The richest person in America was worth $2 billion in 1982, but in 2019 the richest person, Amazon.com founder Jeff Bezos, was worth about $115 billion. In contrast, the bottom 90 percent hold almost three-quarters of America's debt, most of it is wrapped up between credit cards, personal loans, and home mortgages.[27]

The possession of such a high degree of capital has much to do with the opportunities accorded to those who already possess access to great wealth. In the United States, significant wealth provides an exceptional education, a comfortable and valuable home, discretion over doctors and medical procedures without concern for cost, and financial security. The accumulation of wealth is important in that it provides financial freedom to improve opportunity and ensure one's health care. Moreover, the access to large pools of wealth allow for expanding investments by placing money into various assets, which on average grow at a higher rate than income.

ASSET WEALTH AND THE RISE OF FINANCIALIZATION

Asset growth, the key to wealth accumulation, is strongly associated with the rise of financial mechanisms to manage and grow those assets. Since the 1970s economic crises involving the oil crisis, global competition, and stagflation, new relations developed between the private sector and the State in which "a new neoliberal order in which market logics increasingly replace social contracts, and the liquidity of capital [was] prioritized over long-term employment stability."[28] The largest shift in the structure of the American economy during this period was the rise of *financialization*, specifically an economy moving away from manufacturing and service production to financially oriented investment and management strategies, from a manufacture-driven to a finance-orientated economy.

Low growth and high inflation in the 1970s lowered bank profits that had come from extending credit to consumers and businesses. With the lack of investment funds, the federal government raised interest rates to restore profitability of banks, and the United States also opened its doors to foreign investment, receiving an infusion of investment cash from other nations. The inability of the United States to generate its own investment capital was therefore resolved by further globalization of finance, which further fed the financial system.[29]

So although manufacturing and worker productivity had been the traditional means of growing value, now, with the increase in financialization, money could move quickly into or away from profitable investments, without the sunk costs and long-term commitment of establishing and building material infrastructure, sales and distribution flows, or an expanding customer base. This resulted in the expansion of financial markets. Sociologists Ken-Hou Lin and Donald Tomaskovic-Devey summarize, "The combination of a growing demand to maximize profits and minimize fixed capital investment and the increasing profit opportunities born of financial deregulation steered nonfinance firms to look into financial markets."[30] This resulted in a series of deregulations and new policies aimed at unleashing the flow of capital through financial markets.

Overall, *financialization* has become an important term used to delineate the increasing importance of finance, financial markets, and financial institutions to the workings of today's economy and, therefore, to our everyday lives. For example, financialization includes our dependence on credit cards, health care payments, mortgages, and student loans.[31] Indeed, the expansion of consumer credit (personal credit cards, department store cards, longer-term auto loans, etc.) fulfill the basic desire of corporations for increased profits. Given that American population expansion has slowed, businesses seek profits by finding ways to increase the spending of each household. Credit has therefore expanded, allowing each household to purchase more items by extending the terms over years, thereby expanding the percentage of debt.

Corporations and their shareholders saw greater increase in profits, and corporate profits increased at the same time that the net worth of the American household decreased. Corporations increased their reliance on financial income—interest, dividends, and capital gains—rather than production, which excludes wage labor from gains in company revenue. Indeed, in recent times, financial income accounts for more than 40 percent of corporate revenue.[32] And the expansion of credit allowed broader play of experimentation with pools of capital.

Capital flows more easily and abundantly, and the increase in the trade of capital assets fosters new and unanticipated markets for financial vehicles for investments that did not follow the neoclassical assumptions of supply and demand. For example, speculation regarding future value and the risk involved in achieving that value are based on guesses; investors depend on hints, fads, and outright misleading signals to indicate areas of growth or decline that then become institutionalized. Financial innovations prompt new forms of investment speculation. Most certainly, the rise of the internet and the dot.com companies like Amazon and Google would not have emerged without these new dynamics of finance, allowing companies premised on guesses regarding the growth in shareholder value alone to attract investment capital and demand for stock while operating over many years at significant loss.

The decline of labor's share of income occurs at the same time as a surge in extraordinarily high executive compensation. Profitability no longer increases labor's share of income, but it does increase the compensation of top officers, most often through stock shares. This change in sources for executive compensation effectively restructures managerial priorities from growing market share to growing profits wherever they can be made (often short-term), as long as the value of stocks and dividends increase or are at least maintained. The desire to remain profitable encourages executive officers to think of corporations as malleable components made up of various activities, with arenas that can be expanded, contracted, or coopted, all in pursuit of profitable avenues through multifunctionality and cross-industry conglomerates. Human capital, material production, and sales are bundled into "tradable assets that should be evaluated, eliminated, or acquired according to their expected returns."[33] Corporation strategy is placed in the hands of financial strategists who reconceived the nature of the firm such that questions of finance dominate decision making.[34] Shareholder value becomes the primary goal, and is more important than fulfilling needs of workers or consumers.

FINANCIALIZATION AND THE 2007 MARKET CRASH

Financialization is therefore a historical trend that involves an economic shift toward greater reliance on financial motives, financial markets, financial actors, and financial institutions, "a broad-based transformation in which financial activities (rather than services generally) have become increasingly dominant in the US economy."[35] Rather than the typical free-market assumptions, financialization is "a pattern of accumulation in which profits accrue primarily through financial channels rather than through trade and commodity production."[36] Financialization occurs when the economy relies on trade and multiplication of existing capital (where capital represents stocks, bonds, real estate, and other assets, the value of which are determined by trade), which indicates the centrality of shareholder value to the system to corporate governance.[37]

The move toward financialization was intentional as part of a neoliberal shift in American government (see Chapter 6). In 1980, Congress passed the Depository Institutions Deregulation and Monetary Control Act, which did not establish new laws as much as remove old ones. Most importantly, it repealed banking regulations that had been enforced since the Glass-Steagall Act of 1933. It allowed banks to merge, removed regulations over interest paid on savings accounts, permitted credit unions and savings and loans to provide interest on checking accounts, and removed caps on interest rates charged by financial institutions. Nonfinancial firms also engaged in financial activities. The dependence on earnings through financial vehicles grew significantly in the nonfinance sector, particularly in manufacturing, including for companies like Ford, General Motors, and General Electric. Between 1980 and 2007, the finance sector share of profits tripled from 15 percent to 45 percent of all profits in the American economy. [38]

This system only benefits those who are doing the trading and multiplying, and those with enough wealth to invest in the stock market. In the 1960s and 1970s, financial sector profits accounted for between 10 percent and 15 percent of the total profits in the United States. By the 1980s that number was up to 30 percent and after the turn of the twenty-first century, it has increased to over 40 percent of the total profits. [39] One reason that these numbers are so high is because corporations that are "nonfinancial" have become "dependent on financial activities as sources of revenue in recent years" and have been getting more tangible assets to grow. [40] In the 1980s, Reagan-appointed banking regulators provided nonfinance firms clearance to engage in financial activities, yet exempted these new initiatives from regulatory oversight.

To understand the relationship between financialization and the market crash of 2007, Nancy Fraser and Rahel Jaeggi, in their book *Capitalism: A Conversation*, describe how deregulation of financial mechanisms from the 1980s onward resulted in the increase in an array of innovative, increasingly complex, precarious, and fundamentally obscure financial bundles of risks and guesses unmoored by the actual production of tangible goods and services. These complex investments included adjustable-rate mortgages (with teaser rates and balloon payments), mortgage-backed securities (easily traded and based on bundles of mortgage payments and interests), subprime mortgages (higher interest for higher risk borrowers), collateralized debt obligations (based on diversified portfolio of "junk bonds" and other risky securities), and credit default swaps (with payments based on the defaults on corporate bonds). These toxic instruments betrayed faith in the "efficient markets hypothesis" that assured investors that unregulated markets found their accurate pricing based on investors' having processed all relevant information. Yet these new financial products had no history, were vaguely understood, and operated on the whims of available capital seeking opportunity more than a careful consideration of future value. In the end, no one knew how to evaluate them.[41]

Housing was a particularly seductive asset. The desire for homeownership is always greater than the ability to borrow, yet banks had loosened requirements, promoted low-interest "teaser" rates on adjustable loans, and aggressively promoted loans at 125 percent of the cost of the home. Although such loans allowed home buyers to install new appliances, generously furnish rooms, and customize spaces, it also meant that their homes were already financially "underwater," with their debt well exceeding the value of their home. Brokers and bankers were paid via commissions and bonuses, which resulted in conflicts of interests as they urged borrowers into obligations far beyond their means.

Once high-risk borrowers began to default on their mortgage payments and available capital began to contract, the delicate ties between financial relations that had been built on bundles of "packaged" risk started to crumble. The real estate bubble—in which investors would purchase a lower-priced home, complete repairs, do remodeling, and add decoration to "flip" the house for a significant profit a short time later—had inflated the price of homes, resulting in a scramble of hopeful home owners wanting to purchase property before a continued rise in home costs would leave their dreams permanently out of reach. The decline of house buying and the suppression of the mobility of American workers left other industries hurting. Loans for cars, televisions, furniture, and more that had been taken out based on home equity loans were also defaulted. The resulting spiral of the 2007–2009 crash was dramatic and far reaching.

PERSISTENCE OF RACIAL DISPARITIES IN AMERICAN INEQUALITY

Understanding the dynamics of financialization—especially how the expansion of consumer debt benefits those with asset-based wealth in comparison with the great majority of Americans who depend on borrowing to supplement the stagnation of wages—changes our assumptions of how income inequality works. Financialization shapes patterns of inequality. Finance heightens income inequality because returns from financial investment are not reinvested in firms for productive activities but rather to buttress shareholder value, which contributes to the stagnation of wages. Although costs of living continue to go up, wages fail to keep pace, prompting increased indebtedness, creating a nation of borrowers with less available for their own investment, which in turn feeds back into the financial system to the benefit of already established investors. Although wealth can accrue to those who are able to invest, the fees and expertise necessary require investment in and of itself, and small investors require long-term patience of five years or more of nonliquid assets to achieve a measure of benefit from financial investments. Although the use of financial services has increased across all levels of income, only those in the top 20 percent of the income distribution benefit by leveraging their assets through active financial management.[42] Further, pressure to reduce the cost of labor is a primary focus of shareholder-oriented firms, which has resulted in the elimination of pension plans and the reduction of health benefits.[43] The level of income inequality in the United States is now equivalent to that of developing countries such as Iran, China, and Mexico.

Race continues to play a significant factor in income and wealth inequality, and the gap between the prosperous and the impoverished continues to expand. Recall that throughout American history, whites have been the primary group capable of obtaining and maintaining opportunities for wealth; historically, this has been at the expense of, and with the help of, blacks and other minorities, whether it be through the slave trade, the use of slave labor, the exploitation of Chinese immigrants, or one of countless examples of exploitation of blacks and minorities. Because whites are the primary recipients of inherited wealth, whites continue to do well, and the racial differential in wealth continues to increase. Given that wealth is tied to generational opportunities to accumulate wealth, a review of the racial history of the United States as presented in much of this book so far leads us to expect that wealth in nonwhite groups would be lower than for whites; in actuality it is *far* lower, with black and Latino families being twice as likely to have no wealth.[44] Because the neoliberal economy now places the burden of success on individuals, there are few initiatives that recognize the historic injustices placed on nonwhites. The inability to accrue wealth is interpreted as a moral failing rather than a systemic problem.

The extent of racial inequality is well documented. A thorough overview of contemporary racialized wealth inequality is found in *Toxic Inequality: How America's Wealth Gap Destroys Mobility, Deepens the Racial Divide, and Threatens Our Future*, in which Thomas Shapiro provides harrowing evidence for inequality. He notes that "the typical African-American family today has less than a dime of wealth for every dollar of wealth owned by a typical white family."[45] The $147,000 median wealth of a white family compares with a median wealth of $3,500 for a black family and $6,500 for a Latino family; that is, whites have twenty-two times the wealth of Latinos and forty-one times that of blacks in America.[46] Even more harrowing is that this disparity seems doomed to continue because of the severe lack of economic mobility in America.

This "toxic inequality" is due to the "historic and rising levels of wealth and income inequality in an era of stalled mobility, intersecting with a widening racial wealth gap."[47] The bottom half of the United States has been declining sharply in wealth since the 1980s, a direct result of policies supported by Reagan (see Chapter 6).[48] White families in the United States make up 90 percent of the national wealth, as compared with Latino families, which hold 2.3 percent, and black families, which hold 2.6 percent.[49] For every dollar of wealth owned by the typical white family, the median black family owns only five cents.[50] Getting an education is not enough: older, single black women with a college degree have $11,000 in median wealth; in contrast, single white women with a bachelor's degree have a median wealth of $384,400.[51]

To grasp the nature of wealth inequality, Shapiro uses the metaphor of a ladder, with five wealth quintiles representing each rung. Although the numbers show a general upward trend of income over the generations (many Americans are wealthier than their parents were at their age), this does not necessarily mean families are generally improving. First, the cost of living today is much higher than it was in the past such that, although children may have more money than their parents did, they are required to spend more of it. Second, as Shapiro notes, "the rungs of the ladder are getting farther apart, and it is becoming harder to move from one quintile to another."[52] The majority, 66 percent, of those raised at the bottom of the ladder remain on the bottom two rungs, and 66 percent of those at the top of the ladder *also* remain at the top of two rungs. And there is a racial difference in the ability to move: half of blacks raised in the bottom remain stuck there compared with only one-third of whites. Whites are far more likely to leave the bottom rung over a generation compared with African Americans, most of whom will remain at the bottom over many generations. In part, this is due to advantages conferred by elite college education, which is built on a long history of the ability to participate in extracurricular activities, to pay for tutors, to live in better areas with better public schools, to afford private schooling, to provide opportunities for unpaid internships, to take test-prep courses, to take standardized tests multiple times, and to apply to wide variety of schools. As Shapiro writes,

> [I]t is important to see clearly and concretely the kinds of opportunities, privileges, and cumulative advantages that wealth confers, as well as the mindset that makes privilege seem natural. Opportunities are, in fact, integrally connected to resources, which is not to say that health, head starts for children, and a good life are exclusive domains of the wealthy. One cannot deny, however, how much of the ecosystem of wealth and privilege improves the probability of attaining better life chances.[53]

Although we know that wealth is concentrated at the top of the financial ladder, we do not always recognize the patterns of financial resources, social networks, and cultural capital.

Lack of financial progress is frequently attributed to laziness, stupidity, or deficient cultures, but such explanations leave out that historic injustices are "baked into" the circumstances of minorities, suffering the consequences of a history where they were kept away from certain professions and excluded from networks that contribute to access to opportunities for wealth. As noted previously, one of the most important means to accumulate wealth in American society is through investing in the housing market. Houses are generally understood to be an appreciating asset, and investing in a house can increase a family's financial stability. Indeed, home equity accounts for two-thirds of net wealth for the middle 60 percent of Americans.

However, as a result of the suppression of black wealth accumulation, blacks face challenges in the housing market. In 2014, 70 percent of first-time buyers were white, whereas only 9 percent were black.[54] White families are given two times more financial help to purchase homes than blacks. Also, Shapiro found that "families are likelier to build wealth in predominantly white neighborhoods, especially high socioeconomic-status ones, while black and Latino neighborhoods more often saw greater home value volatility or declines."[55] Shapiro writes, "African Americans were eight times more likely than white residents to live in high poverty neighborhoods, and Latinos were five times more likely."[56] People living in low-opportunity neighborhoods pay higher mortgage rates and face harsher legal judgments. Even if black and Latino families work hard enough to invest in a house, the value of the houses they can afford are not as stable as white-owned houses. Historically, the practice of "redlining" meant that black families moving into a neighborhood would often result in white families leaving, and the value of homes would decrease. The effects of redlining continue to be felt today.

Neighborhoods also affect educational attainment because more desirable neighborhoods tend to hold value because of the proximity of high-quality schools. Children who benefit from these neighborhood schools are more likely to pursue secondary education, obtain bachelor's or master's degrees, and secure a job with benefits, all of which contribute to the accumulation of greater wealth than their parents. Shapiro writes, "[C]hildren from highest-income families were eight times more likely than children from low-income families to obtain a bachelor's degree by age twenty-four."[57]

Also, unemployment is far higher among nonwhites than whites, which means the "official" unemployment rate that is reported in news media is misleading. In 2014, the unemployment rate was 5.8 percent, but the unemployment rate that included part-time workers who wanted full-time work as well as those who were only marginally attached to the workforce was considerably higher at 11.5 percent. These two numbers tell very different stories. For example, a clever research design was done on résumés. When submitting résumés, the only difference between candidates was the race that would typically be associated with their names. African-American names were less likely to receive callbacks on job applications; they needed to send 50 percent more résumés to receive a callback. Even white men with criminal records received more responses than black men without them. Unemployment is more frequent and prolonged for blacks than it is for whites.

The greater challenge of employment has consequences for members of the family who do work. Thomas Shapiro finds that families overcome the limitations on their incomes by increasing the number of hours or the number of jobs they work or the number of family members working. Although nearly half of African-American adults provided assistance to their parents, only 16 percent of whites did.[58] These approaches only benefit in the short term. When both parents work, there are no adults at home providing enrichment for children, which adds stress for the parents and adds the burden of care for each child.

Another avenue to accumulate wealth and financial stability is through employment benefits such as pensions and retirement plans. Racial minorities find it more difficult to find employment with such benefits. Shapiro found that 55 percent of black workers and 38 percent of Hispanic workers in 2009 had retirement plans in comparison with 65 percent of white workers.[59] White families in 2013 on average "had seven times more in retirement savings than African-American families and eleven times more than Hispanic families."[60] Lower-end jobs that necessitate more than one wage earner are often without health or retirement benefits, raising the potential for financial emergencies and leaving little or no monies for future inheritance. White Americans are more likely than black Americans to hold stable jobs that allow for the accumulation of wealth.

In the end, Shapiro effectively demonstrates that discussion of the accumulated privileges of wealth does not constitute an attack on a person's character. It is possible to make sacrifices, work hard, and feel accomplished, yet recognize that one's own starting line was far ahead of others. The structural arrangements of privilege that create opportunities to accumulate wealth, whether through better access to job opportunities, investment, or preferential taxation, allow whites to better maintain their wealth and pass it on to their children.

RICH PEOPLE'S SOCIAL MOVEMENTS AGAINST TAXATION

Rich People's Movements: Grassroots Campaigns to Untax the One Percent by Isaac William Martin discusses taxation (with a focus on income taxes), tracing the history of support, resistance, and implementation, as seen previously (see Chapter 6). The elite show a tendency to ignore the need for government in favor of keeping most (if not all) of their millions and billions in income. Through programs like Social Security, Medicare, Medicaid, and the welfare system, the U.S. government provides some assistance to those who qualify. In rich people's movements, the elite act as outsiders, demanding policies to further benefit themselves. In members of rich people's movements, the primary fear is fear of the "tyranny" of the democratic majority (see Chapter 6).[61] Elites are troubled that the impoverished will become envious and rise up against them. Many of the wealthy believe they have a "special moral worthiness," are "persons of admittedly superior ability," and are "trustees for the public."[62] Members of these movements believe they have successfully navigated the financial system, and they believe the opportunity for others to similarly figure out paths to wealth are available. There is no excuse for those who have not. The wealthy elite are more likely to support Republican candidates who will lower their taxes "at the expense of discretionary public programs that serve the poor, veterans, and schoolchildren."[63]

Social scientists are accustomed to thinking of social movements as emerging from the marginalized or dispossessed—as in the Civil Rights movement or the movement for lesbian, gay, bisexual, transgender, and queer rights. Usually, movements are aimed at stimulating change and are led by the disempowered; the collective action draws support from a larger population, which helps to overcome the relative weakness of marginalized groups. Social movements mobilize people to affect political power and provoke the elite to make changes. Rather than voicing their demands in moderate tones, avoiding extremes to appeal to the sentiments of the majority, the "spokespeople for these [rich people's] movements speak up frankly and unabashedly in favor of more economic inequality,"[64] similar to Tea Party supporters (see Chapter 5). The wealthy seek to influence politicians and their economic policies, providing lawmakers with their own policy proposals. Radical proposals allow for negotiations, such that conservative bills are viewed as moderate in comparison.

Rich people's movements, which often focus on the elimination of income taxes, have occurred in every historical era, although they cluster at particular times. More recently, the American Legislative Exchange Council (ALEC) and the Chamber of Commerce are two prominent organizations that organize and promote decisions regarding issues like health care or public schools from the perspective of corporate interests. The broader agendas of these organizations resemble far-right, neoliberal agendas: cutting "entitlements" like Social Security, unemployment insurance, and food stamps; shrinking public funding for schools; opposing paid sick leave and workplace safety regulations; and undermining unions and their political voice.[65] Organizations like these, with access to extensive resources and lobbyists, overshadow the voices of working families.

The wealthy minority have accumulated so much capital that they have effectively accumulated significant power and influence in our political system that is wildly disproportionate to their size in the population of the United States. Therefore, *economic* inequalities inevitably lead to *political* inequalities. For example, groups in society with less economic sway have substantially less voice in American democracy. Corporate lobbying totals about $2.6 billion per year, far outpacing the lobbying capacity of organizations representing a majority of Americans. According to Elisabeth Jacobs, "For every $1 spent on lobbying by labor unions and public interest groups, large corporations and their associations spend $34."[66] Members of the lower class are unable to attract attention by giving sizable financial donations, and they are less inclined to participate in political processes compared with members of the middle and upper classes. Thus democracy "does not respond to the preferences of those at the bottom of the economic distribution."[67]

The minority that holds the majority of wealth is aware of the vast socioeconomic disparities that exist but shows little concern for changing broader systems to spread the benefit of their expanded wealth. The great majority—86 percent—of wealthy Americans are aware of the wage gap but a majority also do not support anything they would interpret as wealth redistribution.[68] Top wealth and income holders feel they are deserving of their economic success. Any efforts to redistribute wealth in America, most notably in the form of increased corporate taxes, is seen as a form of stealing; yet for the most part, corporate elites accumulate their wealth at the expense of public programs that could assist the great majority who are challenged. Political leanings and concrete legislation are more likely to work in favor of the elite who contribute significantly to political campaigns.

In the early nineteenth century, plantation owners had most of the wealth within the United States. These plantation owners felt betrayed by the government when proposals threatened to free slaves, which motivated them to go to war. As wealth passed down through families, so did their conservative sentiment. They reaped the most benefits from capitalism and through their contributions to certain politicians and political movements sought to maintain their influence. They mobilized their wealth into campaign contributions to secure political sway to protect the basis of their wealth.

More recently, under the influence of elite Americans, the Republican Party adjusted tax codes in America so that tax expenditures largely favor the top economic classes. The after-tax income of wealthy Americans continues to rise while more Americans are stuck on the bottom of the economic spectrum. Republicans frame their actions to cut taxes for the wealthy as part of a broader effort to reduce government spending and put money directly in the pockets of the middle class (see Chapter 6); however, independent analysis affirms that the greatest benefit by far goes to the wealthiest, where the combination of large wage and investment income combine with significant drops in the tax rates to produce a massive windfall to those making the most in our country. For example, a family making $80,000 per year with a composite tax rate of 14 percent would pay $11,500 in income taxes; in contrast, an asset-rich family who received the same $80,000 from $1.6 million in investments would pay only $765.[69] The difference? Tax rates on capital gains are much lower than wage-earner income.

Such wealth inequality overlaps with political issues of inequality because economic wealth grants political influence. Economic policy in the United States has recently been greatly influenced by a movement powered by the country's wealthiest citizens. The wealthy elite lobby for tax loopholes, and then hire accountants and lawyers to maximize them, deducting the cost of their services. Although white evangelicals fear losing their position in society to the increasing minority in America, these elite Americans fear losing their wealth to public social programs, mainly sponsored by the Democratic Party. In 2012, "more than 60 percent of all personal campaign contributions came from less than 0.5% of the population."[70] These "megadonors" sway the political system through the access they gain to power by providing campaign funding.

The distribution of wealth is not only concentrated among individuals, it is also concentrated among corporations. Since the 2007 market crash, corporations in America have become even more powerful with the help of the 2010 Supreme Court ruling made in *Citizens United v. Federal Election Commission*, which classified corporations as individuals for all intents and purposes relating to monetary policy regarding campaign finance.[71] Since the *Citizen's United* ruling, corporations and corporate lobbies are able to spend unlimited amounts in elections—and do so anonymously. This change gave corporations the ability to have even more influence on politics than they already had by not capping the amount that they could contribute to a campaign. On average, corporations donate to political campaigns more than ten times more than labor unions, the primary representative body advocating for better wages and economic conditions for middle- and lower-class Americans. A corporation can identify a candidate who will push policies to benefit them and fund their campaign to victory. The loosening of campaign finance regulations further accentuated the need to appeal to "special interests." And with political campaigns costing more, there is an increased reliance on private donors over general support from the political party.

With the top of the economic hierarchy, the proverbial 1 percent, taking on tremendous political influence, the "rich-get-richer" dynamic is further perpetuated. Not only does the majority of America not have access to most of the nation's wealth, they also do not have opportunity to make political changes. The rich support policies that most benefit themselves. As historian Ronald Formisano writes, "The concentration of wealth is unhealthy for democracy and, in fact undermines republican government—raising a plutocracy in its stead."[72]

POWER AND THE CONCENTRATION OF WEALTH

Wealth is a guiding factor in a person's life. One's wealth determines the quality and quantity of an individual's life benefits, opportunities, and protection, whether earned or inherited. Wealth determines the quality of one's future. Wealth provides a safety net for families. Wealth provides long-lasting advantage. But wealth is far more likely among certain racial groups than others. Shapiro shows that "a child born into a wealthy family is more than six times as likely to become a wealthy adult than a child born into a poor family."[73] And in terms of keeping one's wealth, tax policies matter. Wealth is taxed at a lesser rate than direct income, so that those who rely solely on income pay more in taxes while those who gain income from the dividends or sale of assets keep more of their wealth than those who obtain income through wages. Because of lobbying and leveraging of their wealth to push for favorable policies, tax expenditures continue to favor wealthy, white Americans, and they continue to seek reductions that would further advantage those already wealthy Americans.

Supreme Court Justice Louis Brandeis once said, "[W]e must make our choice. We may have democracy, or we may have wealth concentrated in the hands of a few, but we can't have both." The wealthiest Americans, the economic elite, are associated with neoliberal principles, advocating free-market ideology. Plutocrats—wealthy leaders who govern on behalf of the wealthy—laid the foundation for a structure of Christian-grounded capitalism that continues to yield profits in particular directions, while harvesting political and social support for ideals. This development took place well before the 1970s, but since then, policies favoring deregulation, increasing the flows of capital, and the expansion of consumer debt together fostered the financialization of our economy, which benefits asset-based wealth over the increase of wages and provision of practical financial assistance when needed. Donald Trump's 2016 election is a pivotal point in the development of capitalism legitimated by Christian Libertarianism and an affirmation of a nation that affirms distributing opportunities to "true" Americans, those who deserve to belong within our borders.

Chapter 9

IDENTITY POLITICS AND EVANGELICAL SUPPORT

Trump's White Christian Nationalism

At the annual meetings of the American Sociological Association in 2017, Janelle Wong, a professor of political science at the University of Maryland, shared new data gathered by a team of more than eighty scholars on race, religion, attitudes, and identity from more than ten thousand US respondents.[1] Her research revealed two outstanding patterns: (1) white evangelicals are far *more* likely than all other racial-religious groups to believe "whites" face more discrimination than *any* other group (including Mexicans and Muslims), and (2) white evangelicals are far *less* likely compared with all other groups to believe *any* other group faces significant discrimination (including Mexicans and Muslims). The tables and charts were conclusive and jaw dropping. I heard gasps in the room on seeing the extent of the gap in perception. This reaction was significant because everyone in the room—all international experts on race and religion—knew this mismatch in perceptions on discrimination to be a significant development. The perception of white evangelicals had become exceedingly skewed in relation to the actual discrimination faced by racial and religious minorities in America every day.

Such attitudes reflect the ideological framework that bolsters support for President Trump's policies. The list of attempted legislation and executive orders by the Trump administration builds on and further

accentuates white evangelical presumptions: the Muslim ban on refugees from the Middle East; an office out of Department of Homeland
Security pushing to keep families safe from crimes committed by undocumented immigrants; a speech at Liberty University touting religious freedom sponsored by its president, Jerry Falwell Jr. (the son of
Jerry Falwell Sr., founder of the Moral Majority); the Justice Department's focus on suing universities with affirmative-action programs
deemed to discriminate against whites; the pardoning of Sherriff Joe
Arpaio of Arizona who was found to be in contempt for systematically
ignoring a court order to stop detaining people based on racial profiling;
and more. As controversial and divisive as these acts have been, 64
percent of white evangelicals believe that Trump has united America.[2]

Perhaps most telling was the white evangelical reaction to Trump's
response to the violence occurring at a Unite the Right "alt-right" rally
in Charlottesville, Virginia. What happened August 12, 2017, was truly
historic.[3] A few hundred white supremacists wearing Nazi uniforms,
mimicking Hitler, and carrying signs with white-nationalist slogans and
symbolic paraphernalia paraded through Charlottesville's neighborhood
streets. They carried clubs, shields, and torches; took over a park; and
surrounded themselves with other white people carrying guns and rifles
dressed in military gear. This rally was an attempt to organize fragmented hate groups, groups that work toward taxes, public policies, private
businesses, and public schools that act in racially exclusionary ways.
Many of these people came from a significant distance to stage this
"rally." The fear of that day was not so much the presence of the white
supremacists themselves but rather the public and forthright promotion
of their hateful beliefs. Were these sentiments becoming mainstream in
America? To visibly counter such a possibility, local residents, supported by progressive clergy and antifascist volunteer groups, quickly
organized themselves, walked together, made their way to the site, and
spoke out against the demonstration on behalf of their community.
They made themselves a presence to let that hate group and the public
know that such demonstrations of hate should not be tolerated. The
ensuing clash ultimately resulted in the intentional killing of Heather
Heyer, a white demonstrator against white supremacy.

Trump's public response to the rally and Heyer's death was ambiguous at best. Days later, he read prepared remarks to "condemn in the
strongest possible terms this egregious display of hatred, bigotry, and

violence"—yet went "off script" to quickly emphasize that the hatred, bigotry, and violence were present "on many sides, on many sides." He then added, "What is vital now is a swift restoration of law and order." Dozens of Democratic and Republican members of the House of Representatives and the Senate criticized the ambiguity of Trump's statement, refusing to grant moral equivalency between white supremacists and the demonstrators against hate, and they issued their own statements. In contrast, social media posts from white nationalists and neo-Nazis themselves viewed Trump's words approvingly. The creator of the Nazi website *The Daily Stormer* stated, "Trump comments were good. He didn't attack us. . . . He said he loves us all." The neo-Nazi blog also noted Trump's refusal to respond when a reporter asked about white nationalists who supported him: "No condemnation at all. . . . When asked to condemn, [Trump] just walked out of the room. Really, really good. God bless him." In the coming days, columnists, clergy, and commentators of all sorts stressed forceful denunciations of the alt-right.

Members of Trump's Evangelical Advisory Board remained largely silent during the entire episode. Member Jerry Falwell Jr. said, "One of the reasons I support him is because he doesn't say what's politically correct, he says what's in his heart." Although Falwell Jr. was supposed to be defending Trump on the Sunday talk shows, critics believe all he did was further implicate his racism. Despite glaring criticism and in contrast to nearly every other demographic group, 70 percent of white evangelicals persist in believing that Trump's behavior has had no impact on white supremacist groups (for example, 78 percent of black protestants believe that Trump's behavior does encourage these groups)[4].

The seemingly ironic support of Trump among white conservative evangelicals, despite Trump himself violating moral standards (e.g., lying, bullying, lack of sympathy, extramarital affairs) usually associated with Christianity can only be explained by their confidence in his support for their own attitudes. Avoiding mainstream news outlets (with the exception of Fox News) and favoring Christian media (like Pat Robertson's Christian Broadcasting Network), Trump continues meetings with key white evangelical leaders, providing them access and influence to the White House and to conservative policy initiatives in Congress, and, perhaps most importantly, to assist in nominations for

Supreme Court judges who will restrict immigration, expand "religious liberty" (support for preferential treatment by white evangelical initiatives), and further limit abortion to undermine *Roe v. Wade*. These political priorities are not concerned with Trump's *piety* but with his enactment of *policy*.

THE UNEXPECTED ORTHODOXY OF DONALD J. TRUMP

Discerning the underlying legitimation that propelled and sustains Donald J. Trump in his presidency is an ongoing topic of conversation—whether with the policy analyst on cable news or with my neighbor next door. For example, I recently had dinner with a group of social scientists at my institution where the conversation inevitably turned to politics. They knew exit polls from the 2016 election revealed that Trump had received overwhelming support (81 percent) from white evangelical or "born-again" Christians.[5] Yet these academics were sincerely confused since the months leading up to the election revealed a morally compromised candidate who never confesses or asks for forgiveness, is unaware of idiomatic speech among evangelicals (e.g., "Two Corinthians"), and has no concrete religious affiliations and therefore a lack of understanding of basic doctrine or liturgical practice. As historian John Fea observes, "Prior to his decision to run for office, very few Americans, including American evangelicals, were even aware that [Trump] was anything but a profane man—a playboy and adulterer who worshiped, not at the throne of God, but at the throne of Mammon."[6] Since the election, the new president continues to be criticized as untruthful, radically narcissistic, and unsympathetic to those facing poverty or prejudice—yet white evangelicals stay with him.[7]

My colleagues asked: *How can these Christians support such an obviously un-Christian person?* They believed that evangelicals needed to be convinced that Trump was not actually worth their allegiance because examples abound of Trump's failure to meet any definition they held of *Christian*—even a "baby" Christian. But I disagreed, letting them know that what they needed to grasp was a properly sociological understanding of religious orthodoxy.

Many otherwise educated colleagues in the social sciences with little training in the study of religion view religious orthodoxy as consisting of morally upright actions like being "loving," "truthful," and "sexually pure." Yet as a sociologist of religion, I knew that Trump's white evangelical support required an understanding of religious orthodoxy that included more than just individualistic virtues. For example, Sorcha Brophy points out in an article published in the journal *Sociology of Religion* that religious communities are accustomed to managing a wide range of interpretive practices and beliefs, citing an array of previous sociological research showing how common discrepancies between prescriptions of religious traditions and actual practice actually are.[8] For Brophy, being orthodox is primarily about acting to preserve a group's identity over time. Therefore, orthodox orientations are defined not only with an eye toward their past but also, and perhaps more importantly, toward projections regarding their future. As Brophy writes, "these actors are centrally concerned with maintaining their practices and beliefs *in the future.*"[9]

White evangelicals neither obscure nor ignore their religious convictions when they declare their allegiance to the forty-fifth president. In fact, their actions indicate a preeminent concern with upholding orthodoxy. In the case of President Trump, *observers should focus on discerning the orthodoxy of an actor who is perceived as religiously legitimate primarily because he engages in actions in support of religiously defined group interests rather than as a result of statements of belief or piety of behavior.* While fear, nostalgia, racial resentment, and white nationalism have all been analytical pieces of the Trump support puzzle scholars have been weaving together since November 2016,[10] a critical aspect of Trump support is to assert, rather than deny, that he is indeed unexpectedly religiously orthodox in the conduct of his presidency.

EXPANDING THE ANALYTICAL SCOPE OF RELIGIOUS ORTHODOXY

In her award-winning article "Orthodoxy as Project," Brophy makes clear that, although groups that enforce orthodoxy may appear homogeneous, they actually exhibit great internal diversity.[11] Those who misread white evangelicals seem to miss that evangelicals are so concerned about the loss of orthodoxy that they are willing to accommodate variation in *orthopraxy*, that is to say the accomplishment of orthodoxy in practice. As Brophy makes clear, "orthodox communities are centrally concerned with resisting a decline from orthodoxy."[12] Further, she encourages us to examine "how these communities engage in future-oriented projects, theorizing, anticipating, and responding to current issues in light of perceived future threats to organizational identity."[13] I agree. Although evangelicals are surprisingly heterogeneous, their assertion of unity with President Trump is a bulwark against the seeming deterioration of a valued, and highly racialized, religious orientation.[14]

President Trump himself is not a devout Christian; his white evangelical supporters concede that they do not see Trump as a strong, ideal Christian when they make statements like, "We're not electing a pastor, we're electing a president." Yet he resonates with a majority of white evangelicals and continues to do so while in office. Research has shown that conservative white evangelicals had felt that their interests were excluded from the Obama presidency and that their religious convictions were under attack (see Chapter 7).[15] Indeed, perceived marginalization has long been central to evangelical identity.[16]   In contrast, Trump declared himself early on as a defender of their interests. In January 2016, in a speech delivered to a packed auditorium at Liberty University, Trump said, "We're going to protect Christianity." Trump went on, saying, "You look at the different places, and Christianity, it's under siege. I'm a Protestant. I'm very proud of it. Presbyterian to be exact. But I'm very proud of it, very, very proud of it. And we've gotta protect, because bad things are happening, very bad things are happening. . . . We have to band together. . . . Our country has to do that around Christianity." Later that year, at a rally at Oral Roberts University, Trump said, "There is an assault on Christianity . . . on everything we stand for, and we're going to stop the assault." Trump generates strong support among white evangelicals, even among those who do not attend church, because of his willingness to enforce their convictions through the apparatus of the State.[17] As Franklin Graham declared in a 2018 interview, "I never said he was the best example of the Christian faith. He defends the faith."[18]

Since roughly 70 percent of Americans identify as Christian, certainly they do not all vote the same way. Although the majority of Christians do not vote the same way, and not all branches of Christianity are the same when it comes to politics, white evangelicals are far more important in today's American politics than other Christian denominations.

Of the 25.4 percent of evangelicals that identify as such, 76 percent identify as white—meaning 19 percent of Americans who identify as white are evangelical.[19] In terms of politics, white evangelicals make up 26 percent of the electorate, a percentage that has remained the same since 2008.[20] Of these white evangelicals, 81 percent voted for Donald Trump in the 2016 election. Therefore, white evangelicals made up roughly 21 percent of the American population that voted for Trump.[21] Only 60 percent of the electorate voted, and Trump captured 46.1 percent of the votes.[22] Doing the math, we can see that almost half of Trump's base was made up of white evangelicals. Who are these white evangelicals? And what accounts for their support for Trump?

White evangelicals have made up a consistently large chunk of the GOP base. And evangelical faith communities mobilize to support conservative politics. During the 1960 presidential election between John F. Kennedy and Richard Nixon, Billy Graham used his platform to mobilize evangelicals against Kennedy, a Catholic. Graham feared the influence of the Pope on Kennedy's policies. Harold John Ockenga, an evangelical peer of Graham, similarly urged evangelicals not to aid the movement toward "Roman Catholic domination of America" by electing Kennedy. In 1960, 60 percent of evangelicals voted for Nixon, 69 percent did so when he ran again in 1968, and 84 percent did in 1972.[23] Later, 78 percent of white evangelicals voted for George W. Bush in 2004, 74 percent for John McCain in 2008, and 78 percent for Mitt Romney in 2012.[24] White evangelicals have consistently voted Republican over the past four elections, and in similarly high numbers in the 2016 election. Indeed, more white evangelicals voted for Trump than any other previous GOP candidate since Nixon. And despite rumors that these supporters are nominal evangelicals who are inactive in their faith, evidence shows that those who attend church most frequently have the highest rates of voting for Trump.[25] The data clearly reveals that devout Christians were more supportive of Trump's presidential bid than anyone else. White evangelicals have much more organizational influence within the Republican Party, and the GOP actively leverages church-based evangelical networks to promote their candidates.

However, after seeing what a Trump presidency looks like, and the various controversies surrounding his behavior, support among white evangelicals still remains strong. As of August 2019, 77 percent of white evangelicals approve of President Trump's job performance, an approval rating almost twice as high as that of the general public, which stood at 40 percent and has generally remained in the low 40s.[26] The difference between evangelical and general support is not unusual—72 percent of white evangelicals approved of George W. Bush, exceeding the general public's approval at 54 percent—but the degree of difference is extraordinary.

White evangelicals have consistently voted Republican over several decades now and remain loyal regardless of their actions; this has been especially true during the Trump presidency, a reality that has distressed many people, particularly because of the outrageous and unapologetic behavior that bluntly cuts across the sensibilities of many people, including a minority of sincere, highly vocal, and more politically moderate and progressive evangelicals. And conservative white evangelicals became even *more* approving of objectionable acts since Trump's election.

In 2011, during the Obama presidency, the Public Religion Research Institute (PRRI) asked voters about their support for "immoral" politicians, specifically if "an elected official who commits an immoral act in their personal life can still behave ethically and fulfill their duties in their public and professional life." Sixty-one percent of white evangelicals said, "No." Not only did the majority condemn immorality, they exhibited the lowest tolerance of all religious groups (Catholic, white mainline Protestant, unaffiliated). In contrast, and only five years later, in October 2016—after explosive revelations of Trump's previous liaisons and crude talk of his groping women ("Grab 'em by the pussy. You can do anything."), just weeks before the presidential election, PRRI asked voters the *same question*. They found a dramatic shift. With candidate Trump in view, the proportion of white evangelicals who said private immoral conduct did not prevent elected officials from fulfilling their public duties had flipped to 72 percent—a shift of over forty-two points. White evangelicals were now the most tolerant of unethical conduct of all religious groups, and even all Americans in general.[27] This explains why approval remained high at 71 percent at the start of impeachment hearings.[28]

Remarkably, many evangelicals do not see themselves as partisan or even political. The conservatism of their politics is obscured in their religious life. Lydia Bean makes this striking point in her book, *The Politics of Evangelical Identity: Local Churches and Partisan Divides in the United States and Canada.*[29] Bean finds that, although direct political talk was not observed in American churches, evangelicals in US congregations "enforced an informal understanding that good Christians voted Republican."[30] Since the National Association of Evangelicals was founded in 1943, evangelicals have aligned themselves with the Republican Party because the Democratic Party was too soft on crucial issues, like Communism, and too closely allied with religious minorities, like Roman Catholics. Not only did evangelicals become politically dominant over the twentieth century, Bean writes, "American evangelicals enthroned themselves as the nation's unofficial established religion."[31] Implicit support of the Republican Party prompts votes for Trump, even when some of his specific positions, like his apparent openness to the LGBTQ community, go against the grain.

According to research by Steven Brint and Seth Abrutyn published in *Journal for the Scientific Study of Religion*, there are three compelling explanations for the link between evangelicals and conservative politics: religiosity, traditional morality, and gender ideology.[32] *Religiosity* is the generalized level of personal commitment, and is linked to several behaviors like frequency of church attendance and amount of Bible reading per week, and to attitudes like belief in the inerrancy of scripture and in an afterlife. Since religion influences beliefs on how one is supposed to live life, those with high religiosity desire to bring their political beliefs in sync with their religious beliefs. The evangelical vote, then, reflects support for values that are urged and affirmed in their religious devotion. Second, those holding to a more traditional morality, which affects attitudes on a variety of issues reflecting lifestyle and personal conduct, tend to see social change as a threat to traditional ways of life. Republicans have generally held an idealized image of personal conduct and see them as important for all people—a general moral standard applied to everyone regardless of personal religious convictions. Traditional morality also tends to be nostalgic, believing that prior eras were more in keeping with high standards, a sentiment that can be seen in Trump's campaign catchphrase, "Make America Great Again." Third, gender ideology provides an orientation for idealizing relationships between parents and between parents and their children. Evangelicals have long held male-dominated family power structures and encourage male-oriented social and political action. The masculinity of Trump—and perception of the wrongly aggressive feminism of

Hillary Clinton—contributed to his appeal among white evangelicals. Voting for Trump instead of Clinton and electing a man instead of a woman maintains the patriarchal power structure that evangelicals believe is expected by the Bible. The common theme tying these elements together is the expectation among white evangelicals of what they want to see politicians as willing to fight for.

NOT WHAT YOU BELIEVE BUT WHAT YOU FIGHT FOR

An image widely circulated through social media shows Donald Trump sitting at his desk in the Oval Office, signing a piece of legislation; he is backed by a ghostly figure of Jesus Christ whose arms are reaching around Trump, with a hand guiding the president as he signs the paper. This piece of art went viral, generated millions of impressions, and is perhaps the most prominent visual legitimation of Trump's presidency as guided by God. The picture is ambiguous, but it sacralizes support for his presidency, saying his actions actualize the purposes of God on earth. Of course, President Trump is not recognized as religious for his doctrinal beliefs or church involvement but rather for his endorsement of sentiments that align with the white evangelical political right. The most important issue for white evangelicals is not profession of belief but rather support for policy initiatives that would enforce white evangelical priorities in all sectors of government. For example, those who identify as evangelical and belong to an evangelical tradition are more likely to support reduced environmental regulations and tax cuts more than those who simply self-identify as evangelical.[33]

Although America functions under the broad assumption of a separation between church and state, in many ways the influence of religion has grown as certain groups have become more particular in their agendas and more active in advocating for them. For example, it was not until well into the twentieth century that the phrase "In God We Trust" was inscribed on our currency and in the halls of Congress and that "under God" was placed in our classrooms through the Pledge of Allegiance; both alterations were thanks to a group of powerful, white Christians.[34] But the belief that America was founded as a Christian nation is quite recent. As historian Joseph Moore explains,

[T]he United States is a more Christian nation today that it was when the Founders wrote the Constitution. We trust God on our coins (1864) and paper money (1955). The Post Office no longer opens on Sunday (1912). Students pledge allegiance to a nation "under God" (1954) and spend government loans and grants to study theology at religious schools (1944, 1965). An entire government office focuses on helping religious charities use tax money (2001). Presidents Bush and Obama both called for national days of prayer each year they were in office, something President Jefferson refused to do and President Madison did once but later regretted. All of this represents the creation of something new, not the continuation of something old.

For the Covenanters of early America, a radical Scotch-Irish Presbyterian sect originating in the mid-1600s, "the United States was not founded as a Christian nation, because slavery was in the Constitution and Jesus was not."[35] Well into the nineteenth century, aggressive lobbying by the National Reformed Association hoped to convert the United States into a Christian nation by pushing adoption of the "God Amendment," a constitutional amendment that would explicitly acknowledge God, declare submission to His son Jesus, and place the nation under the Bible's authority. Although the God Amendment was introduced by Charles Sumner on the Senate floor in 1863, it died in committee. Nevertheless, energized by the total emancipation of the enslaved in 1865, Covenanters and Reformed Presbyterians believed that perhaps America could finally *become* a Christian nation by asking for forgiveness of its slave past and thereby deliberately excise its unchristian legacy.[36] The God Amendment continued to be introduced by sympathetic congressmembers several times more over the following decades, all the way into the 1980 presidential candidacy of Illinois congressman John Anderson, but it never gained traction. The initiative was firmly rejected by the Reagan administration.

The God Amendment was never adopted, yet the Covenanters inspired the rationale for today's Christian nationalism. Around 1980, theologian Francis Schaefer, an evangelical polemicist who fought against "secular humanism, rediscovered Covenanter Samuel Rutherford and argued that the Founding Fathers had intended "We the People" to really mean "We the *Christian* People."[37] Jerry Falwell and other prominent leaders took up this perspective, and now conservative, white evangelicals today feel tied to a nostalgic, seemingly more pious past and believe that the nation is exceptional in the eyes of God. Therefore, these same evangelicals fight against forces they view as tainting the purity of American identity, forces that include immigration, nontraditional gender roles, and same-sex marriage. So whereas evangelical movements of the more recent past have latched on to politicians like Ronald Reagan in hopes of establishing a stronger Christian presence in public policy (see Chapter 6), the politician of choice for white evangelicals today is the brash, hard-hitting, and seemingly unintimidated Donald J. Trump.

Based on many years as an observer of evangelicalism in America,[38] I believe that today's evangelical conservatives have given up on spiritual revival as a means of change. Even in the recent past, *conversion*—a change of heart and mind that is the fruit of repentance and spiritual regeneration—was thought to be the means by which America would become a morally upright nation: change enough individuals, and the change on a personal level would result in broad change on a collective level. The politics of Ronald Reagan endorsed this understanding among the Moral Majority; as recently as George W. Bush, such sentiment still reigned. However, the accumulated frustrations of not being able to ease their sense of religious decline, their continued legal struggles against abortion and gay marriage, and the overwhelming shifts in popular culture promoting much less religiously restrictive understandings of personal identity have prompted politically active religious actors to take a far more pragmatic stance.

Revivalism has been abandoned as a solution to changing society. Their goal is no longer to persuade the public of their religious and moral convictions; rather, their goal has become to authoritatively enforce behavioral guidelines through elected and nonelected officials who will shape policies and interpret laws such that they cannot be so easily altered or dismissed through the vagaries of popular elections. It is not piety but policy that matters most. The real triumph is when evangelical convictions become encoded into law.

Borrowing Max Weber's conceptual framework, white evangelicals have turned away from the charismatic authority of the Church in favor of the rational-legal authority of the State.[39] They view themselves as a shrinking group that needs the protection of the State. Although the pulpit can still mobilize the faithful, white evangelicals understand that they are too few to rely on churches alone to influence politics, so they embrace the State to curb changes they fear, holding government accountable to do so on their behalf.

Of course, the State is viewed as a legitimate instrument for asserting a distinctively conservative Christian privilege because they remain fixed on the belief that America is a nation chosen by God and built by Christians.[40] In their eyes, a national identity that coincides with the tenets of Christian morality will be showered with blessings from above and will prove to be still more prosperous. So on January 20, 2017, when Donald Trump placed his own hand on the Bible and was sworn into office, it represented a significant victory for moral crusaders who had been fighting to rescue America—a move that would advance government-enforced initiatives to further purify America, that would be rooted in Christian values, and that, if successful, would be rewarded by the hand of God himself.

TRUMP THE FIGHTER

On September 28, 2018, Liberty University's President Jerry Falwell Jr. put out a Tweet saying:

> Conservatives & Christians need to stop electing "nice guys". They might make great Christian leaders but the US needs street fighters like @realDonaldTrump at every level of government b/c the liberal fascists Dems are playing for keeps & many Repub leaders are a bunch of wimps!

Similarly, a T-shirt from a Trump supporter that went viral in 2016 simply states, "Jesus Died For You—Trump Lives For You." I suggest that a truer meme would say, "Trump *Fights* For You."

White evangelical news media widely report that President Trump has "kept his word" about issues that matter most, like the prolife agenda. On the campaign trail in 2016, Trump stated that women having an abortion should be criminally prosecuted. Even after this remark was "walked back" with comments that "abortionist" doctors should instead face punishment, his words spoke volumes. The antiabortion movement remains staunchly allied with the Republican Party. This was especially obvious during the 2016 election, when prolife voters overwhelmingly supported Donald Trump, even though he is not a traditional conservative Christian candidate.[41] He has five children by three women, and since becoming president, Trump has not regularly attended church. However, Trump's support from the Christian base has nothing to do with his religious status. A majority of prolife supporters voted for Trump not because Trump embodied Christian values but because they trusted that Trump would protect prolife interests when elected. Furthermore, while Trump represents a prolife promise to many conservative Christians, he also represents a fundamental shake-up of the establishment, especially to evangelical Christians who lost faith in the government in the 1970s. The ultimate goal of the antiabortion movement is not only to outlaw abortion, but to make America great again, by returning it to the prosperous, godly nation that they believe it once was. Prolife activist Marjorie Dannenfelser put it in the simplest of terms when she said, "to make America great again, *Roe* must go; abortion must end."[42]

Historian John Fea coined the term "Court Evangelicals" to characterize the coterie of particularly prominent white evangelical supporters, those who have cozied up to Trump (e.g., Richard Land, Jim Bakker, Paula White, James Dobson, Franklin Graham, Ralph Reed, Gary Bauer, Mark Burns, Robert Jeffress, Greg Laurie, and Jerry Falwell Jr.), even flattering him, apparently working to remain in close proximity so they can access the power of the State and gain his favor to implement their own conservative agenda.[43] According to Fea, Court Evangelicals have made a strategic calculation, believing that the opportunity to affect executive decisions of government is more important than the potential soiling of their reputations in being associated with Trump's "un-Christian" actions. Certainly, the attempt to overturn the *Roe* ruling and overturn the legality of abortion has been a primary goal.

The nomination of Judge Brett Kavanaugh to the Supreme Court and aggressive support for him during his controversial hearings in 2018 further affirmed Trump's support for white evangelical concerns and energized this political base. The Trump administration has also pushed for a narrow definition of "religious liberty," one that favors upholding religious conviction of conservative Protestants as sufficient justification for refusing service to gays or for receiving federal funding despite a failure to follow established guidelines against discrimination. More examples could be added; suffice to say that the integrity and witness of

Christianity are being defined not by private morality but by the heavy-handed imposition of a public agenda.

Again drawing on Brophy's discussion of orthodoxy, white evangelicals, like other orthodox communities, embrace a "spectrum of standards," meaning that different standards are expected for individuals based on their perceived proximity to the ideological center of their group.[44] The tension with Trump is palpable: as a public figure, it is important that he strongly support the political interests of white evangelicals; yet as a person with no prior investment in evangelical activities or organizations, he is only marginally expected to uphold conventional standards of piety. Some prominent evangelicals like James Dobson suggest that Trump is a "baby Christian," meaning a Christian with little experience of maturity, to explain the apparent lack of Christian behavior. Clearly, white evangelicals do not see Trump as a strong, ideal Christian; yet because they struggle to justify supporting someone who does not espouse the Christian values associated with their religious identity, they must make accommodations for Trump. Recognizing his moral deficiencies, white evangelicals recognize that Trump is not a man of high moral character and have thus adjusted their stance on the type of morality required in public office to accommodate their political priorities.

Trump is orthodox because he actively works to protect orthodoxy, even when he fails to be a very good Christian. Brophy's analysis further affirms that members of orthodox communities readily accept that some core members create uncomfortable tensions when aggressively working to preserve key aspects of orthodoxy (as when ultraconservatives are labeled "mean-spirited"). Forceful action deemed impolite, uncaring, and certainly "not politically correct" is itself justifiable. As demonstrated by the Falwell quote cited previously, some of Trump's supporters assert that his being a religious "outsider" allows him to fight even more aggressively for the causes they hold dear. As outspoken Baptist pastor and Trump advocate Robert Jeffress declared in April 2016, "Frankly, I want the meanest, toughest son of a gun I can find. And I think that's the feeling of a lot of evangelicals. They don't want a Casper Milquetoast as the leader of the free world."[45]

In the end, perhaps the unexpected orthodoxy of Donald Trump is not so unexpected after all, especially given the many ways he appeals to the priorities of white evangelical voters. He presented a campaign platform—served with a pugilistic attitude of strength—to a religious group among whom it deeply resonated, a group whose support continues despite his widely publicized controversies in office. He's a fighter on their behalf, and their enthusiasm for him upholds the righteousness of his stance. Sarah Diefendorf recently wrote, "Today, US white evangelicals do not necessarily need political candidates who are going to carry their understanding of Christian values into personal actions but instead want candidates who will help them defend their identities and public cultural influence."[46] Given this observation, it is entirely plausible to suggest that *the greater the threat of religious decline, the greater the expansion of acceptable orthodoxy*—as long as those actions are perceived to protect and enhance orthodoxy rather than further diminish it. Preliminary indicators seem to affirm this point. As Trump himself said in an exclusive interview with the Christian Broadcasting Network a few days before the November midterm elections in 2018, "I know they're very happy with me. We've seen they're very happy."

MOBILIZING THE STATE TO MAKE AMERICA HOLY AGAIN

White evangelical influence on politics and society is deeply rooted in America. In many ways, these same evangelicals have fought for a long time against forces they believe taint the purity of American identity. John Fea writes that the Trump presidency is "the latest manifestation of a long-standing evangelical approach to public life."[47] White evangelicals have sought to strengthen the nation's connection to God through policies that attempt to purify American identity and cast it on a firmer spiritual foundation. Despite the woes of falling church attendance, the rise of secularism, exits by members to becoming religiously unaffiliated "nones," and the frequent claim of general religious decline, the power of religion is implicit to the success and continual support of Donald J. Trump. That Trump generates such strong support among white evangelicals, even among those who do not attend church, shows the continued relevance of white evangelical religious identity to American politics.

Among the central imperatives of white evangelicals is a resolution of anxieties emerging from "liberal" political movements throughout the twentieth century, stoking their fervor as reactionary conservatives, taking up the desire to save America by becoming active in government and promoting policies and politicians that best serve Christian interests.[48] Trump interprets himself in this light. At a private meeting of white evangelical leaders in August 2018, he described the political left as consisting of dangerous people, warning that Democrats "will overturn everything that we've done, and they'll do it quickly and violently"—that is, if Republicans lose their majority in Congress in the upcoming midterm elections. In this elaborate meeting, Trump attributed resistance to his presidency as motivated by his support for white evangelicals, saying, "The level of hatred, the level of anger is unbelievable. Part of it is because of some of the things I've done for you and for me and for my family, but I've done them." Occasions like this demonstrate that white evangelicals have the ear of the President, with regular meetings and consultations in the White House. Trump said, "They really have silenced you. But now you're not silenced anymore." In the same meeting, one minister looked to the president and said, "Now we have a warrior at the helm who is willing to stand up and fight."

White women had a fundamental role in building this new, more combative Christian right. Their attitudes and political viewpoints came as a reaction to social change. It would seem that white evangelical women would have been deeply offended by Trump's multiple marriages, documented and highly public infidelities, and, most famously, the *Access Hollywood* tape released in 2016 of a dialogue between television host Billy Bush and Donald Trump:

> Trump: You know, I'm automatically attracted to beautiful [women]—I just start kissing them. It's like a magnet. Just kiss. I don't even wait. And when you're a star, they let you do it. You can do anything.
>
> Bush: Whatever you want.
>
> Trump: Grab 'em by the pussy. You can do anything.

Yet data show that a majority of white evangelical women voted for Trump. Moreover, the higher their church attendance, the more likely they were to vote for Trump such that white evangelical women who attend church more than once a week showed a slightly higher level of support (87.5 percent) than white evangelical men (85 percent).[49]

The support from white evangelical women for Republican candidates has been long established. Concerned Women for America (CWA) is one of the most prominent organizations explicitly oriented around the political mobilization of white evangelical woman. CWA is a lobbying group founded by Beverly LaHaye, which is intent on reminding America that "the feminists do not speak for all women in America."[50] Lobbying the U.S. government, LaHaye's work shows "the ways in which the modern religious right has relied on women's leadership even as traditionalist gender ideologies would seem to limit women to the domestic sphere."[51] With strong women helping inspire the conservative movement, Christian ministers began preaching the "doctrine of complementarianism" instead of the "doctrine of wifely submission."[52] This means that instead of wives submitting to their husbands as their husbands submit to God, both men and women are submissive to God with roles that are different but equally important. This was a massive step for the respect of women in the new Christian Right, leading them to closely align with Republican Party politics. Perhaps the most prominent recent manifestation of CWA's brand of gendered conservatism is found in Sarah Palin, the conservative Republican candidate for vice president in 2008. As Emily Johnson states in her book *This Is Our Message: Women's Leadership in the New Christian Right*, "Palin's choice to identify as a 'conservative feminist'" forces a "reinterpretation of the feminist label."[53]

The focus of white evangelicals has been to mobilize the mechanisms of the State to enforce their convictions. The center of intervention is the American legal system. One of the most important developments in the American legal system over the past fifty years has been the commitment of the Christian Right, aided by the sympathy and energy of white women evangelicals, to influence both legal rhetoric and law itself. This is now known as the Christian legal movement (CLM), a movement defined by its defense of religious liberties within the United States.[54] The CLM is motivated by a conviction that conservative Christian religious freedoms have been under attack in America.

The CLM's efforts to change the legal system are carried out by Christian Conservative Legal Organizations (CCLOs).[55] The CLM is therefore defined by the actions of CCLOs, translating the issues of the traditional Christian Right—religious freedom, sanctity of life, and defense of a traditional marriage—into matters to be strategically resolved through the courts and broader legal system.[56] In the book *Defending Faith: The Politics of the Christian Conservative Legal Movement*, Daniel Bennett writes that the CLM may be the most expansive yet least understood effort to actualize the imperatives of the Christian Right through the apparatus of the State. Bennet writes that the most common issue pursued by CCLOs is that of religious liberty, accounting for 40 percent of all press releases publicizing their activity.[57] The phrase *religious liberty* is misleading because its implementation by CCLOs is skewed toward only Christian interests. Although advocacy for religious liberty is generally oriented toward Christians, the theme of religious liberty allows CCLOs to present their advocacy in positive and inclusive language, allowing CCLOs to maintain on the surface an insistence that religious liberty is pursued in the name of all religions. Yet most fail to give support for any religious tradition outside of Christianity, are almost exclusively advocating for Christianity's presence in the public realm, and are critical of other religious traditions like Islam.

CCLOs mobilize supporters and attract generous donations by positioning Christians as an endangered minority. For example, CCLOs promoted the idea of the "war on Christmas." The war on Christmas (a perception that Christians cannot say "Merry Christmas" in public and "secular" spaces) stems from the notion that it is no longer "politically correct" to recognize Christmas in the civic sphere, another symptom of America's decline into secularism. Side-stepping issues of pluralism, the war on Christmas presumes that American culture had rested on Christianity and that a basic assumption of U.S. culture was being compromised in a way that marginalized Christianity. Charles LiMandri of the Freedom of Conscience Defense Fund admitted that his organization is "trying to preserve a Judeo-Christian culture that permeates society."[58] Indeed, the majority of CCLOs are attempting to uphold a culture of conservative Christianity not on the basis of informal norms but in a manner that makes such actions obligatory and concrete, with backing from legal precedent. According to Bennett, "[T]hese groups, by and large, do not consider their work to be mere legal advocacy; they consider it to be instrumental in shaping and (eventually) winning the culture for their faith."[59]

Among CCLO initiatives, defending the sanctity of heterosexual marriage and discrimination over and against the LGBTQ community has been fundamental. Twenty-eight states banned same-sex marriage from 2000 to 2008, thirteen in 2004 alone. This broad opposition to same-sex marriage is again framed as an expression of religious liberty. So, although broader society, including white evangelicals as a group, have become more accepting of the LGBTQ community, CCLOs have maintained a mission to craft arguments against gay marriage through the court system. Those arguments are exemplified in the story of Kim Davis, a state clerk for Rowan County, Kentucky. When the Supreme Court struck down state bans against gay marriage, Davis was expected to fill out marriage licenses for gay couples, meaning it was her duty to sanction marriage for same-sex couples. The decision was made on a Friday, and on the following Monday, Davis announced that she would no longer fill out marriage licenses for any couples, saying, "It is my deep conviction and belief that God ordained marriage between a man and a woman. I can't be a part of this."[60] Predictably, lawsuits followed, and in spite of arguing that she was simply expressing religious freedom, Davis wound up in jail for a short time for violating a federal order to issue marriage licenses. Her situation captured the attention of the CLM, and Mike Huckabee, who was at that time seeking the Republican nomination for President, used her arrest as proof of "the criminalization of Christianity in America."[61] When Davis was released from jail several days later, both Huckabee and fellow candidate Ted Cruz were there to show their support, effectively making Davis something of a martyr for the religious convictions of the Christian Right.

THE FIGHT AGAINST ABORTION AND THE CHRISTIAN LEGAL MOVEMENT

The most important legal battle taken on by conservative Christian legal organizations is most certainly the fight against abortion. Although concern over abortion grew gradually, since 1980, the antiabortion movement has aligned itself with the Republican Party, while the Democratic Party largely supports abortion rights. In the Republican Party, white Christians make up 73 percent of the demographic, and a 2018 Gallup poll indicates that 74 percent of Republicans consider themselves "pro-

life." Fewer than one-third of Democrats are white Christians, however, and 71 percent of these Gallup poll respondents consider themselves "prochoice."[62] This striking polarization in the abortion debate is
the result of nearly a century of developments in the political arena.
Theologian Francis Schaeffer is credited as locking in opposition to
abortion as a white evangelical cause, framing abortion through his
writings and a high-quality film series titled *Whatever Happened to the
Human Race?* as a cultural tipping point that would lead not only to
infanticide and euthanasia but also to the deterioration of traditional
gender roles.[63] Schaeffer's panache was particularly effective. As historian Steven P. Miller makes clear, Schaeffer's intense intellectual tone
made him appear progressive, but "his aesthetics really were apologet-
ics," combining "an open door style with a case-closed dogmatism that
betrayed his fundamentalist roots. . . . Schaeffer was a reactionary, not a
proto-postmodernist."[64]

The prolife movement became potent in part because Schaeffer and
others drew on the same vocabulary of struggles for domestic civil
rights and global human rights, those values for human life that inspired
the movement for African-American freedom, the feminist movement,
antiwar protests, and LGBTQ rights. A human fetus became known as
"a pre-born person."[65] Antiabortion advocates may champion ideas of
freedom and "right to life," but this rhetoric screens their ambitions to
realize a pure Christian America. Much of the history of the antiabortion movement has relied on the direct suasion of young people, mostly
in churches but also in schools and various public forums and events, to
keep them sexually pure and abstinent until marriage, and to train them
as upholders of Christian morality, using pictures of dead babies, conversion testimonies, and Bible verses shared in deeply emotional language—all of which are used to convey a message that abortion and
anything that leads to it is inherently sinful. Now, a decisive pivot to the
courtroom, crafting legal arguments to support it and nominating conservative judges to rule in their favor, has been the driving force behind
more recent antiabortion activism.

The adoption of rights-based language by both Catholics and evangelicals helped the larger antiabortion movement appeal to both sides
of the aisle and initially attract bipartisan support. The Republican Party was not always home to the antiabortion movement. In the 1960s, the
Democratic Party, which historically fought for human rights in the

Civil Rights movement and in its opposition to the Vietnam War, still viewed abortion as a right. But Catholics argued that opposition to abortion should be seen as more consistent with their liberal sentiments, saying that "the most 'liberal' cause is protecting other people's lives,"[66] beginning with the unborn. During this time, Democrats advocated for increased social spending for health insurance for unwed mothers and free day care centers. Some believed it would not be enough to aid those with unplanned pregnancies to cope with their increased financial obligations. By legalizing elective abortion and subsidizing the expenses, not only would lower-income women be helped but also the growth of the United States' population would be moderated, particularly if abortions were incentivized for women. The proposal fell in line with Lyndon B. Johnson's Great Society and the War on Poverty, while "[t]he prolife message was antithetical to that goal."[67]

With a fiscally restrictive platform, many Republicans felt that the policies that Democrats were advocating were socialist and went against their ideals, especially given the continued stigma against communism in the wake of the second Red Scare of the 1950s. Greater spending on programs for babies and their mothers would mean greater taxation of all Americans; this, of course, was anathema in the eyes of neoliberal thinkers as an infringement on taxpayer freedom—the right to not pay taxes that they viewed as exploitative.

On the other hand, the Republican Party initially advocated for abortion rights for both financial and freedom-based reasons. As the politically progressive and morally driven abortion debate of the 1960s centered on increasing the welfare of all and advancing quality of life (including for the unborn), "many young conservatives and college Republicans supported abortion law reform, especially if they identified with the libertarian wing of the conservative movement."[68] The libertarian Republican sentiment changed following *Roe v. Wade*, when many Republican interest groups adapted their narrative to a rights-based argument to avoid conflict with their fiscal platform. The Catholic church eventually joined forces with white evangelicals, hoping to create a nonsectarian movement. A broader antiabortion movement alongside the unlikely ally of the GOP would ensure greater political pressure to advance their agenda.

In the book *The Rights Turn in Conservative Christian Politics: How Abortion Transformed the Culture Wars*, professor of political science

Andrew Lewis describes the development of the antiabortion move-ment. Unlike Catholics, abortion was not always a key issue for conser-vative evangelicals, despite the fervor with which they argue against it today. Evangelical elites would choose an "easy" political issue—that is, one that can be argued from the pulpit—and use that issue to unite and mobilize their base. In the mid-twentieth century, these issues largely revolved around religion in schools and obscenity: evolution, school prayer, and porn magazines.[69] Notable evangelical leader Jerry Falwell engaged in a lengthy libel lawsuit designed to restrict free speech.[70] However, these issues were largely a losing cause for evangelicals. On the basis of First Amendment rights, the Supreme Court (and many lower courts) rejected evangelical pleas to preserve "American" values in schools. Even obscenity laws, long championed by the Christian right as a way to save society and further the Christian moral agenda, were slowly being loosened in the name of free speech. Despite the slowly changing court precedents, evangelical leaders continued to put their trust in the fact that, although they might lose any particular court battle, they would eventually win the war.

In the early 1970s, evangelicals began to rapidly lose faith in the US government. Although Christian antiabortion activism was not yet the powerhouse it is today, evangelical leaders felt that 1973's *Roe v. Wade* decision was a major blow to their platform. Furthermore, in the after-math of the Watergate scandal, evangelicals lost trust in the govern-ment along with the rest of the country. In response, "nineteen relig-ious organizations . . . formed the Religious Committee for Integrity in Government (RCIG) to respond to Watergate and support campaign reform efforts," announcing that "Watergate was a moral crisis."[71] This newfound conservative Christian mistrust in government allowed evan-gelical leaders to push their antiabortion agenda despite the *Roe* deci-sion. Instead of respecting the court, they now saw the court as open to challenge and the ideologies of the judges as open to much greater scrutiny.

Abortion became a primary issue for Jerry Falwell as well as other church leaders like Billy Graham and Francis Schaeffer. However, even through the 1970s, many evangelicals still supported limited abortion rights. Over time, the fervor of the few prolife evangelical activists seeped into the teachings of the churches. Within evangelical culture, antiabortion activism became the norm such that being "prolife" was now a de facto requirement of being a good Christian, and voting for "prolife" candidates became a Christian obligation. Voter guides, hand-outs that preselected the right candidates in local, state, and federal elections, were passed out in churches across the nation, leveraging the abortion debates into a formidable political force.

The *Roe v. Wade* case was a major catalyst for the Christian Right to focus more intensely on legal matters, which ultimately led to more focused involvement in politics.[72] Alongside Catholic activists, evangeli-cals adopted their rights-based rhetoric. And having learned their les-son from the many defeats of their midcentury Christian activism, evan-gelical leaders this time advocated *for* rights rather than *against* them. As Andrew Lewis writes, "They champion individualist free speech principles and lean on liberal legal precedents, taking positions that would have been unthinkable to evangelical forbearers, including Jerry Falwell."[73]

Although the evangelical stance on abortion is undoubtedly political, and voter guides became a standard "resource" passed out in church services, many evangelical churches work hard to maintain a brand of apoliticism while advocating for the prolife agenda. These evangelical leaders preach about the dangers of politics and assert a position of political neutrality, trying to side-step any potential political polariza-tion, while quietly cementing an "informal understanding that good Christians vote Republican."[74] As Lydia Bean finds, there is no "explicit persuasion or deliberation" involved in most evangelical churches, but rather conservatism is normalized "through implicit cues about what political affiliations are" for devout evangelical Christians.[75] Just as ev-angelical church leaders disguise their political preferences with relig-ious rhetoric, the prolife movement uses rights-based language to sep-arate itself from association with Christian ideas regarding sexual purity that became increasingly unpopular among Americans.

Not only did rights-based rhetoric make the abortion debate more accessible to the general public, it also joined evangelicals and Catho-lics. In the book *Defenders of the Unborn: The Pro-Life Movement before Roe v. Wade*, historian Daniel Williams writes that Catholics framed their antiabortion position in the language of human rights, specifically the individual right to life.[76] Evangelicals and Catholics had long diverged on their understanding of Christian doctrine. However, they agreed on most moral issues, especially regarding sexual promiscuity. Remember that the antiabortion movement began as a primarily Catholic cause. The Catholic church attacked abortion on the grounds that it, "along with contraception, sterilization, and euthanasia, [was] one of the pagan and irrational philosophies based on modern creeds of unlimited sex indulgence."[77] Additionally, abortion was an issue of inalienable rights that would destroy "the essential dignity of man as a child of God and destined for God in heaven."[78] If legalized, abortion, "[i]n their view[,] . . . was a step toward the eugenic and genocidal policies of the Nazis."[79] Evangelicals were attracted by the success of Catholic rights-based rhetoric, and Catholics welcomed evangelical allyship because they needed to widen the scope of their cause to exert as much political power as possible. What started as a progressive Catholic cause evolved to include evangelicals and align with the Republican Party. In its desire to enact a constitutional amendment that would reverse *Roe*, this coalition found the support of Reagan and the larger Republican Party.

Up until the Supreme Court's historic ruling on *Roe v. Wade*, the joint Catholic-evangelical antiabortion movement had focused its efforts on swaying public opinion in their favor and winning legislative battles regarding abortion reform in local court systems. Many antiabortion campaigns centered their efforts around claims that elective abortion was exploitative of women as it allowed a male-dominated society "to evade its responsibility to care for pregnant women who were in need" and instead pressured women to kill unborn fetuses to regain the acceptance and satisfaction of that society.[80] The movement proposed that, rather than force women to engage in a practice that antiabortion advocates considered to be comparable to genocide, society itself should work toward accommodating women facing unplanned pregnancies by offering services such as "subsidized adoption" and "health insurance for unwed mothers."[81]

In addition to the use of provocative rhetoric to explain the unjust nature of abortion, prolife proponents also enlisted the help of new ultrasound technology to provide the public with graphic images of the unborn fetus. The antiabortion movement was enthused by the prospect that fetal photography had the power "to convince the public that every abortion killed a human baby."[82] Ultrasounds revealed that unborn fetuses possessed "distinctively infant-like features," which were dissected or forcefully expelled from the body during an abortion procedure.[83] With the use of groundbreaking embryonic photographs and vivid, emotionally charged rhetoric, the antiabortion movement desperately attempted to convince Americans that the unborn fetus qualified as a human life, and abortion not only denied the fetus basic, inalienable rights but also ostracized and disrespected women.

In the time following *Roe v. Wade*, the antiabortion movement had to quickly realign its strategies to preserve its relevance and adapt to the new ruling. The Supreme Court had legalized abortion on the grounds that "the constitutional right to privacy gave women a right to an abortion" and that there was not sufficient evidence "to confirm prolifers' claim that fetuses had legal rights."[84] Because both of these rulings refuted central tenets of the antiabortion arguments, the movement immediately recognized that its only chance at survival was to reverse the court's decision.

Roe v. Wade signaled for both evangelicals and Catholics that "the American state no longer [supports], in any meaningful sense, the laws of God."[85] For many devout antiabortion proponents, the government was "a legitimate instrument for asserting a distinctively conservative Christian privilege," which is why for them, the most effective way to combat *Roe v. Wade* was to use the government to enact a human life amendment (HLA). The amendment would permanently protect the country against the dangers of legalized abortion, but it would also reaffirm Christian values, which many antiabortion advocates believed the Supreme Court's decision had violated. The antiabortion movement concentrated on supporting congressional and presidential candidates who supported the HLA. Antiabortion policy supporters knew that if they were to pass the HLA, they would need mainstream, consistent support. Republican candidates, on the other hand, wanted to be elected into political office, even if it meant reliance on single-issue voters. This mutually beneficial relationship combined antiabortion activists with new Republican politicians.[86]

Although both Democrat and Republican candidates alike seek election into political office, the Republican candidates and their agenda more closely aligned with conservative Christian privilege and neoliberal ideals. Unlike the cohort of antiabortion Democrats who were advocating for greater spending on supportive social programs, the majority of conservative Christians sided with neoliberal-Libertarian conservatives in promoting tax cuts and reductions in social spending. Conservative political support of the HLA and antiabortion policy combined with a neoliberal fiscal agenda cemented the mainstream antiabortion movement's place in the Republican Party.

Roe v. Wade established that women have the right to have an abortion, but it also stated that states have the right to determine when to protect the possibility of life. The conversation quickly shifted on securing state versus federal power over abortion. Continuing the *Roe* debate over states' control of abortion, the Supreme Court issued a consequential decision in 1992, *Planned Parenthood of Southeastern Pennsylvania v. Casey*. The wording of the *Casey* decision established that states were barred from putting a "substantial obstacle" in front of a woman trying to get an abortion.[87] This led to experimentation with regulations by state legislatures on abortion laws, particularly the extent of accessibility required. CCLOs welcomed the *Casey* decision because it provided a legal foothold on the issue of abortion. "Sanctity of life" became the spearhead of CLM's ultimate goals.

CCLOs now fight for the sanctity of life, namely defending prolife against prochoice advocates. A major win came more recently in the 2014 Supreme Court case of *Burwell v. Hobby Lobby*. The *Hobby Lobby* case was essentially a response to the 2010 Affordable Care Act (ACA), because ACA guidelines mandated that health insurance include coverage for contraceptives, which conservative evangelicals claimed could be used to assist in abortion. Hobby Lobby, a private company with conservative Christian ownership, argued that the obligation to provide coverage for contraception violated their right to freedom of religion.[88] The Supreme Court decided in favor of Hobby Lobby, which now meant that not only corporations but also religious institutions would be granted amnesty from government regulations that violate their religious beliefs.

More importantly, the decision in the *Hobby Lobby* case means that the actions of businesses and whole corporations over their workers could be determined by the religious convictions of their owners. The president of the National Association of Evangelicals summarized the triumphant tone taken by conservative Christians, saying, "Business owners in America should be able to run their businesses according to their religious faith and values."[89] Thus, through the use of legal advocacy by CCLOs, the Christian Right made significant strides in legitimating their power in the corporate sector both in pressing the issue of religious liberty as well as taking a bold step toward allowing the State to protect the sanctity of life.

EVANGELICALISM, ECONOMICS, AND CONTEMPORARY CHRISTIAN LIBERTARIANISM

Although the fight against abortion is a core feature of Trump support, another important aspect of evangelical support remains economics. In general, evangelicals tend to reside on the middle and lower end of the economic spectrum, with many white evangelicals feeling as if they are "left behind financially."[90] The perception of financial struggles among white evangelicals allowed them to be open to outsider perspectives, and the billionaire entrepreneur Trump qualified for them as someone who may know how to better the economic fortunes of everyday Americans. Thus, when Trump presented a "different economic vision,"[91] it struck a chord with evangelicals who identified that a primary reason for their support of Trump involved his views on the economy.[92]

Trump's economic plan was presented as an overhaul of the nation's tax system in which "the rich will not be gaining at all with this plan"— but this was simply not true.[93] Despite its presentation as a "fair plan" benefiting "everyone," later analysis of actual proposals revealed that the intentions and consequences of his economic plan were obscured, and that Trump's plan for reforming taxation, like all neoliberal proposals, would actually greatly benefit wealthy elites and large corporations. The result is increased wealth retained by elites, which, as has been discussed in Piketty's analysis (see Chapter 8), proves to be significant in a financial system increasingly affected by the rise of inherited wealth.[94]

Although the economy and Christianity may seem to many like two separate, unrelated entities, many conservatives intertwine these concepts to create a spiritually motivated perspective on finance, a white Christian Libertarianism (see Chapter 5).[95] The GOP has managed to capture votes from what appears to be two opposed bases: religious interests and corporate interests. The puzzle for sociologists and for the public at large is to make sense of how the two align (see Chapter 6). After all, corporate interest orients around the profit motive and the suppression of corporate regulation. Surely religious interest is wholly different from this: morality before money, Bible before the bank, and decency above all else. Indeed, most expect religious interest to center on opposition to progressive social issues such as abortion and LGBTQ rights.

In November 2016, a LifeWay Research poll found that 87 percent of white evangelicals believed that the economy is "very important" when deciding on how to vote (only terrorism outranked the economy at 89 percent). When asked what single issue was of most importance, the top answer among white evangelicals was "improving the economy." "National security" came second, "personal character of the candidate" third, and "supreme court nominee" came fourth. Abortion hardly made the list at 4 percent. Although white evangelicals care about religious issues, the majority prioritize their vote based on considerations of the economy, not the Bible or other social issues.[96]

Both white and black evangelicals strongly believe that an individual can work in God's will to alleviate the problems of this country. However, black churches interpret America's problems in a social sense based on their histories of oppression by whites. In contrast, white churches interpret America's problems economically as a result of the slipping of their "social prestige" and "good order" that they have felt in the country, a sense of place that has most often ignored the oppression of blacks and other minorities. Nancy MacLean summarizes their attitude: "[I]ndividual liberty is a higher good than racial equality."[97] This individual liberty, in theory, could be used to promote the success of others; however, as seen in the work of Philips-Fein, most interpretations of the Bible are formed toward a social good, and white evangelicals have shown a historic tendency toward emphasizing a more individualistic, ego-centered, self-serving good. Especially in prosperity gospel theology, profit is seen as a good in itself; money is a means to allow God to work. The power of success in their finances allows them to help themselves and then to assist others with the overflow of their prosperity (see Chapter 5).

Evangelicalism is said to be based on an individual relationship with God; similarly, neoliberal capitalism is said to be based on the freedom to pursue individual profit; the connection is made simple: monetary freedom—the ability to exert one's influence on buying, investing, and selling in whatever way one chooses—allows evangelicals to pursue their destiny as part of their individualized connection to God. Generally speaking, evangelicals have great confidence that all people have the capacity to improve their lives "on the basis of accepting Jesus Christ as their personal savior."[98] Evangelical belief in individual ability to better oneself leads to "individual morality as the solution to moral problems with free market ideology and antistatist impulses."[99] So white evangelicals care about the economy, but not in the same way as corporations care about it. Although corporate interests support the profit motive as a matter of course, white evangelicals see the profit motive as a moral good against communism (or socialism), consistent with the desire of God. This orientation was forged early in the twentieth century (see Chapters 5 and 6). Remember, James Fifield, a Protestant minister, claimed that "the blessings of capitalism come from God."[100]

In the mid-twentieth century, evangelicals tied themselves closer to the Republican Party via conservative businessmen (see Chapter 5). Lydia Bean writes, "[R]ight-wing businessmen adopted a new strategy: funding evangelical institutions that promised to make Christians into political conservatives as part of their religious socialization."[101] Such investments gave evangelicals like Billy Graham the leverage to build media (mostly radio) empires, allowing them to broadcast their political and conservative views to a mass audience.[102] The result of these theo-economic views regarding poverty and prosperity is that the wealthiest individuals have a deeper connection to God. In the eyes of an evangelical who trusts these ideas, a man of immense wealth, like Donald Trump, has, by virtue of his riches, been endorsed by God.

God himself supposedly takes a hands-on approach when it comes to economic prosperity. In his book *Redeeming America: Piety and Politics in the New Christian Right*, Michael Lienesch quotes George Grant, who says, "All throughout the Bible, the pattern is clear: God punishes the rebellious, making them a scattered, homeless people."[103] Social welfare is wrong in part because it keeps people from seeking their help and strength from God himself. Another statement comes from John Eidsmore:

> God at times uses poverty as a test for believers, as he did with Job. It may be said that God puts some believers through a "poverty test" and others through a "prosperity test." There are some whom God will never allow to become wealthy, because he knows they could never handle wealth. . . . There are others whom God will never

allow to become poor, because he knows they could never handle poverty.[104]

Ultimately, a "secular, bureaucratic state" that evades the consequences of poverty is a danger as it results in the "dismantling of an entire ethic based on individual responsibility to family, church, community, commerce, and—above all—God."[105]

These free enterprise–inflected theologies do not remain in the pews; rather, they have consequences for public policy. Not only does this theologically tinged logic perpetuate negative views of the welfare systems and the poor but it also teaches that any sort of government regulation in the economy is a direct interference with God's plan. This belief is in agreement with Libertarian economic principles consistent with the image of a free market. An alliance is formed between fiscally conservative capitalism and evangelicalism. Ultimately, God decides who is prosperous and who is not.

The neoliberal interpretation of Christian doctrine that is characteristic of Christian Libertarianism has proved politically useful to corporate interest. White evangelicals give support to corporate desires, while corporations help support and fund the social issues of concern to the religious right. The relationship may benefit corporate interests more, given that the fight to cut taxes has been far more successful than the fight to criminalize abortion or same-sex marriage. Nevertheless, these believers carved a new path for interpreting finances from the biblical cannon under the conditions of modern capitalism, a societal system not anticipated by the scriptures. This does not bother modern-day biblical interpreters who assume the timeless applicability of the scriptures and who read into the richness of the biblical narrative lessons that fit neatly into the dominant economic environment of the United States. Of the many points they extract, none has been as pivotal as the idea that one's economic prosperity, or the lack of it, is a cause-and-effect result under the general principles of life established by God. Whether attaining wealth or falling into poverty, both are manifestations of the will of God working itself out in the lives of people. Success is correlated with the visible effects of personal salvation; poverty is associated with punishment for a failure to follow the dictates of God.

MAKE AMERICA A WHITE AND
CHRISTIAN NATION AGAIN

All of these elements are powerful aspects of white evangelical support for the Trump presidency. Although most recognize the priority given to antiabortion sentiment, this discussion reveals how white evangelicals also connected with the Trump campaign's focus on the economy.[106] Emphasizing the intent to create an economy that benefits "America first," regardless of potential outcomes, is consistent with white evangelical identity. However, perhaps the aspect of the America-first economy that best resonated with evangelical identity, even if not readily identifiable by evangelicals themselves, is Trump's strong nationalist sentiment. In short, the identity politics of today's Trump supporters is perhaps best summarized as *white Christian nationalism*.[107]

Christian nationalism has been implicated among evangelicals for most of the twentieth century, beginning with a reaction against communism, intertwining religion and country based on "the claim that America is a 'Christian nation.'"[108] The conservative white evangelical movement in America is fixed on the belief that America is a nation chosen by God and built by Christians. In their eyes, a national identity that coincides with the tenets of Christian morality will be showered with blessings from above and will prove to be even more prosperous. While playing into the character of a political outsider, as Lydia Bean writes, white evangelicals draw on narratives of Christian nationalism to blame liberals for American moral decline.[109]

Trump is seen as the last gasp of white Christian Americans who believe the culture of the United States is shifting.[110] Trump catered to evangelical fear that Christianity was declining in America. Patriotic and nationalist attitudes are intertwined, allowing "Make America Great Again" to be received as a religious sentiment, especially when in 2016 evangelicals felt "like America [was] becoming a more difficult place for them to live."[111] In September 2014, 42 percent of white evangelicals felt that it was more difficult for them in the United States; by June 2016, that figure moved up to 46 percent—almost half of white evangelicals now believed it was increasingly difficult to be an evangelical Christian in their own country.[112]

Central to the political orientation of white evangelicals is who should be considered "truly American." For the majority of conservative evangelicals, members of religious minority groups cannot be properly American. Pew Research found that 57 percent of white evangelical Protestants said that it is very important to be Christian to be truly American.[113] The implication of such beliefs is that only "true Americans" have the right to rule America, a belief that buttressed attacks against the presidency of Barack Obama. Recall that, although Obama is a US citizen and a Christian, the "birther" movement repeatedly accused Obama of having ties to the Muslim faith and of being born in Kenya, which they believed made him not only unsuitable but disqualified to lead the United States (see Chapter 7). For many, the Obama presidency dislodged the moral foundation of America, a foundation assumed to rest on white evangelical Christianity. These sentiments feed directly into contemporary controversies regarding immigration to the United States.

ANTIIMMIGRATION AS A CONSEQUENCE OF WHITE CHRISTIAN NATIONALISM

In electing President Trump on the heels of the first African-American president, white evangelicals sought out a person who would support their values and presumptions. A key aspect of Trump's campaign was his rhetoric against immigrants and immigration, especially with respect to Mexican and Muslim immigrants. Trump's position on terrorism was the most identified reason for supporting him, with 80 percent of evangelicals citing this as significant; 66 percent also agreed on his stance on immigration.[114] Trump's views on terrorism and immigration can certainly be tied to a Christian nationalist sentiment.

Xenophobic and racist sentiments were clearly evident in Trump's widely televised and well-documented rallies, events that occurred both before and after his election. On entering the presidency, Trump immediately implemented even stricter policies on refugees, those who migrate to avoid violence or persecution, slashing the quota of how many could enter the United States by more than half. For example, data from the United Nations High Commissioner for Refugees shows that in 2016 the United States resettled about 97,000 refugees; in contrast, in 2017, America resettled only 33,000 refugees—the lowest total since 2002, immediately following the September 11 terrorist attacks. The sudden change is a sharp contrast to our contemporary history, and the cuts continued.

The year 2017 was the first time since the adoption of the 1980 United States Refugee Act that the United States admitted fewer refuges than the rest of the world. America has historically taken far more refugees than any other country. Over the past forty years, three million of the more than four million refugees resettled worldwide were taken in by the United States.[115] But by the end of 2018, the number was restricted even further, with only 22,491 refugees resettled in the United States, well under the established refugee ceiling set by Trump of 45,000.[116] For 2019, Trump set the ceiling even lower at 30,000 with actual resettlement much lower still.[117] For 2020, the annual cap was slashed even further, to a new low of only 18,000.

The president's administration appeals to fairness, saying that such people need to metaphorically "get in line" and "wait their turn," using proper channels to secure permission to enter the United States. But as sociologist David Scott Fitzgerald observes, "Restrictionists invoke the principles of fairness to claim that asylum seekers are 'queue jumpers' who should have gone through the proper legal channels to arrive. At the same time, governments [like the United States] deploy remote controls to shut down almost all legal avenues to seek protection," a phenomenon that has been called "the paper curtain."[118]

Other policies have a similar tone, including an outright ban on entry by residents of several Muslim-majority countries and the retraction of an Obama-era program that allowed 59,000 Haitian refugees to legally reside in the United States following the 2010 earthquake.[119] These policies have great approval among white evangelicals, tied as they are to fear of Muslims and the desire to protect the United States against terrorism. Surveys show 76 percent approval for these policies among white evangelicals.[120]

To understand the dynamics of shifting immigration laws, one must understand the dynamics of hyperincarceration in America and how criminalization shapes approaches to immigration. In her book *From Deportation to Prison: The Politics of Immigration Enforcement in Post–Civil Rights America*, Patrisia Macías-Rojas writes that as Reagan's war on drugs kicked into full gear in the 1980s, incarceration rates rose dramatically and particularly affected the black population through disparate sentencing.[121] Soon, the American prison system began to run out of room for all of the people who were being arrested. According to Macías-Rojas, this lack of space created "a need to pull noncitizens out of regular prisons in order to create space for newly criminalized people of color."[122] The need for additional bed space for the swelling prison population led Congress to order the Immigration and Naturalization Service (INS) to target noncitizens with convictions for deportation.[123] So, the lack of beds to house domestic criminals led the US government to be more punitive against immigrants and more aggressive with the amount of deportations that were being carried out. Migration control become more punitive, and new enforcement priorities and criminal alien classifications attached a greater stigma of criminality to immigration. As criminality was attached to blackness, now it found resonance with immigrants as well, fostering the same approaches of management of the undocumented.[124]

For most of the twentieth century, criminal prosecutions were rarely undertaken for immigration offences, and the criminal justice system operated separately from the immigration system as part of the US labor force (see Chapter 4).[125] Latinos have long dealt with being viewed as being perpetually foreign, despite the fact that Hispanics have lived in some regions of the United States longer than the white population (see Chapter 2). Immigration enforcement did not focus on crime but on labor. However, the war on crime and the generous funding allotted to agencies to fight crime motivated a shift, such that the INS (the precursor to Immigration and Customs Enforcement [ICE]) switched its focus to fighting crime as well. With massive funding for crime control moving into the Department of Justice, the INS framed its enforcement actions in budget requests (which had been considered administrative rather than criminal) through a new prosecutorial language of fighting crime.[126]

Linking criminality to immigration continued in 1986 with the Anti–Drug Abuse Act, which further justified deporting migrants charged with drug offenses. Eventually, Congress voted to increase funding both for detention bed space and for prosecuting immigration offenders as criminals.[127] This allowed immigration authorities to prosecute immigrants in criminal courts instead of the immigration courts to avoid allowing illegal migrants to be released on parole and to criminally prosecute those who violated their deportation orders. Immigration was no longer a labor problem, it was an issue of national security. In short, the overflowing (and mostly black) prison population played an important role in bringing about many of the changes to immigration enforcement, from detention and processing to the current issues of criminalization and deportation along the southern border of the United States.

Although the content of the debate on immigration is different than the debate about the sanctity of life, a common thread exists between abortion politics and the battle to radically restrict immigration, namely, the need to focus legal battles on a state and local level. The legal battle regarding immigrant deportation shifted from the federal or national level to the local and state level in the 1990s when local and state enforcement agencies greatly expanded their involvement in immigration and deportation. This localization occurred as a result of the diffusion of immigrants across the country away from customary landing spots to new destination cities and to rural areas that had not experienced such diversity previously; thus legal immigration battles shifted to local arenas.[128] Furthermore, as it relates to Trump's intense conflicts with Democratic members of Congress and legal action from immigration advocates with using ICE, the laws Trump hoped to implement could only succeed with the cooperation of local and state governments.

According to Hana Brown, a professor of sociology at Wake Forest University, ICE could deport at best around four percent of all undocumented immigrants; however, if the federal government is able to secure cooperation from the more than six hundred thousand local law enforcement agents across the country, the odds of deporting undocumented immigrants is much higher. Of course, this need for the federal government to coopt local law enforcement has produced passionate conflicts regarding the politics of immigration, skewing communities for or against deportation and affecting the elections of local sheriffs and assessment of the efficacy of local police forces.

The criminal stigma of migration in the mind of Americans that developed in the decades since the 1965 Hart-Celler Act paved the way for Donald Trump's xenophobic rhetoric against immigrants. Immigration policy is a major part of Trump's agenda, and it is one of the issues most often emphasized in his public discourse. Throughout his campaign and during his presidency, Trump has framed immigrants as murderers and drug dealers, as people who are coming to steal the jobs of honest, hard-working Americans; his rhetoric is powered by his overarching talking point of building "The Wall." He has also empowered agencies, such as ICE, to take drastic and at times morally questionable measures against immigrants, including "speedy" removals deporting long-term US residents when they attend school or visit a hospital, intentionally separating families, placing children in large detention centers, holding detainees indefinitely, and relocating children to American families without their parents' consent.[129] ICE's budget increased by 50 percent under Trump, and it deported nine hundred immigrants in the first nine weeks of the Trump presidency.[130] Legal matters around immigration are now at the forefront of both American law and politics, making it a central aspect of the Trump administration through the political support it still garners from his supporters and the political opposition to his presidency.

RELIGIOUS FERVOR FOR TRUMP AND RELIGIOUS RESISTANCE TO TRUMPISM

Although some white evangelicals persist in a narrative of being excluded, ostracized, or even "oppressed" by the secular culture, the cozying of white evangelicals with the Trump administration (similar to other associations seen in previous administrations, including Nixon, Bush, and even Clinton), the most recent iterations of relationships, shaping of policy, and appointing of judges friendly to conservative white evangelical priorities points to a current thriving of conservative evangelical plutocracy in America. White evangelicals resonate with the slogan "Make America Great Again," a process that calls for the nation to support a white, Christian core. One of the central imperatives among white evangelicals is the anxiety in response to liberal political movements throughout the twentieth century, which has stoked the fervor of reactionary conservatives, creating the desire to save America and to elect officials that seem to remake the nation to best serve Christian interests.

For example, among many evangelicals, educating their children to value Christianity is important, and efforts by state and federal governments perceived to remove religious influence in public education and other public arenas becomes a rallying point. Even more intense are Christian Reconstructionists—Christians who advocate for the rebuilding of the state with a strict religious agenda. They seek to place their adherents into influential positions in private and public offices, vote according to particular values, and reframe secular institutions to be in line with religious imperatives. Christian Reconstructionists seek to obliterate the separation of church and state, crafting the U.S. government into a theocracy.[131] Through initiatives both subtle and extreme, the conservative evangelical right is firmly rooted in a desire to purify American identity into an explicitly Christian one, and a Christianity of a particular type.[132] Trump's support of white Christian nationalism draws the support of these highly committed and highly mobilized conservative Christians.

The flow of attention and financial opportunities have resulted in a windfall for donations to those evangelicals who are Trump-aligned politicians, have Trump-friendly ministries, and produce Trump-prophesying books and movies. Today, Trump supporters can purchase a $45 gold coin minted with a picture of Trump and King Cyrus on the front, supporting a theologically prophetic notion that Trump is the modern day Cyrus, who is willing to use his executive power to give preferential and providential treatment to white evangelicals even without being a conservative white evangelical himself.[133] Wealthy and propertied white evangelicals gain the most from the Trump presidency in that the administration not only affirms their moral imperatives but also their economic desires for favorable tax subsidies and reduction of what they consider to be obstructive regulations.

Still, it is important to note that not every evangelical approves of Donald Trump. As historian Molly Worthen writes, after his first Muslim ban, opposition arose from several groups "who lamented the [executive] order's unbiblical abandonment of refugees."[134] His continued attitudes expressing not only a great insensitivity but also resentment and disdain to a great many groups in America has provoked a reaction from many quarters of evangelicals and "ex-evangelicals." The extent of white evangelical support has prompted discussions, conferences, and even books regarding the definition of *evangelical* in the wake of the 2016 election.[135] A few distinctive voices have become conspicuous.

Christian leaders like Rachel Held Evans became even more prominent through her writings, speeches, interviews, and even threads on Twitter speaking against Trump policies and the white evangelical ideology that support them.[136] Her sentiments reflect the belief that white evangelical support for Trump has resulted in the loss of their spiritual legitimacy. One passionate statement posted by John Pavlovitz titled "Dear Church, Here's Why People Are Leaving" describes the loss of moral legitimacy as the reason why church attendance is failing in the United States. Pavlovitz writes that the church is silent, neglecting "human rights atrocities," "unprecedented religious hypocrisy," and "political leaders who are antithetical to the heart of Jesus"; Pavlovitz calls this silence "moral laryngitis." Amid the many failings of the church, Pavlovitz writes, "Your silence right now is the last straw." He continues:

> They've been waiting for you to oppose the separation of families,
> to declare the value of black lives,
> to loudly defend LGBTQ people,
> to stand alongside your Muslims brothers and sisters
> to denounce the degradation of the planet—
> to say with absolute clarity what you stand for and what you will not abide.

Pavlovitz calls for white evangelicals to have the moral courage to stand up for the oppressed, to partake in the pluralism of the world, and to embrace a more expansive, and more generous, gospel message. Christian activist Shane Claiborne began to speak more forcefully in 2018, saying, "I'm not anti-Trump. I'm pro-Jesus. And everything Trump seems to stand for is anti-Jesus." Later that year, he tweeted, "Yes, I'm troubled by Trump. But I'm more troubled by the Christians who support him."[137] John Fea, a historian who has long attempted to correct mistaken notions of Christian nationalism that have become a fundamental conviction among white evangelicals, wrote an insightful book, *Believe Me: The Evangelical Road to Donald Trump*, which is intended for a Christian audience and reveals the unsavory history of white evangelical politics.[138] Despite the force of such statements by he and others, white evangelicals opposing Trump and his policies remain a minority.

The political left opposing Trump and his policies also includes a group similar to white evangelicals—black evangelicals. They share many of the same characteristics but differ in political affiliation. Generally speaking, black evangelicals attend church as often as white evangelicals and have similar rates of religious intensity.[139] Yet a key difference is that black evangelicals remain connected to the long history of racial oppression in America.[140] They do not support the abstract and ahistorical notions of hard work and perseverance as the key to opportunity and wealth. So, although they place their faith in a God who saves, they also believe that local, state, and federal governments have a choice to make: either continue to promote policies that further extend the wealth of a tiny minority of white elites, or consciously put policies in place that assist those in need; that recognize and overcome injustices to historically oppressed groups; and that provides relief to all people, regardless of race, creed, or sexual orientation, to actualize the benefits of education, employment, medical care, and security for the future of themselves and their children.

As impeachment hearing began in October 2019, prominent white evangelical supporters of Trump once again spoke out on his behalf. In the midst of a multicity evangelistic crusade, Franklin Graham urged prayer against the Democrats and for the president, ignoring reports of potential abuse of power and asserting the need to keep Trump in office. Trump himself said to reporters outside the White House that "the biggest pastors" had called to encourage him, telling him, "We've never seen our religion, or any religion, so electrified."

Chapter 10

CONCLUSION

Ethnoreligious Structures of Inequality in the Trump Presidency

Well into the administration of the forty-fifth president, many Americans freely admit to having felt blindsided by the unexpected triumph of Donald J. Trump. Moreover, they remain in awe of his constituency's ongoing endorsement of Trump's behavior and policy-making. This is largely due to a widespread underestimation of the political authority of a crucial group of voters: white evangelical Christians. The steady liberalization of society and social policy has given weight to the assumption that the link between conservative religious beliefs and American politics has diminished to the point of irrelevance. However, Trump's recent election highlights the previously unseen influence of white evangelicals on American politics and, perhaps more importantly, the deeply rooted relationship between conservative evangelical belief and the political and economic landscape of the United States.

A broader understanding of American history lessens the shock still experienced by many regarding the 2016 election; such an understanding draws continuities that reveal support for Trump as less of a surprise and more consistent with historical trends. The goal of this book has been to help readers acknowledge the existence, development, and consequences of ethnoracial and religious structures of political and economic power in the United States. By providing a historic context for the Trump presidency, the book constitutes an exploration of American society that draws together racial, economic, and religious dynamics. The overarching themes throughout the chapters provide some overview on the significance of race, class, and religion in shaping the political climate of the United States. Those themes are the salient influence of whiteness as a powerful yet often unseen undercurrent, the consistent yet legitimated economic inequities, and the variety of conservative evangelical manifestations that have supported particular programs and positions. The selective historical moments brought together in this narrative are heuristic, and the implications intentionally suggestive and provocative. I expect that more data and disciplined, systematic, and rigorous research and analysis will bring greater nuance and complexity to the legitimation of Donald Trump and his policies. In anticipation of future research, the book intends to stimulate questions on issues to be pursued. As such, my hope is that we will see more work focused on distinctively sociological issues at a macro level of analysis that includes dynamics of continuing relevance on race, class, and religion as curiously intertwined.

Those in political authority make decisions, and various interests are affected by those decisions. In discerning the outcome of the election, the voting patterns of the wealthy are fairly easy to explain as the wealthy clearly benefited from the proposed policies of candidate Trump. But the voting patterns of evangelicals seem harder to explain, if they are approached from the standpoint of their explicitly religious convictions alone. However, when looking at the broader patterns of history and recognizing that white evangelicals share certain racial and economic sentiments formed over a long period in the United States, the racialized political force of wealthy whites and their willingness to align with evangelicals reveals the operations of American plutocracy. Not all white evangelicals are wealthy, yet a large portion of America's propertied upper class resonates with the Christian nationalism of white evangelicals, an orientation that itself has gone through successive changes over time. Moreover, the unforeseen conjunction of libertarian principles with conservative Christianity successfully generated a powerful framing of religious identity and political policy, resulting in the ascendance of white Christian Libertarianism (see Chapter 5).

Evangelicalism has gone through dramatic changes since the Great Awakening, especially during the waves of activism in the mid-twentieth century. Evangelicals have continued to build bridges to elected officials and legislative powers to pursue advantages that benefit them. Evangelicals had generally emphasized the individual's obligation to intensify one's own personal religious commitment, carrying the particular priorities of evangelicalism into their personal convictions. Evangelicals have long believed that American culture has spiritually atrophied, that the family unit has broken down, that understandings of the Bible have been lost, and that secular government structures hinder religious flourishing. Because the Spirit of God dwells within individuals, the intervention of God works through individuals. Yet, as church attendance declined and the saliency of religion waned, evangelicals turned to political structures to enact their influence and establish an order to society deemed to be desired by God himself. Evangelicals uphold an illusion of historical constancy in belief and practice instead of acknowledging their intentional engagements in politics to stem the uncomfortable tide of social change they see as working against their interests.

As such, evangelicalism today might be defined more accurately not as a theological orientation but as a political one, oriented around coalitions of voluntary nonprofit organizations whose members have a common cause for which they seek to influence public policy and effect their political control. As of this writing, the buzzwords *socialism*, *open borders*, and *infanticide* have become the triad on which white Christian conservative political mobilization has coalesced. Together, they constitute a challenge to the white Christian conservative assumption of a "true" America, the God-intended political order, one that is capitalist, wary of foreign influence, and conscious of the loss of traditional conservative Christian values.

By presenting himself as a defender of Christian religion, Trump gained the support of white evangelicals who were willing to overlook his prejudices and personal failings. By standing up for white evangelical Christians and producing legislation that aligns with their priorities, Donald Trump made himself the official protector for the evangelical community. Although many Christian leaders openly admit that Trump is not a good Christian, they continue to affirm and promote him, strengthening and expanding his white evangelical base of support. For the sake of expediency, many white evangelicals readily admit that typical moral niceties can be sacrificed in the pursuit of sanctioned political desires.[1] Ralph Reed, founder of the Faith and Freedom Coalition, and a white evangelical insider, has advocated for Trump since his Republican nomination and continues to argue for the urgency of supporting their protector, most publicly in a new book scheduled to publish before the 2020 election titled, *For God and Country: The Christian Case for Trump.* Trump's pugilistic style represents a culmination of the combative tactics of "the Long New Right" stemming from the McCarthyism of the early 1950s, the Barry Goldwater campaign of the early 1960s, the growing conservative activism around the politics of resentment in the 1970s, the smashmouth politics of the 1980s, the brash talk-radio conservatives whose popularity swelled in the 1990s, and the political principles espoused by cable channel personalities on Fox News in the 2000s and beyond.[2] As Daniel Schlozman and Sam Rosenfeld write, "For the Long New Right, the goal to smash liberalism came first."[3]

To the extent that white Christian Libertarianism is mobilized as a base for the Trump presidency, it is not only a religious identity but also a powerful sociopolitical movement representing the desires of a virtuous community influenced by the sentiments that shaped it over time. Their concern is not for the morality of President Trump but for the moral order of the United States. Reflecting the political thought of Protestant reformer Martin Luther, the fallen world is unrestrained, having no intrinsic order, so the State must impose order.[4] Taking power and applying force becomes necessary because the nobility of the State lies in establishing order, what conservative Christians metaphorically deem to be "the sword" of government found in the Apostle Paul's letter to the Romans in chapter 13. It is a political order established by coercion rather than love—although it might be asserted that love prompted the obligation to assert a righteous authority that is ultimately motivated by charity.[5] The coercive push for a desired order is not a rationally derived disposition; it stems from a set of values and discourses embedded within institutional structures that have been coopted by a Libertarian-leaning Republican Party that has sympathy for morally conservative positions as long as they are accompanied by support of free-enterprise business imperatives.

White Christian Libertarianism is itself one of the most important and consequential developments of our contemporary era, conveying an explicit fusing of neoliberalism with white evangelical religious convictions. Just as neoliberalism asserted that humanity is best served by releasing the unobstructed entrepreneurial freedom of the individual, so evangelicals also assert the importance of individual conviction and the ability for Christian conservatives to act on the basis of their religious convictions without hindrance. For evangelicals, the assertion of conviction became especially important in the face of calls to respect persons with nontraditional sexualities, same-sex marriages, non-Christian religious identities, and a woman's decision to terminate a pregnancy. Trump provides even more justification for the entwining of evangelicalism and neoliberalism. Donald Trump's charismatic persona of an all-American, self-made man is sanctioned by their Christian morals. More importantly, Trump's opposition to identity politics further stoked "resentment toward groups that many white Americans believe have benefited disproportionately from liberal establishment politics and long-standing support for the Democratic Party—Blacks and Latinos, immigrants and feminists, queers and especially same-sex couples."[6] Together, these social groups are the enemies of neoliberal-evangelical politics as they seek government "interference" to achieve equality through welfare programs and legislation that protects their identities. Sociologist Penny Edgell argues that Trump's campaign platform was encoded with whiteness, particularly in his tirade against "identity politics," meaning political persuasions and voting habits of various social groups based on their interests in sociopolitical equality.[7] Therefore, Trump also represents the maintenance of the socioeconomic supremacy of white identity, a political priority historically shared by both white evangelicals and neoliberal advocates.

In the Trump era, it appears that the marriage between white evangelicalism, the capitalist elite, and political control have been forged out of a mutual desire for power and protection. Politics involves persuasion, but the impatience of aligning a desired end amid the recalcitrance of existing institutional structures toward a group's definition of "the good" results in unanticipated alliances, partnerships that provide the means to obtain that desired end. To assert that evangelicalism is more truly rooted in spiritual concerns like forgiveness and redemption is to ignore how evangelicals have asserted themselves in actual historical time. Since the beginning of the American republic, with its intertwining of commerce and the institution of slavery, and then the later rise of corporate business models and financialization, evangelicals

largely aligned themselves with capitalist interests. Capitalists welcomed the moral affirmation stemming from sympathetic, business-
friendly white evangelicals. Although asset-rich capitalists are a minority of Americans whose asset-based wealth accumulation is historically
dependent on the exploitation and expropriation of the majority's labor—as evidenced by the long-standing depression in wages in comparison with the astronomical and continued rise of corporate profits and
the increased gap of the wealth of top 1 percent—white evangelicals
from the times of slavery until now have shown that they readily align
with government leaders who are willing to support their policy initiatives. Wealthy neoliberals' and white evangelicals' affinities and grie-
vances unite in a push against government intervention and perceived
overreach, for example, over issues like taxation and religious liberty. As
political theorist Sheldon Wolin wrote, "In its political aspect, a community is held together not by truth but by consensus."[8]

Many conservatives hold on to the idea that the United States once
had a "golden age" of consensus. But such naïve notions of political
community are quickly displaced when recognizing the immense diversity of affinity and interest groups that has always existed in the United
States and taking into account the consequences of differing privileges
and power allotted among those groups. With the inevitability of imper-
fect knowledge and irrational desires, as well as the fear and suspicion
that arise because of the inability to think outside of one's own group
interests, the pursuit of narrow political wins pushes aside concerns for
the common good, substituting the fulfillment of private desires over
the needs of a common citizenship. In this way, the potential investment of political energy into a broad-based hope for mutual happiness
across the whole of society morphs into the mobilization of fighters
thrust into narrow skirmishes aimed at grasping the reins of power.
Ultimately, interest groups in a democratic system can only expect to
achieve what Wolin called "tentative stabilities within a situation of
conflict."[9]

Any political system is an arrangement of power and authority, and
the propertied class in America has long been willing to engage in
manipulations of the political system to maintain its wealth and social
status. Since the days of plutocrats like John C. Calhoun, the wealthy
have made it a pattern to criticize government overreach that would
threaten their status as property owners. At the same time, these same

advocates for government nonintervention actively pursue new legislation to allow the wealthy to effectively maintain and grow their own
monetary assets. (Note that although the United States was founded on
the dispossession of Native American land, the political orientation
among today's economic elite is based in the fear of being subject to
their own dispossession, especially through taxation.) Certainly, one
method the wealthy elite have used to maintain their economic and
political power is through voting systems. Another is through applying
downward pressure for increased taxation of lower income earners. Still
other systems involve releasing protections for workers in the name of
accentuating their freedom (e.g., "Right to Work" legislation) and mobility. Along the way, the burden of privatization places the obligation
on the individual to self-fund their own training, transportation, and
travails, making the individual responsible for his or her own life as a
requirement to build and demonstrate moral character.

Capitalism increases wealth among the very few while increasing
wealth inequality among the many. And it does so with the assistance of
government.[10] Government entities provide permits, favorable interest
rates, generous tax subsidies, permission to extract resources, obtain
lucrative contracts for services, receive protections from foreign interference, and more. And although there is much talk about small business owners, the resources and benefits of government policies have
accrued not only to the wealthiest individuals but also to the wealthiest
corporations. With increased wealth, their influence increases. Consequently, as Larry Bartels concludes, "Economic inequality is, in substantial part, a *political* problem."[11] When the super-rich lobby for their
interests and fund campaigns for politicians willing to enact their interests, the wealthy are able to exercise excessive influence in the
American political system.

So, although capitalism is surrounded by narratives of free exchange,
realistically the operation of businesses is curated by government initiatives and policies designed to protect and stabilize the flow of capital
against the whims of market forces. Countering the protection of capitalist interests will entail a perceived infringement on their "freedom,"
which actually entails loosening the grip of myriad governmental supports for the mechanisms perpetuating their wealth. As Wolin writes,
"[I]t is difficult to fathom how the regulatory state could significantly
improve the lot of the disadvantaged without infringing upon the liberty

of those who control the means of employment, determine the extent of health care, and resist environmental safeguards."[12] Such a policy change toward employers is made all the more difficult given that corporations are given rights of speech and campaign finance that facilitate their political dominance. When corporate interests are sanctioned as political rights (as was most notably affirmed in *Citizens United v. Federal Election Commission* in 2010), they leverage the mechanisms of the State to sway the decision-makers representing the State further toward the service of corporate wealth rather than responding to the popular will.[13] Wolin recognized the manner in which political machinery becomes subservient to the preservation of wealth since "the wealthy have purchased and nurtured political agents to govern for them." Corporations systematically pour millions into legislative battles and electoral campaigns, exaggerating the unequal access wealth provides for motivating political attention to particular problems and preferred solutions. Because such flow of capital is required for politicians to obtain and maintain their platforms, "[s]tate actors become dependent more on corporate power than on their own citizens."[14] Meanwhile, unions have been systematically dismantled since the 1970s, deadening what had been historically the most organizationally powerful advocate for the wages and occupational conditions of working people.[15]

Together, white evangelicals and neoliberals form a new radical right that lifted Trump into the presidency and remained his base of support. These groups believed that both America's Christian heritage and its economic stability were threatened. Both evangelicals and neoliberals have found a strongman who plays to their victimhood and will protect their privileges from further exploitation. Their alignment with Trump was not due to shared religious values but rather to the consolidation of political influence. Nevertheless, in exerting their political influence, evangelicals and neoliberals do so with a righteous defiance against those who hold alternative views, believing that the proper moral order requires them to act with conviction and strength.

In addition, we cannot ignore that voting patterns attempting to actualize a particular moral order in America are racialized because of long-standing patterns of voter suppression. After Republican candidates were swept into office in 2010 in response to the presidency of Barak Obama, the American Legislative Exchange Council (ALEC) developed arguments and proposals to strengthen Republicans' newfound priorities against "voter fraud." These measures did little to expand the right to vote; instead, these initiatives fueled legislators in forty-one states to introduce more than 180 bills to restrict who could vote and how they could vote. Overall, their initiatives worked to reduce the influence of low-income and young people, groups that are more racially diverse and more politically liberal. This complimented a set of other efforts to systematically disenfranchise people from voting at local, state, and federal levels.[16]

American white evangelicals seem unconcerned about such matters as they have largely opted to align themselves with imperatives that the great majority of Republican leaders promote, ignoring what those leaders choose to ignore and unconcerned about what they see as unproblematic. For example, an analysis by Larry Bartels reveals that more politically aware conservatives (indicating their involvement and interest in politics) are more likely to deny the increased gap of income inequality in America; at the same time, these well-informed conservatives acknowledge economic inequality but are less likely to see the income gap between rich and poor as a bad thing and simply assume "some people just don't work as hard."[17] Similarly, while increased information generally results in a sharp decline of support for tax cuts, the same information among conservatives results in no change in their attitude at all. And it's not just economic ideas that are affected by prior ideological commitments. Another example of the partisan effect on interpreting information lies in the assessment of voter fraud. In North Carolina, despite gross anomalies in the 2018 election for District 9 in which Republican Mark Harris, a candidate for the House seat and a white Baptist pastor, hired a campaign consultant who paid his staff to fill out absentee ballots to vote for their own candidate, white evangelicals continued to assume that conservative politics and moral superiority are intertwined. Harris was disgraced and the North Carolina GOP shamed; state officials ordered a new election. Yet in the special election that followed in 2019, Republican voters remained faithful to their party—both President Trump and Vice President Mike Pence campaigned in the state on their behalf—giving victory to the new Republican candidate, Dan Bishop. There is no commentary regarding this gross corruption of the political process among white evangelicals. Instead, concerns regarding Republican-sponsored voter manipulation fell away.

Politics is a means to assert a desired social order, and through political power, groups seek to stabilize situations in a way that is most congenial to them. Trump appears to have direct access to his supporters through campaign rallies, selective media appearances, and steady tweeting on social media, calling for initiatives and issuing decisions (sometimes outright "commands"), without the burden of government bureaucracy. Some analysts speculate that Trump's affinity for autocratic leaders across the world (including Russia's Vladimir Putin, China's Xi Jinping, North Korea's Kim Jong-un, Turkey's Recep Tayyip Erdogan, and the Philippines' Rodrigo Duterte) indicates his envy of their ability to bypass inconvenient checks on his directives. Nevertheless, the Trump government and his supporters smack against the complexity of administratively coordinated institutions, which include the allotted powers constitutionally established across our institutions and the multiple interests presupposed in the vastness of our democratic political apparatus. After all, as Wolin writes, "The main aim of a constitutional form of government is to limit the exercise of political power to prevent its being abused."[18] Checks and balances frustrate the achievement of a desired social order. As seen during the 2019 impeachment inquiry, these checks most certainly frustrate President Trump, motivating his defiance.

Even more, in a democratic system, order is dynamic, and voting results can radically disrupt political systems. The pursuit of a desired political order is risky because the outcome of the final vote in any election is uncertain. This is why claims of "voter fraud" have been used in American history to limit and even sway voting patterns. Some concerns regarding the threat to the vote are overblown, while others are radically minimized, all depending on who benefits from perceptions of the problem with the vote. Among Republican leaders, the disingenuousness of the concern for protecting the American vote has been further exposed by their reluctance to enact meaningful sanctions and protections against Russian influence in US elections, a confirmed foreign influence conclusively investigated by the nation's top intelligence groups, including the Central Intelligence Agency, the Office of the Director of National Intelligence, the Federal Bureau of Investigation, the National Security Agency, the Justice Department, the Department of Homeland Security, the House Intelligence Committee, and the Senate Intelligence Committee.[19] Voter fraud is not a signifi-

cant national problem; foreign influence on our elections, especially
Russian, most certainly is. Yet Republicans do not deem them a significant threat to their interests.

Within a political order, when groups come to believe that a desirable moral order cannot be forged among disparate interests, policies of
repression and expulsion ensue. And when politics becomes nothing
but the pursuit of particularistic interests without shared ideals, ugliness
follows. The troubling aspect of the Trump presidency is that white
Christian Libertarians who align themselves with neoliberal policies
assume that their constructed notion of "American" ideals is absolute,
foundational, and therefore unquestionable. The possibility of viewing
any other political vision as legitimate is lost, and even the suggestion of
a more inclusive moral order is itself a threat. The zeal that energizes
support for Trump simultaneously removes the possibility of political
compromise because acknowledgment of pluralism is gone.[20] A self-
defined virtuous community becomes an openly exclusionary and violent one. As Wolin writes, "absolute power [is] the logical remedy for a
depraved society."[21] It is in this light that American issues of race and
immigration can be viewed as a distinctively political problem.

Racial disparities and racial violence continue today, but voting patterns reveal that not enough people are convinced that the American
political system should be better positioned to address such issues. Despite abundant evidence tracing racial inequality to founding economic
structures, longstanding historic prejudices, and government-backed
racial policies with respect to banking, housing, and education, there is
an insistence that the problem is individual, not systemic, and that
individuals are to blame for their misfortunes. While the ugliest strains
of white supremacy continue to the current day, they often go unchallenged since collective mediations are deemed unnecessary. When people act out of an extreme prejudice that aligns with fears of "white
genocide" and "ethnic replacement," all Americans should take into
account how they legitimate their views. For example, in August 2019, a
gunman with an AK-47–style rifle drove ten hours from Allen, Texas, to
El Paso, along the Southern border, and opened fire at a Walmart,
killing twenty-two people and injuring twenty-four others. It is the
deadliest attack to target Latinos in modern US history. The twenty-
one-year-old killer who confessed to deliberately targeting "Mexicans"
had posted a 2,300-word antiimmigrant manifesto before the attack. In

his writing, he raged against the invasion of legal and illegal Hispanics in Texas, fearing that their votes would make Texas a Democratic stronghold, and said, "If we can get rid of enough people, then our way of life can be more sustainable."[22] Despite those who seek to individualize the problem as one of "mental health," the attitudes are socially derived, have an extensive history, and are maintained both formally and informally by people across the United States. When looking at the mindset of the El Paso gunman, such sentiments may not have pulled the trigger, but they are resourced to provide the motivation and the targets for the bullets.

The issue of immigration continues to be salient for discerning American sentiment and be consequential for the Trump presidency. From 1990 to 2005, the foreign-born population in the United States grew 81 percent, from 19.8 million to 35.7 million.[23] Although Latinos increased 87 percent and Asians 71 percent, the white non-Hispanic population only grew by 2 percent. Demographically, the percentage of foreign born in the United States grew to about 15 percent of the total American population; the last time the United States had such a high percentage of foreign-born residents was in the 1920s—the same period that initiated the aggressive restrictions on immigration (see Chapter 4).[24] It could be argued that, like a temperature gauge, the native-born, white American population has a demographic "trigger" such that when the foreign-born population passes a certain point, aggressive actions are taken to restrict that population from growing further. This is reflected in many of Trump's public statements, like those made at a Pennsylvania rally in May 2019: "Our country is full. We don't want people coming up here. Our country is full. We want Mexico to stop. We want all of them to stop. Our country is packed to the gills. We don't want them coming up." Supporters, many of whom sported red Make America Great Again hats, clapped and cheered in hearty agreement.

When the 1980s brought a surge of appreciation for multiculturalism from the political left, sentiments that sought to honor diversity rather than ignore it, that appreciation brought a level of color-consciousness to the American population accompanied by greater efforts to ensure opportunity and access to historically disadvantaged minority groups. These initiatives, accompanied by greater exposure of diversity in mass media and new government policies, could be seen as either compensation for years of oppression and acknowledgment of the economic, educational, and sociocultural barriers that made it more difficult for members of minority groups to succeed in America, or an attempt to further stimulate the economy by drawing in the buying power of growing segments of the population. Either way, greater consideration and exposure of people of color fueled resentment among many whites, particularly poor whites, who felt these racial recognitions were inequitable.

Racial strains were further accentuated under the presidency of Ronald Reagan, who revitalized American nationalism but neglected the concerns of minorities, further worsening race relations in the United States. In the 1970s, before Reagan's election in 1980, Reagan had capitalized on a technique that most politicians had already grasped: "demonizing Latino immigrants and illegal migration" has "political advantages."[25] Like Donald Trump, Reagan argued that illegal immigrants were coming into the United States in overwhelming numbers and that Americans ultimately paid for them, which caught the attention of many voters. As has been seen in the rhetoric of other presidents, the use of fear and "loss of control" narratives were effective in mobilizing broad support in the white electorate.[26]

When Barak Obama was elected in 2008, this new president disrupted the historically legitimized practice of white superiority, appearing to sidestep the racial hierarchy and defy historically saturated definitions of American leadership. Research suggests Obama's occupation of the presidency evoked among whites a form of cognitive dissonance, in which his accomplishments were placed in opposition to ideas previously engrained. The election of the first black president was a warning sign to white supremacists that their version of American values were endangered. The urgency to bring the country back to normalcy is tidily summarized in the Trump campaign's key phrase: Make America Great Again. Both a vague promise but also a strong statement of value, the phrase seized on white frustration in the face of an increasingly nonwhite majority. As seen in the narrative of this book, this same discomfort was evident after emancipation, in the restrictive immigration policies of the late nineteenth and early twentieth centuries, and in the struggles over integration during the Civil Rights movement. The sentiments that propelled Trump's candidacy are consistent with racial tensions seen across American history.

In the wake of the presidency of the first black president of the United States, race relations have worsened. People with white nationalist and antiimmigrant attitudes have been emboldened, and they display those attitudes more overtly at the same time that the issue of mass incarceration and police abuse of blacks has been thrust into the public eye. After the attacks of September 11, 2001, George W. Bush was convinced that a properly constructed and religiously inflected multiculturalism was compatible with conservative values; he sought to distinguish between the Islamic mainstream and the radical Islamic fringe. But his efforts to promote tolerance of Muslim Americans failed, and anti-Muslim and anti-Arab Islamophobic sentiment continued to rise among many groups of Americans. And although Bush had reached out to Latinos in the South and Southwest, Obama accelerated the rate of deportations on the one hand while passing by Executive Order new protections for long-term undocumented migrants called DREAMers who were brought to the United States as young children and know only the United States as their country and thus hope to obtain legal residency based on their deep immersion in American culture.

Since political systems involve the management of boundaries, the many unresolved issues of race in the United States impinge on the many unresolved issues of immigration. In 2016 and the years leading up to Donald Trump's election, rhetoric surrounding immigration was based on fear and the supposed unfairness of giving benefits to immigrants that are unavailable to struggling white Americans. One can readily see the resonance between the unfairness attributed to immigrants and the unfairness attributed to newly freed blacks in the Reconstruction period (Chapter 3). Trump famously villainizes immigrants and blames them for America's problems, thus rallying white voters and appealing to their nativism. Immigrants are the scapegoats for America as a white nation. Trump will be the white nation's protector, best exemplified by his aggressive efforts to build The Wall at the Southern border.

Yet in accomplishing his protection, Latino families are separated at the border, driving children into the foster care system while their parents, who crossed the border to seek asylum in the United States, are labeled as criminals and sent to jail. One can see the similarities between the Dillingham Commission (see Chapter 4) and Donald Trump's presidential campaign in that they both determined who was fit for citizenship within the United States and prevented certain people from entering the United States based on their country of origin. Similarly, Trump prevented immigrants from seven countries (Iran, Libya, Somalia, Syria, Yemen, North Korea, and Venezuela) from entering the United States on the basis of their nationality and assumed threat to the United States. Based on notions of a perceived immigration problem, Trump effected further restrictions on refugees and other legal migrants, and nonwhite, non-Christian individuals living in the United States are subjected to degradation.

By implementing a "zero tolerance" policy,[27] the Trump administration actualizes a "zero migration" policy, taking policies that had been created to deter specific groups and applying them to every group. As professor of law Shoba Sivaprasad Wadhia concludes, when it comes to banning and deportation, "[e]veryone is a priority."[28] In all instances, "security" is the master frame for not just limiting immigration but halting it altogether. As Donald Trump tweeted in June 2018, "We cannot allow all of these people to invade our Country. When somebody comes in, we must immediately, with no Judges or Court Cases, bring them back from where they came."

Our national immigration policies not only have the capacity to be different, they actually can be quite accommodating and generous, wholly dependent on the right political will. Look at the case of Cuban refugees. US policy toward Cuba since the Kennedy administration reveals the phenomenal capacity of the United States to accept a large number of refugees without advance notice or preparation. In 1960, President Kennedy directed his Cabinet Secretary of Health, Education, and Welfare, Abraham Ribicoff, to implement the following (all italics from the original):[29]

- Provide all possible assistance to *voluntary relief agencies* in providing *daily necessities* for many of the refugees, for *resettling* as many of them as possible, and for securing jobs for them.
- Obtain the assistance of both private and governmental agencies to provide useful *employment opportunities* for displaced Cubans, consistent with the overall employment situation prevailing in Florida.
- Provide supplemental funds for the *resettlement* of refugees in other areas, including transportation and adjustment costs to the

new communities and for their eventual return to Miami for repatriation to their homeland as soon as that is again possible.

- Furnish financial assistance to meet *basic maintenance requirements* of needy Cuban refugee families in the Miami area as required in communities of resettlement, administered through
  Federal, State, and local channels and based on standards used in
  the community involved.
- Provide for *essential health services* through the financial assistance program supplemented by child health, public health services, and other arrangements as needed.
- Furnish Federal assistance for *local public school operating costs*
  related to the unforeseen impact of Cuban refugee children on
  local teaching facilities.
- Initiate needed measures to augment *training and educational
  opportunities for Cuban refugees*, including physicians, teachers,
  and those with other professional backgrounds.
- Provide financial aid for the care and protection of unaccompa-
  nied children—the most defenseless and troubled group among
  the refugee population.
- Undertake a *surplus food distribution program* to be administered by the county welfare department, with surplus foods distributed by public and voluntary agencies to needy refugees.

The sheer comprehensiveness of assistance and support for infrastructure provided on behalf of Cuban refugees, especially considering the
length of time the program was sustained, is breathtaking. From 1960
to 1980, arrangement for migrants from the island benefited approxi-
mately one million Cubans (including my own parents who met and
married in the United States, where I was born a year later). Until 1973,
support included US-financed "Freedom Flights" that carried 265,000
Cubans directly to the United States. Until January 2017 (the month
President Trump took office), the "wet foot, dry foot" policy allowed
Cubans without visas whose feet reached US soil to officially enter. All
of these refugees were provided a wide range of social services without
having been previously screened abroad. And after one year of residence, Cuban refugees were eligible for lawful residence in the United
States, a major step toward obtaining full citizenship.[30]

The contrast in tone from the Kennedy administration to the Trump administration is striking.[31] For example, the Reforming American Immigration for Strong Employment (RAISE) Act, introduced and upheld by Donald Trump, prioritized wealthy and highly educated English-speaking immigrants over those trying to reunite with family. Rather than consider humanitarian needs, the bill focused on the tangible benefit immigrants would bring into the United States. It also explicitly reduced the annual distribution of green cards awarding permanent legal residence by 50 percent, from one million to just over five hundred thousand. In part, the RAISE bill of 2017 sought to cut waves of legal immigration by limiting the allowance of children and spouses of legal immigrants who could enter the United States. Although family reunification had been a major priority of immigration policy for decades, it was now given a dark shadow. The term "chain migration" had been a demographic concept indicating the linking of children to their parents through family reunification; now, under harsh tones of threat and danger, "chain migration" has been uttered by Trump as if it were a grand conspiracy, a hidden loophole that migrants have used to take advantage of the system. In reality, by discouraging family reunification, the RAISE bill would have pushed legal immigrants who had been hired by American companies to work in the United States to fulfill specific roles to self-select in going back to their home countries in order to be with their families. Although the bill did not pass, the structure and character of the attitude toward immigration that informed its construction is indicative of the attitude of the Trump administration.

Trump's nativist ideology fueling initiatives like the RAISE bill speaks to deep cultural strains among Americans, a bedrock of sentiment that had been forged throughout the entirety of the history of the United States. Trump's use of coded language to accentuate notions of criminality among nonwhites and the foreign born perpetuated fear and bolstered support for Trump, the president who vowed to protect white Christian Americans (see Chapter 9). As Gary Gerstle writes, immigration has become "a policy site onto which Americans [project] their fears about the nation's alleged enemies."[32]

In the end, the most pressing political question seems to be: who is a true American? The voters and the enacted policies of their elected officials continue to define American identity through their actions and

the imperatives they affirm and enforce. As such, America may continue to veer toward increasingly white minority—birth and death rates
clearly indicate the inevitable shift of fewer whites in the United
States—as the base of American citizenship, with the highest tiers of
status and privileges due them. The imagination of political order is
constricted to be based on compulsion and constraint, as Wolin writes,
"the transformation of government from an instrument to serve human
needs and alleviate human distress into a system increasingly geared
towards punishment and control."[33] To the extent that white evangelicals leverage their political power to ensure this happens, they justify
State-sponsored, religiously sanctioned violence.

White evangelicals have long sided with a far too restrictive definition of American citizenship. What is so frustrating to groups like Christian Libertarians oriented around religiously derived interests, is that
the "truth" of their position is thought to be flawless. Political order
should reflect their supposed truths, even when available evidence is
contrary to their assertions. As Bartels summarizes, "careful logical arguments running from factual premises to policy conclusions are unlikely to persuade people who are ideologically motivated to distort or
deny the facts."[34]

The confidence of the rightness of their position, which they believe
is reflective of the metaphysical structure of reality, encourages them to
welcome all others, even those who do not share their religious convictions, who are willing to work in support of their goals—as long as they
do not challenge their premises. The securing of partnership affirms the
rightness of their position, even though the actual substance of ideals
and objectives between factions in the coalition are quite different.
Even more, the desire for partnership for the sake of power leaves
religious groups vulnerable to the manipulations of groups that ostensibly support their initiatives but are actually using the anchoring power
of their infrastructure and networks to forward their own agenda. As
John Fea assessed, "It's time to take a long hard look at what we have
become."[35]

It should be noted that many white evangelicals will not easily recognize themselves in these pages. Reluctant to attend rallies, volunteer for
campaigns, or otherwise actively engage in political issues, their passive
citizenship is typically expressed more so through the familiar ministries
of the churches they attend, the conservative Christian television and

radio networks they consume, and the partisanship they channel into the voting booth. They do not believe themselves to be political actors, and certainly not those who have exercised cruelty, deception, or self-benefit in the exercise of their political will. Such "value voters" insist that Trump and his policies (including child separations at the border) have accomplished "a lot of good things." As "respectable evangelicals" they insist that the most morally objectionable political actors in the Trump administration are exceptions: "it's not us."[36]

At the same time, they hold on to their innocence by distance, fervently defend his policies, and declare they would vote for him again. Survey results from the Public Religion Research Institute (PRRI) released in October 2019 found that white evangelicals who are Republican and Republican-leaning Independent are among the most unified in support of Trump, with 82 percent saying they favor him to be his party's nominee.[37] They reveal the modern circumstances of political engagement, a shift from the active member of Plato's *polis* where every citizen is actively involved to instead granting discretion to a delegated power, entrusting decisions to a distant executive power who is presumed to represent their values. Like the absentee landlord, the messiness of actual government is assigned to others whose day-to-day decisions do not matter as long as they can regularly assure us of a semblance of stability and right order. Politics is left to others to allow the freedom to pursue private activities without hindrance, not just work and family but also the pleasures of leisure. As Wolin states, "The average voter, overwhelmed by the number and magnitude of social problems, retreated into apathy and the diversions of mass entertainment."[38] This is how an abstract allegiance to Christian nationalism among well-meaning "value voters" translates into inaugurating and legitimizing a vast, yet particularistic, political system that is coopted by neoliberal purposes and perpetuates an unjust racial hierarchy.

Still, many Americans engage in struggles to successfully break the long-term momentum of white privilege and pursue a more expansive sense of our collective identity that acknowledges everyone who is already here; that has been attempted through fits and starts; that would more broadly inspire a more generous vision of who belongs and who can access the full benefits of social, economic, and political participation of the good life that can be made possible for all in our country. Among them are the religiously unaffiliated (the religious "nones") who now compose a larger percentage of the American population than white evangelicals. Emerging data reveal that their political attitudes are more progressive and their embrace of initiatives to address race- and class-based inequities is considerable.[39] Even within Christianity, challenges to the presumptions of whiteness and neoliberal-libertarian approaches to wealth continue their long-term trajectory of addressing injustice.[40] Moreover, the global center of Christianity is also shifting toward a more global and more colored constituency, which may affect the American church.[41] Importantly, some evangelicals of color within the United States—including Mark Charles, Soong-Chan Rah, and Jemar Tisby—are taking even greater responsibility for educating their white evangelical brethren on the historic injustices in their country, highlighting racial and economic abuses with which the American church has been complicit, abuses that go against core principles of justice and mercy embedded within Christian doctrine.[42]

Whether change is accomplished through the growth of the religiously unaffiliated or, perhaps, with an unforeseen change in the dominant tone of American Christianity remains to be seen. And if no significant shift occurs, white Christian Libertarianism will remain the default stance for a highly influential political coalition whose force will significantly shape what becomes America.

NOTES

PREFACE

1. Martí 2020.
2. Martí 2019.
3. Mulder, Ramos, and Martí 2017; Ramos, Martí, and Mulder 2018; Ramos, Martí, and Mulder forthcoming.
4. Mulder and Martí 2020.

CHAPTER 1. THE UNEXPECTED PRESIDENT

1. Initial and exemplary efforts were made by sociologist John L. Campbell and historian John Fea; see Campbell 2018 and Fea 2018.
2. Weber 1978.
3. In the United States, the panethnic category of "Asian" includes multiple subgroups. Although Chinese, Korean, Indian, and Japanese groups have relatively high incomes, the majority of Asian groups, including Cambodian, Laotian, and Vietnamese groups, do not share in that prosperity. The distinction occurs because the motivations for migration and the circumstances of their education and employment involve different historical trajectories. An excellent discussion on Asian-American achievement can be found in Lee and Zhou (2015).
4. Bonilla-Silva 2017.
5. Wormald 2015.
6. "Most White Evangelical Protestants Say It Is Very Important to Be Christian to Be Truly American," Pew Research Center, January 31, 2017.

https://www.pewglobal.org/2017/02/01/faith-few-strong-links-to-national-identity/pg-02-01-17_national-identity-4-01/.

7. "Election 2016: Exit Polls," *New York Times*, November 8, 2016. https://www.nytimes.com/interactive/2016/11/08/us/politics/election-exit-polls.html.

8. Parker and Barreto 2014.

9. "Trump Holds Steady After Charlottesville; Supporters Think Whites, Christians Face Discrimination," *Public Policy Polling*, August 23, 2017. http://www.publicpolicypolling.com/main/2017/08/trump-holds-steady-after-charlottesville-supporters-think-whites-christians-face-discrimination.html.

10. Holilnger and Gushee 2000.

11. Lienesch 1996.

12. Newman 2007.

13. Marsden 2006: 87.

14. Newman 2007: 89.

15. Marsden 2006: 93–94.

16. Parker and Barreto 2014.

17. Lienesch 1996.

18. Lienesch 1996: 119.

19. Phillips-Fein 2009.

20. Bean 2014: 63.

21. Phillips-Fein 2009: 73.

22. Silverman 2017.

23. Miller 2016.

24. Schlozman 2015: 94–95.

25. Echolls 2017.

26. Wormald 2015.

27. Clement and Green 2011.

28. Parker and Barreto 2014: 89.

29. Parker and Barreto 2014: 155. See also Bonilla-Silva 2017.

30. Jones 2016.

31. "Support for Trump Rose with Embrace of White Identity," *New York Times*. https://www.nytimes.com/interactive/2017/08/24/opinion/100000005388503.embedded.html.

32. "Trump Holds Steady."

33. Pew Research Center, "Persistent partisan, demographic gaps in Trump job approval." August 16, 2019. https://www.people-press.org/2019/08/16/most-democrats-are-excited-by-several-2020-candidates-not-just-their-top-choice/6-26/.

34. Fox News Poll results, October 6-8, 2019.

35. Pew Research Center, 2017 Religious Landscape Study.https://www.pewforum.org/religious-landscape-study/.

36. Worthen 2017.
37. Recent book-length discussions can be found in Baradaran 2017, Kendi 2016, Lee 2019, Okrent 2019, Painter 2010, and Rothstein 2017.
38. Smith 2017.
39. Schwadel and Smith 2019.
40. Phillips-Fein 2009: 74. See also Kruse 2015.
41. Lienesch 1996.
42. Lienesch 1996: 110.
43. MacLean 2017: 81.
44. Lienesch 1996: 123.
45. Dulk and Joustra 2015.
46. Putnam and Campbell 2012: 255.
47. Lienesch 1996: 117.
48. Lienesch 1996: 127.
49. Lienesch 1996: 11.
50. Phillips-Fein 2009: 73.
51. Dahl 2018: 68–72; Ostler 2019: 203;Williams 2003: 28.
52. Kousser and McPherson 1982: 150.
53. Fea 2018: 5.

CHAPTER 2. DEEP CULTURAL BACKGROUND ON RACIAL INEQUALITY

1. Aptheker 1943.
2. Baptist 2014.
3. Foner 1970.
4. Guyatt 2016: 3.
5. Painter 2010: ix.
6. Painter 2010: 36.
7. Painter 2010: 40.
8. Painter 2010: 42.
9. Painter 2010: 103.
10. Gerbner 2018.
11. Painter 2010: 80.
12. Painter 2010: 87.
13. Painter 2010: 202.
14. Painter 2010: 164.
15. Painter 2010: 167.
16. Painter 2010: 164.
17. Litwack 1961.

18. Guyatt 2016: 34.

19. Jones-Rogers 2019: xiiii.

20. Jones-Rogers 2019: 17.

21. Jones-Rogers 2019: xiv.

22. Jones-Rogers 2019: 25.

23. Jones-Rogers 2019: 31.

24. Jones-Rogers 2019: 54.

25. Jones-Rogers 2019: 127, 131.

26. Jones-Rogers 2019: 82.

27. Jones-Rogers 2019: 108.

28. Jones-Rogers 2019: 200.

29. Jones-Rogers 2019: 2.

30. Jones-Rogers 2019: 6, 16.

31. Jones-Rogers 2019: 69–70.

32. Jones-Rogers 2019: 79.

33. Jones-Rogers 2019: xvii.

34. Jones-Rogers 2019: 156–57.

35. Jones-Rogers 2019: 201–202.

36. Found in François Jean Chastellux's 1828 book, *Travels in North America, in the years 1780–81–82*, 296. https://archive.org/details/marquistravels00chasrich/page/n6.

37. Guyatt 2016: 192.

38. Guyatt 2016: 127.

39. Abraham Lincoln, Speech on the Dred Scott Decision, presented in Springfield, Illinois, on June 26, 1857. https://teachingamericanhistory.org/library/document/speech-on-the-dred-scott-decision/.

40. Thomas Jefferson, *Notes on the State of Virginia* (New York: Furman and Loudon, 1801), 214. Space does not permit a full examination of Jefferson's attitudes in relation to his relationship with his black slave, Sally Hemings. See Nicolaisen 2003.

41. Guyatt 2016: 126.

42. Guyatt 2016: 2.

43. Guyatt 2016: 33.

44. Guyatt 2016: 7.

45. Guyatt 2016: 5.

46. Fredrickson 1981.

47. Dahl 2018: 13.

48. Wolfe 2006.

49. Dahl 2018: 89.

50. Ostler 2019: 98–100.

51. Ostler 2019: 98.

52. Washington quoted in Dahl 2018: 40.
53. Ostler 2019: 99.
54. Vateel quoted in Ostler 2019: 100.
55. Ostler 2019: 203.
56. Jefferson quoted in Dahl 2018: 33.
57. Dahul 2018: 70.
58. Ostler 2019: 204.
59. Marshall quoted in Ostler 2019: 204.
60. Dahl 2018; Ostler 2019.
61. President Jackson's Message to Congress "On Indian Removal," December 6, 1830. Records of the United States Senate, 1789–1990: Record Group 46. Records of the United States Senate, 1789–1990, National Archives. https://www.ourdocuments.gov/doc.php?doc=25
62. Ostler 2019.
63. See de Tocqueville 2000: 25–26.
64. See Haselby 2015: 312.
65. Tocqueville quoted in Dahl 2018: 90.
66. Dahl 2018.
67. Dahl 2018: 65.
68. Paraphrased sentence from *Federalist* #2 quoted in Dahl 2018: 65.
69. Dahl 2018: 101.
70. See Dahl 2018: 49–50.
71. Dahl 2018: 107.
72. González 2009.
73. Maffly-Kipp 1994; Menchaca 2001.
74. Alonzo 1998; see also Gonzáles 2009.
75. Telles and Ortiz 2008: 75.
76. De León 2010: 17; see also Telles and Ortiz 2008: 78.
77. González 2009:84; Telles and Ortiz 2008: 75.
78. González 2009: 83.
79. Del Castillo 2002: 48.
80. Del Castillo 2002: 49.
81. Alonzo 1998: 147.
82. See Barton 2006: 2; Jackson 2000: xii, 59; Kessell 2002: xiv.
83. Butts 1997: 224.
84. Butts 1997: 224
85. Butts 1997: 223.
86. Machado 2003.
87. De León 2010: 20.
88. Montejano 2010: 123.
89. González 2018.

90. Dahl 2018: 114–15.

CHAPTER 3. RACIALIZED POWER AND CONSTRAINTS OF FREEDOM AFTER SLAVERY

1. Lockett 1991; Magness and Page 2011.
2. Vorenberg 1993: 22–45.
3. Delbanco 2018.
4. Fehrenbacher 2001.
5. Finkelman 2018.
6. Goldstone 2011: 37.
7. See Foster 1987.
8. Wilson 2009.
9. Dabney 1867.
10. Dabney 1867: 24–27.
11. Dabney 1867: 26.
12. Baradaran 2017.
13. Baradaran 2017.
14. Baradaran 2017:25–26.
15. Anderson 2017: 20.
16. Anderson 2017: 20.
17. Anderson 2018.
18. Frymer 2017: 142.
19. Loewen 2005.
20. Baradaran 2017.
21. Stampp 1965: 196.
22. Wilson 2009: 110.
23. Gillette 1979.
24. Luxenburg 2019.
25. Foster 1987.
26. Wilson 2009: 63.
27. Wilson 2009: 36.
28. Cox 2003; Foster 1987.
29. Wilson 2009: 22, 39.
30. Wilson 2009: 48.
31. Wilson 2009: 42–45.
32. Wilson 2009: 167.
33. MacLean 1994.
34. Fredrickson 1981: 93.
35. White 2018: 122.

36. Goldstone 2011: 36.
37. Maggor 2017.
38. Goldstone 2011: 134–35.
39. Bateman, Katznelson, and Lapinski 2018.
40. Foner 1970.
41. Frymer 2017.
42. Dahl 2018: 134.

CHAPTER 4. A "TRUE AMERICAN" IDENTITY

1. Frymer 2017.
2. Tichenor 2002: 66–67.
3. Tichenor 2002: 68.
4. Gerstle 2017.
5. Crèvecoeur's letters are widely available online. For example, see "What Is an American?" Letter III of *Letters from an American Farmer*, 1782. http://americainclass.org/sources/makingrevolution/independence/text6/crevecoeuramerican.pdf.
6. Kerber 1997; Vecoli 1996. Also, consistent with patriarchal rule, citizenship was passed from the father to his children, not from the mother.
7. Painter 2010: 133.
8. Painter 2010: 103.
9. Painter 2010: 133.
10. Okrent 2019: 42.
11. Painter 2010: 104.
12. Painter 2010: 203.
13. Kelkar 2017.
14. Tichenor 2002.
15. Chang 2019.
16. Tichenor 2002: 91.
17. Nancy Fraser distinguishes between the "exploited" labor of whites versus the "expropriated" labor of nonwhites in her analysis of the development of capitalism. See Fraser 2016; Fraser and Jaeggi 2018.
18. Tichenor 2002: 90–91.
19. Tichenor 2002: 87–113.
20. Gerstle 2017: 105.
21. Okrent 2019.
22. Okrent 2019: 92–97.
23. Ross 1901.
24. Whitman 2017; Wilde and Danielsen 2014.

25. Benton-Cohen 2018.

26. Okrent 2019: 61–62.

27. Hall quoted in Okrent 2019: 118.

28. Gerstle 2017: 94.

29. Perlmann 2018.

30. Tichenor 2002: 147.

31. Okrent 2019: 330–31.

32. Okrent 2019: 339.

33. Hernandez 2010.

34. Tichenor 2002.

35. Ignatiev 1995.

36. Higham 1955.

37. Tichenor 2002: 78–79.

38. Gerstle 2017: 7.

39. Gerstle 2017: 71.

40. Gerstle 2017.

41. Fox 2012.

42. Painter 2010.

43. Williams 2003: 80.

44. Rothstein 2017.

45. Rothstein 2017.

46. The literature on differential segregation of racial groups affecting inter-racial social interaction is extensive. One excellent source is Charles 2003.

47. Williams 2003.

48. Moreno 2008; Trotter Jr. 2009.

49. Golash-Boza 2015: vii.

50. Golash-Boza 2015: vii.

51. Massey and Pren 2012: 3.

52. Tichenor 2002: 174.

53. Massey and Pren 2012.

54. Massey and Pren 2012.

55. Macías-Rojas 2016.

56. Macías-Rojas 2016: 46.

57. Gillette 1979.

58. Minion 2018.

59. Massey and Pren 2012: 6.

60. Minian 2018: 215.

61. Minian 2018.

62. Golash-Boza 2015: 168.

63. Golash-Boza 2015: 257.

64. Macías-Rojas 2016.

65. Okrent 2019: 394.
66. Warren 2019.
67. Jennifer Hochschild, quoted in Gerstle 2017: 356.

CHAPTER 5. BUSINESS-FRIENDLY EVANGELICALISM

1. Haselby 2015.
2. Foster 2002.
3. Phillips-Fein 2009: x.
4. Emerson and Smith 2000.
5. Grem 2016; Kruse 2015; Mulder and Martí 2020; Phillips-Fein 2009.
6. Haddigan 2010; Kruse 2015; Lynerd 2014; Martí 2020.
7. Rachel Martin, "Trump Hosts White House Dinner For Evangelical Supporters" *National Public Radio*, August 29, 2018. https://www.npr.org/2018/08/29/642871570/trump-hosts-white-house-dinner-for-evangelical-supporters.
8. Mulder and Marti 2020.
9. Trachtenberg 1982; White 2017.
10. Baradaran 2017.
11. Lew-Williams 2018.
12. Martínez 2018.
13. Grem 2016; Kruse 2015; Mulder and Martí 2020; Phillips-Fein 2009. Haddigan 2010; Kruse 2015; Lynerd 2014.
14. Emerson and Smith 2000.
15. Bean 2014: 30; Kruse 2015: 28. Bean also details how the founding of organizations that range from Campus Crusade for Christ to Pepperdine University could be traced to a conservative Christian effort to socialize university students to become political conservatives as a component of their religious identity.
16. Phillips-Fein 2009: 72.
17. Phillips-Fein 2009: 4.
18. Phillips-Fein 2009: 72.
19. Philips-Fein 2009: 221.
20. Philips-Fein 2009: 69.
21. Phillips-Fein 2009: 222.
22. Philips-Fein 2009: 72.
23. Phillips-Fein 2009: 73.
24. Lienesch 1996: 5.
25. Weber 1968.
26. Phillips-Fein 2009.

27. Philips-Fein 2009: 75.

28. Bean 2014.

29. Dochuk 2010.

30. Dochuk 2010: 166. See also Ruotsila 2015; Sutton 2014.

31. Tamara Keith, "How 'Positive Thinking' Helped Propel Trump to the Presidency," *National Public Radio*, January 19, 2017. http://www.npr.org/2017/01/19/510628862/how-positive-thinking-helped-propel-trump-to-the-presidency.

32. Mulder and Martí 2020.

33. Mathews 2017; Mulder and Martí 2020.

34. Ingersoll 2015.

35. Grem 2016.

36. Wacker 2014.

37. Schlozman 2015; Schlozman and Rosenfeld 2019.

38. Bean 2014: 86.

39. Fea 2016.

40. Data based on Pew Research Center's 2014 Changing Religious Landscape Study. https://www.pewforum.org/2015/05/12/chapter-3-demographic-profiles-of-religious-groups/.

41. Lienesch 1996: 6.

42. Johnson 2019.

43. Ingersoll 2015; Shupe 1989. Schlozman 2015: 77.

CHAPTER 6. THE ESTABLISHMENT OF FREE-MARKET CONSERVATISM

1. Ronald Reagan. "Remarks at the Annual Convention of the National Religious Broadcasters," January 30, 1984. https://www.reaganlibrary.gov/research/speeches/13084b.

2. Scholzman 2015: 77–106.

3. See Fea 2018: 51–52.

4. Smith 1998: 89.

5. Evans 2008.

6. Kotz 2015: 11.

7. Phillips-Fein 2009.

8. Jones 2014: 63.

9. MacLean 2017: 81.

10. MacLean 2017:xxxii.

11. MacLean 2017:xxv.

12. MacLean 2017:9.

13. MacLean 2017:79.

14. MacLean 2017:57. See also Forrester 2019: 108–109, 233.

15. MacLean 2017:35.

16. MacLean 2017:76.

17. MacLean 2017:142.

18. See Crouch 2011; Davies 2014; Harvey 2005; Larner 2000; Mirowski and Plehwe 2009; Peck 2010.

19. Glickman 2019: 20.

20. Palley 2012: 145.

21. "How Popular Is Donald Trump?" *FiveThirtyEight*. https://projects.fivethirtyeight.com/trump-approval-ratings/.

22. Forrester 2019: 228.

23. Rawls quoted in Forrester 2019: 7.

24. Forrester 2019: 59.

25. Rawls quoted in Forrester 2019: 25.

26. Harvey 2005: 2.

27. Harvey 2005: 64.

28. Harvey 2005: 66.

29. MacLean 2017: xxiv.

30. Harvey 2005: 3.

31. Faricy 2015. See also Bartels 2016: 62–73.

32. Faricy 2015: 180.

33. MacLean 2017: 215.

34. MacLean 2017: 213.

35. Slobodian 2018: 17.

36. Sandel 1996.

37. MacLean 2017: 69.

38. Schlozman 2015.

39. Glickman 2019: 17.

40. Forrester 2019: 204.

41. Krippner 2011.

42. Krippner 2011: 81.

43. Blanchard, Branson, and Currie 1987.

44. "Historical Highest Marginal Income Tax Rates." *Tax Policy Center*, Urban Institute and Brookings Institution, January 19, 2019. www.taxpolicycenter.org/statistics/historical-highest-marginal-income-tax-rates.

45. Blanchard, Branson, and Currie 1987.

46. "Historical Highest Marginal Income Tax Rates." *Tax Policy Center*, Urban Institute and Brookings Institution, January 19, 2019.

www.taxpolicycenter.org/statistics/historical-highest-marginal-income-tax-rates.

47. Schalch 2006.
48. Gribben 2015.
49. Phillips-Fein 2009: 225.
50. Phillips-Fein 2009: 225.
51. Balmer 2006.
52. Scholzman 2015: 90-101.
53. Schlozman 2015: 95-96.
54. Mulder and Martí 2020.
55. Phillips-Fein 2009: 72. See also Dochuk 2019.
56. Phillips-Fein 2009: 234.
57. Scholzman 2015: 215.
58. Phillips-Fein 2009: 74.
59. Pistor 2019.
60. Weber 1978.
61. Kotz 2015: 9.
62. Pistor 2019: 19.

CHAPTER 7. REACTIONARY POLITICS
OF THE TEA PARTY

1. Parker and Barreto 2014: 209.
2. Ross and El-Buri 2008.
3. Data from a September 1, 2015, press release from Public Policy Polling. https://www.publicpolicypolling.com/wp-content/uploads/2017/09/PPP_Release_National_90115.pdf.
4. Parker and Barreto 2014: 154.
5. Parker and Barreto 2014: 155.
6. Lienesch 1996.
7. Parker and Barreto 2014.
8. Lienesch 1996.
9. Parker and Barreto 2014: 198.
10. Layman, Kalkan, and Green 2014.
11. Lafer 2017: 11.
12. Liu 2011.
13. Liu 2011.
14. Braunstein and Taylor 2017.
15. Lafer 2017: 10.
16. Braunstein and Taylor 2017: 55.

17. Dochuk 2012: 15.
18. Dochuk 2012: 17.
19. Campbell and Putnam 2011.
20. Parker and Barreto 2014: 78.
21. Sullivan 2017.
22. Dochuk 2012: 18.
23. Dochuk 2012: 18.
24. Parker and Barreto 2014: 52.
25. Parker and Barreto 2014: 53.
26. Parker and Baretto 2014: 29.
27. McAdam and Kloos 2014.
28. Maxwell and Shield 2019. See also Black and Black 2002.
29. Maxwell and Shield 2019: 11.
30. Knuckey 2005.
31. Parker and Baretto 2014: 165.
32. Parker and Baretto 2014: 163.
33. Parker and Baretto 2014: 153–54.
34. Data on percentage of foreign-born immigration population in the United States from 1900 to 2015 is available online from Jynnah Radford and Luis Noe-Bustamante, 2019, "Facts on US Immigrants, 2017: Statistical Portrait of the Foreign-Born Population in the United States," Pew Research Center. https://www.pewhispanic.org/2018/09/14/facts-on-u-s-immigrants/#fb-key-charts-first-second-gen.
35. Cox, Lienesch, and Jones 2017; Hochschild 2016.
36. Parker and Barreto 2014: 87.
37. Tesler 2016: 183.
38. Abrajano and Hajnal 2015.
39. Parker and Baretto 2014: 35.
40. Parker and Baretto 2014: 194–96.
41. Parker and Baretto 2014: 6.
42. Parker and Baretto 2014: 153.
43. Parker and Baretto 2014: 169.
44. Parker and Baretto 2014: 104.
45. Parker and Baretto 2014: 41.
46. Parker and Baretto 2014: 123.
47. Parker and Barreto 2014: 39, 69–70.
48. Parker and Barreto 2014: 34.
49. Parker and Baretto 2014: 172.
50. Gerstle 2018: 262.
51. Iyengar, Lelkes, Levendusky, Malhotra, and Westwood 2018.
52. Fea 2018: 15–25.

53. Cox, Lienesch, and Jones 2017.

54. Alyssa Foster, "Speaks Volumes Anti-Racism Activist and Educator Jane Elliot Speaks to White Citizens," YouTube. https://www.youtube.com/watch?v=xUlqTNwm-mk.

CHAPTER 8. INCREASED CONCENTRATION OF ELITE WEALTH THROUGH ASSET GROWTH

1. MacLean 2017.
2. Palley 2012.
3. The mechanisms regarding globalization are well beyond the scope of this text and are difficult to summarize briefly. For insights, see Kotz 2015; Krippner 2011; Palley 2012.
4. Kotz 2015; Palley 2012.
5. Piketty 2014.
6. Piketty 2014.
7. For example, see LiPuma 2017.
8. Lafer 2017: 6. See also Patten 2015.
9. Faricy 2015.
10. These and other figures can be found on the website inequlity.org.
11. Eisinger 2017.
12. Formisano 2015: 55.
13. Formisano 2015: 14.
14. Solow 2017: 58.
15. Jacobs 2017: 520.
16. Jacobs 2017: 522.
17. Jacobs 2017: 515.
18. Solow 2017.
19. Solow 2017.
20. Boushey, DeLong, and Steinbaum 2017: 54.
21. See Bartels 2016; "Income Inequality," Inequality.org, https://inequality.org/facts/income-inequality; and information published by the Social Security Administration, https://www.ssa.gov/cgi-bin/netcomp.cgi?year=2017.
22. Solow 2017.
23. "Wealth Inequality in America," *YouTube*, www.youtube.com/watch?v=QPKKQnijnsM.
24. Kotz 2015: 110.
25. Kotz 2015: 99.
26. Formisano 2015: 12.

27. Hacker and Pierson 2010. See also the continually updated Bloomberg Billionaires Index at https://www.bloomberg.com/billionaires/.

28. Lin and Tomaskovic-Devey 2013: 1292.

29. Tomaskovic-Devey and Lin 2011.

30. Lin and Tomaskovic-Devey 2013: 1292.

31. Davis 2009; Davis and Kim 2015; Krippner 2011; Tomaskovic-Devey and Lin 2011.

32. Lin and Tomaskovic-Devey 2013.

33. Lin and Tomaskovic-Devey 2013: 1292.

34. Crotty 2003; Fligstein 2001.

35. Krippner 2011: 2; see also Davis 2009; Kotz 2015.

36. Krippner 2005: 174.

37. Davis 2009; Froud, Johal, Leaver, and Williams 2006; Hutton 1996.

38. Tomaskovic-Devey and Lin 2011.

39. Krippner 2011: 28.

40. Krippner 2011: 28.

41. Fraser 2016.

42. Fligstein and Goldstein 2015.

43. Davis and Kim 2015: 212.

44. "Income Inequality in the United States," Inequality.org, https://inequality.org/facts/income-inequality.

45. Shapiro 2017: 15.

46. Figures from "Facts," Inequality.org, https://inequality.org/facts/.

47. Shapiro 2017: 18.

48. Shapiro 2017: 13.

49. Bruenig 2014.

50. Zaw, Bhattacharya, Price, Hamilton, and Darity 2017.

51. Zaw, Bhattacharya, Price, Hamilton, and Darity 2017.

52. Shapiro 2017: 43.

53. Shapiro 2017: 131.

54. Shapiro 2017: 56.

55. Shapiro 2017: 46.

56. Shapiro 2017: 75.

57. Shapiro 2017: 26.

58. Shapiro 2017: 102–103.

59. Shapiro 2017: 47.

60. Shapiro 2017: 118.

61. Martin 2013: 3. See also MacLean 2017.

62. Martin 2013: 7.

63. Faricy 2015: 144.

64. Martin 2013: 7.

65. Lafer 2017: 15.
66. Jacobs 2017: 524.
67. Jacobs 2017: 522.
68. Jacobs 2017: 523.
69. Shapiro 2017: 154.
70. Lafer 2017: 7.
71. *Citizens United v. Federal Election Commission*, 558 US 310 (2010).
72. Formisano 2015: 19.
73. Shapiro 2017: 26.

CHAPTER 9. IDENTITY POLITICS AND EVANGELICAL SUPPORT

1. This data was eventually published in Wong 2018.
2. Q: Overall do you think Trump has done more to (unite the country), or has done more to (divide the country)? Washington Post-ABC News, September 18–21, 2017. Published October 20, 2017, *Washington Post*. https://www.washingtonpost.com/politics/polling/overall-trump-country-country/2017/10/20/eb44369c-a0dc-11e7-b2a7-bc70b6f98089_page.html#
3. Stolberg and Rosenthal 2017.
4. "Fractured Nation: Widening Partisan Polarization and Key Issues in 2020 Presidential Elections," *PRRI*, October 21, 2019. https://www.prri.org/research/fractured-nation-widening-partisan-polarization-and-key-issues-in-2020-presidential-elections/.
5. "Election 2016: Exit Polls," *New York Times*, November 8, 2016. https://www.nytimes.com/interactive/2016/11/08/us/politics/election-exit-polls.html.
6. Fea 2018: 4.
7. Jones, Cox, Griffin, Najle, Fisch-Friedman, and Vandermaas-Peeler 2018.
8. Brophy 2016; see also Martí 2008, 2010, 2015; Martí and Ganiel 2014.
9. Brophy 2016: 125.
10. See Djupe and Claassen (2018) for an excellent resource bringing several explanatory mechanisms together. A commendable assessment is also found in Fea 2018.
11. Brophy 2016.
12. Brophy 2016: 127.
13. Brophy 2016: 141.
14. See Edgell 2017.
15. Parker and Barreto 2014.
16. Smith 1998.

17. An emerging literature is revealing not only why personally pious Americans are able to support a notoriously impious man but also why "secularized evangelical discourse" as a form of "public religious expression" is supported by a majority of Americans who do not belong to white Evangelical subculture. See Delehanty, Edgell, and Stewart, 2019; Stewart, Edgell, and Delehanty, 2018; Whitehead, Perry, and Baker 2018.

18. "Franklin Graham: Trump 'defends the faith,'" *Axios*, November 25, 2018. https://www.axios.com/franklin-graham-donald-trump-6b18159f-d481-48e2-9eb3-ea48f4eb26aa.html.

19. Wormald 2015.

20. Martínez and Smith 2016.

21. Martínez and Smith 2016.

22. Begley 2016.

23. Williams 2012.

24. Renaud 2017.

25. Smith 2017.

26. Pew Research Center, "Persistent partisan, demographic gaps in Trump job approval." August 16, 2019. https://www.people-press.org/2019/08/16/most-democrats-are-excited-by-several-2020-candidates-not-just-their-top-choice/6-26/.

27. Data reported by PRRI in 2016, "Backing Trump, White Evangelicals Flip Flop on Importance of Candidate Character: PRRI/Brookings Survey," *Public Religion Research Institute*. https://www.prri.org/research/prri-brookings-oct-19-poll-politics-election-clinton-double-digit-lead-trump/. A *New York Times* graphic was widely shared; see Thomas B. Edsall, 2017. "Trump Says Jump. His Supporters Ask, How High?" September 14, 2017. *New York Times*. https://www.nytimes.com/2017/09/14/opinion/trump-republicans.html

28. Fox News Poll results, October 6–8, 2019.

29. Bean 2014.

30. Bean 2014: 62.

31. Bean 2014: 27.

32. Brint and Abrutyn 2010: 329.

33. Lewis and De Bernardo 2010: 122.

34. Kruse 2015.

35. Moore 2016: 1.

36. Moore 2016: 120–35.

37. Moore 2016: 155.

38. First approached in Martí 2005, and then more recently in Martí 2016, 2017, 2018, and Mulder, Ramos, and Martí 2017.

39. On the distinction between charismatic authority versus rational-legal authority, see Weber 1978.

40. Whitehead and Perry, 2020; Whitehead, Perry, and Baker 2018.

41. Smith 2017.

42. Brown 2019.

43. Fea 2018: 99–131.

44. Brophy 2016: 13.

45. Robert Jeffress, cited in Fea 2018: 33.

46. Diefendorf 2018.

47. Fea 2018: 6.

48. See Ruotisa 2015.

49. Shellnutt 2017.

50. Johnson 2019: 1.

51. Johnson 2019: 91.

52. Johnson 2019: 8.

53. Johnson 2019: 145.

54. Bennett 2017.

55. Bennett 2017.

56. Bennett 2017: 4.

57. Bennett 2017: 48.

58. Bennett 2017: 36.

59. Bennett 2017: 144.

60. Bennett 2017: 68.

61. Bennett 2017: 82.

62. "'Pro-Choice' or 'Pro-Life,' 2018 Demographic Table," May 1–10, 2018, *Gallup.* https://news.gallup.com/poll/244709/pro-choice-pro-life-2018-demo-graphic-tables.aspx.

63. Schlozman 2015: 104–105.

64. Miller 2016: 51–52.

65. Schlozman 2015: 207.

66. Williams 2016: 165.

67. Williams 2016: 101.

68. Williams 2016: 101.

69. Lewis 2018: 32.

70. Lewis 2018: 30.

71. Lewis 2018: 36.

72. Bennett 2017: 88.

73. Lewis 2018: 57.

74. Bean 2014: 62.

75. Bean 2014: 87.

76. Williams 2016.

77. Williams 2016: 10.

78. Williams 2016: 10.

79. Williams 2016: 38.
80. Williams 2016: 150.
81. Williams 2016: 205.
82. Williams 2016: 135.
83. Williams 2016: 135.
84. Williams 2016: 202.
85. Williams 2016: 207.
86. Williams 2016: 233.
87. Bennett 2017: 89.
88. Bennett 2017: 87.
89. Lewis 2018: 119.
90. Renaud 2017.
91. MacLean 2017: xxix.
92. Smith 2017.
93. Kiely 2017.
94. Boushey, DeLong, and Steinbaum 2017: 55.
95. Martí 2020.
96. Renaud 2017.
97. MacLean 2017: 94.
98. Brint and Abrutyn 2010: 334.
99. Carwana 2010: 317.
100. Phillips-Fein 2009: 73.
101. Bean 2014: 30.
102. Grem 2016.
103. Lienesch 1996: 126.
104. Lienesch 1996: 126.
105. Dochuk 2012: 16.
106. Martin and Inskeep 2017.
107. Whitehead, Perry, and Baker 2018.
108. Jenkins 2017a.
109. Bean 2014: 79.
110. Glaude 2017; see also Jones 2016.
111. Lipka 2016.
112. Lipka 2016.
113. Stokes 2017.
114. Smith 2016.
115. Connor and Krogstad 2018.
116. Rush 2018.
117. Wadhia 2019: 98–115.
118. Fitzgerald 2019: 45, 59.
119. Wadhia 2019: 7–28, 72–75, 123–25.

120. Smith 2017.

121. Macías-Rojas 2016.

122. Macías-Rojas 2016: 15.

123. Macías-Rojas 2016: 22.

124. Macías-Rojas 2016: 22.

125. Macías-Rojas 2016: 59.

126. Macías-Rojas 2016: 62.

127. Macías-Rojas 2016: 81.

128. Jones and Brown 2019.

129. Wadhia 2019: 79–97.

130. Figures based on research-in-progress presented by Hana Brown (Sociology, Wake Forest University) at presentation at Davidson College on March 20, 2019.

131. Shupe 1989.

132. For a passionate argument from a white evangelical Christian perspective, see Buzzard 1983.

133. Barrett-Fox 2018.

134. Worthen 2017.

135. A good example of a post-2016 Trump election book negotiating the label evangelical is an edited volume, Labberton 2018.

136. For an overview of Rachel Held Evans's short life, see Dias and Roberts 2019 and Griswold 2019.

137. Mealer 2018.

138. Fea 2018.

139. Comparisons can be made by comparing attenders of white evangelical churches and historically black churches through data and reports from the Pew Research Center's US Religious Landscape Survey. https://www.pewforum.org/religious-landscape-study/.

140. Griswold 2018; Wong 2019.

CHAPTER 10. CONCLUSION

1. Wolin 2004: 57. Note that Wolin's expanded *Politics and Vision* is a heuristic resource for articulating the dynamics of political community in this chapter.

2. See Scholzman and Rosenfeld 2019; Rosenwald 2019.

3. Scholzman and Rosenfeld 2019: 6.

4. Wolin: 2004: 142.

5. Wolin 2004: 95, 107.

6. Edgell 2016.

7. Edgell 2017.
8. Wolin 2004: 58.
9. Wolin 2004: 60.
10. Formisano 2015.
11. Bartels 2016: 3.
12. Wolin 2004: 532.
13. Bartels 2016: 2; Wolin 2004: 536.
14. Wolin 2004: 589.
15. Bartels 2016; Greenhouse 2019.
16. MacLean 2017: 231; see also Anderson 2017.
17. Bartels 2016: 124–35.
18. Wolin 2004: 348.
19. Yourish and Griggs 2018.
20. Bruce 2000.
21. Wolin 2004: 147.
22. Key details and several sources are available through Campbell 2019.
23. Wong 2017.
24. Connor and Budiman 2019.
25. Massey and Pren 2012.
26. Kellner 2007.
27. Wadhia 2019: 108–12.
28. Wadhia 2019: 41.
29. As summarized by Commissioner of Social Security, Walter Mitchell. See Mitchell 1962.
30. Fitzgerald 2019: 102–104.
31. See Wadhia 2019.
32. Gerstle 2017: 95.
33. Wolin 2004: 577.
34. Bartels 2016: 133–34.
35. Fea 2018: 165.
36. Gloege 2018.
37. "Fractured Nation: Widening Partisan Polarization and Key Issues in 2020 Presidential Elections," *PRRI*, October 21, 2019. https://www.prri.org/research/fractured-nation-widening-partisan-polarization-and-key-issues-in-2020-presidential-elections.
38. Wolin 2004: 513.
39. Jenkins 2019.
40. See Barger 2018.
41. Hackett and Grim 2011.
42. See Charles and Rah 2019; Tisby 2019.

BIBLIOGRAPHY

Abrajano, Marisa and Zoltan Hajnal. 2015. *White Backlash: Immigration, Race and American Politics*. Princeton, NJ: Princeton University Press.

Alonzo, Armando. 1998. *Tejano Legacy: Rancheros and Settlers in South Texas, 1734–1900*. Albuquerque: University of New Mexico Press.

Anderson, Carol. 2017. *White Rage: The Unspoken Truth of Our Racial Divide*. New York: Bloomsbury.

———. 2018. *One Person, No Vote: How Voter Suppression Is Destroying Our Democracy*. New York: Bloomsbury.

Aptheker, Herbert. 1943. *American Negro Slave Revolts*. New York: Columbia University Press.

Baker, Joseph O., Andrew L. Whitehead, and Samuel L. Perry. 2018."Make America Christian Again: Christian Nationalism and Voting for Donald Trump in the 2016 Presidential Election." *Sociology of Religion* 79 (2): 147–71.

Balmer, Randall. 2006. *Thy Kingdom Come: How the Religious Right Distorts the Faith and Threatens America*. New York: Basic.

Baptist, Edward E. 2014. *The Half Has Never Been Told: Slavery and the Making of American Capitalism*. New York: Basic Books.

Baradaran, Mehrsa. 2017. *The Color of Money: Black Banks and the Racial Wealth Gap*. Cambridge, MA: Belknap.

Barger, Lilian Calles. 2018. *The World Come of Age. An Intellectual History of Liberation Theology*. New York: Oxford University Press.

Barrett-Fox, Rebecca. 2018. "A King Cyrus President: How Donald Trump's Presidency Reasserts Conservative Christians' Right to Hegemony." *Humanity & Society* 42 (4): 502–22.

Bartels, Larry M. 2016. *Unequal Democracy: The Political Economy of the New Gilded Age*, 2nd ed. New York and Princeton, NJ: Russell Sage Foundation and Princeton University Press.

Barton, Bruce. 1925. *The Man Nobody Knows*. Indianapolis, IN: Bobbs-Merrill.

Barton, Paul. 2006. *Hispanic Methodists, Presbyterians, and Baptists in Texas*. Austin: University of Texas.

Bateman, David A., Ira Katznelson, and John S. Lapinski. 2018. *Southern Nation: Congress and White Supremacy after Reconstruction*. Princeton, NJ: Princeton University Press.

Bean, Lydia. 2014. *The Politics of Evangelical Identity: Local Churches and Partisan Divides in the United States and Canada*. Princeton, NJ: Princeton University Press.

Beauchamp, Zack. 2015. "The Racist Flags on Dylann Roof's Jacket, Explained." *Vox*, June 18, 2015. https://www.vox.com/2015/6/18/8806633/charleston-shooter-flags-dylann-roof.

Begley, Sarah. 2016. "Hillary Clinton's Final Popular Vote Lead is 2.8 Million." *Time*, December 20, 2016. Time.com/4608555/Hillary-clinton-popular-vote-final/.

Bennett, Daniel. 2017. *Defending Faith: The Politics of the Christian Conservative Legal Movement*. Lawrence: University Press of Kansas.

Benton-Cohen, Katherine. 2018. *Inventing the Immigration Problem: The Dillingham Commission and Its Legacy*. Cambridge, MA: Harvard University Press.

Black, Earl, and Merle Black. 2002. *The Rise of Southern Republicans*. Cambridge, MA: Harvard University Press.

Blanchard, Olivier Jean, William Branson, and David Currie. 1987. "Reaganomics." *Economic Policy* 2 (5): 15–56.

Bonilla-Silva, Edwardo. 2017. *Racism without Racists. Color-Blind Racism and the Persistence of Racial Inequality in America*, 5th ed. Lanham, MD: Rowman & Littlefield.

Boushey, Heather, J. Bradford DeLong, and Marshall Steinbaum, eds. 2017. *After Piketty: The Agenda for Economics and Inequality*. Cambridge, MA: Harvard University Press.

Braunstein, Ruth, and Malaena Taylor. 2017. "Is the Tea Party a 'Religious' Movement? Religiosity in the Tea Party versus the Religious Right." *Sociology of Religion* 78(1): 33–59.

Braunstein, Ruth, and Malaena Taylor. 2017. "Is the Tea Party a 'Religious' Movement? Religiosity in the Tea Party versus the Religious Right." *Sociology of Religion* 78(1): 33–59.

Brint, Steven, and Seth Abrutyn. 2010. "Who's Right about the Right? Comparing Competing Explanations of the Link between White Evangelicals and Conservative Politics in the United States." *Journal for the Scientific Study of Religion* 49 (2): 328–50.

Brophy, Sorcha A. 2016. "Orthodoxy as Project: Temporality and Action in an American Protestant Denomination." *Sociology of Religion* 77 (2): 123–43.

Brown, Lauretta. 2019. "Pro-Life Leader Marjorie Dannenfelser Tells CPAC: To Make America Great Again, Roe v. Wade Must End." *Townhall*, February 28, 2019. https://townhall.com/tipsheet/laurettabrown/2019/02/28/prolife-leader-marjorie-dannenfelser-to-make-america-great-again-roe-v-wade-must-end-n2542390?190.

Bruce, Steve. 2000. "Zealot Politics and Democracy: The Case of the New Christian Right." *Political Studies* 48(2): 263–82.

Bruenig, Matt. 2014. "The Top 10 Percent of White Families Own Almost Everything." September 8, 2014. *The American Prospect.* https://prospect.org/article/top-10-percent-white-families-own-almost-everything.

Butts, Michéle. 1997. "I Could Realize What Sodom and Gomorrah Might Have Been." *The Journal of Presbyterian History* 75, no. 4 (Winter): 223–34.

Buzzard, Lynn. 1983. "The Evangelical Rediscovery of Law and Politics." *Journal of Law and Religion* 1 (1), 187–201. doi:10.2307/1051077.

Campbell, Alexia Fernández. 2019. "The El Paso Shooter Told Police That He Was Targeting Mexicans." August 9, 2019. *Vox.* https://www.vox.com/2019/8/6/20756750/el-paso-shooter-targeted-latinx-walmart.

Campbell, David E. 2006. "Religious "Threat" in Contemporary Presidential Elections." *The Journal of Politics* 68 (1), 104–15.

Campbell, David E., and Robert D. Putnam. 2011. "Crashing the Tea Party." *New York Times*, August 16, 2011. https://www.nytimes.com/2011/08/17/opinion/crashing-the-tea-party.html.

Campbell, John L. 2018. *American Discontent: The Rise of Donald Trump and Decline of the Golden Age*. New York: Oxford University Press.

Cappelli, Peter. 2000. *The New Deal at Work: Managing the Market-Driven Workforce.* Brighton, MA: Harvard Business School Press.

Carwana, Brian. 2010. "Evangelicals, Democracy, and Values in America." *The Canadian Journal of Sociology/Cahiers Canadiens de Sociologie* 35 (2): 316–23.

Chang, Gordon H. 2019. *Ghosts of Gold Mountain: The Epic Story of the Chinese Who Built the Transcontinental Railroad*. Boston, MA: Houghton Mifflin Harcourt.

Charles, Camille Zubrinsky. 2003. "The Dynamics of Racial Residential Segregation." *Annual Review of Sociology* 29: 167–207.

Charles, Mark, and Soong-Chan Rah. 2019. *Unsettling Truths: The Ongoing, Dehumanizing Legacy of the Doctrine of Discovery*. Downers Grove, IL: InterVarsity Press.

Chinchilla, Norma Stoltz, and Nora Hamilton. 2004. "Central American Immigrants: Diverse Populations, Changing Communities." In *The Columbia History of Latinos in the United States since 1960*, edited by David Gutiérrez, 187–228. New York: Columbia University Press.

Claassen, Ryan L., and Andrew Pvtak. 2010. "The Christian Right Thesis: Explaining Longitudinal Change in Participation among Evangelical Christians." *The Journal of Politics* 72(1): 2–15.

Clement, Scott, and John C. Green. 2011. "The Tea Party and Religion." *Religion & Public Life Project*, Pew Research Center. February 22, 2011. www.pewforum.org/2011/02/23/tea-party-and-religion/.

Coffey, Brandan. 2016. "Which Corporations Control the World?" *Information Clearing House*. June 13, 2016.https://www.internationalbusinessguide.org/corporations/.

Connolly, William E. 2005. "The Evangelical-Capitalist Resonance Machine." *Political Theory* 33(6): 869–86.

Connor, Phillip, and Abby Budiman. 2019. "Immigrant Share in US Nears Record High but Remains below That of Many Other Countries." *Pew Research Center*, January 30, 2019. https://www.pewresearch.org/fact-tank/2019/01/30/immigrant-share-in-u-s-nears-record-high-but-remains-below-that-of-many-other-countries/.

Connor, Phillip, and Jens Manuel Krogstad. 2018. "For the First Time, US Resettles Fewer Refugees Than the Rest of the World." *Pew Research Center*, July 5, 2018. https://www.pewresearch.org/fact-tank/2018/07/05/for-the-first-time-u-s-resettles-fewer-refugees-than-the-rest-of-the-world/.

Cooper, Melinda E. 2008. *Life as Surplus: Biotechnology and Capitalism in the Neoliberal Era*. Seattle: University of Washington Press.

Cox, Daniel, Rachel Lienesch, and Robert P. Jones. 2017. "Beyond Economics: Fears of Cultural Displacement Pushed the White Working Class to Trump." *PRRI/The Atlantic*, May 9, 2017. https://www.prri.org/research/white-working-class-attitudes-economy-trade-immigration-election-donald-trump/.

Cox, Karen L. 2003. *Dixie's Daughters: The United Daughters of the Confederacy and the Preservation of Confederate Culture*. Gainesville: University Press of Florida.

Crotty, James. 2003. "The Neoliberal Paradox: The Impact of Destructive Product Market Competition and Impatient Finance on Nonfinancial Corporations in the Neoliberal Era." *Review of Radical Political Economics* 35(3): 271–79.

Crouch, C. 2011. *The Strange Non-Death of Neoliberalism*. Cambridge, UK: Polity.

Dabney, Robert L. 1867. *A Defense of Virginia and the South*. New York: E.J. Hale and Son.

Dahl, Adam. 2018. *Empire of the People: Settler Colonialism and the Foundations of Modern Democratic Thought*. Lawrence: University of Kansas Press.

Davies, W. 2014. "Neoliberalism: A Bibliographic Review." *Culture & Society* 31(7/8): 309–17.

Davis, Aeron, and Catherine Walsh. 2017. "Distinguishing Financialization from Neoliberalism." *Theory, Culture & Society* 34(5–6): 27–51.

Davis, Gerald F. 2009. *Managed by the Markets: How Finance Re-Shaped America*. New York: Oxford University Press.

Davis, Gerald F., and Suntae Kim. 2015. "Financialization of the Economy." *Annual Review of Sociology* 41: 203–21.

De León, Arnoldo. 2010. *They Called Them Greasers: Anglo Attitudes toward Mexicans in Texas, 1821–1900*. Austin: University of Texas.

de Tocqueville, Alexis. 2000. *Democracy in America*. Chicago: University of Chicago Press.

Del Castillo, Richard Griswold. 2002. *The Treaty of Guadalupe Hidalgo: A Legacy of Conflict*. Norman: University of Oklahoma Press.

Delbanco, Andrew. 2018. *The War before the War: Fugitive Slaves and the Struggle for America's Soul from the Revolution to the Civil War*. New York: Penguin.

Delehanty, Jack, Penny Edgell, and Evan Stewart. 2019. "Christian America? Secularized Evangelical Discourse and the Boundaries of National Belonging." *Social Forces* 97(3): 1283–1306.

Dias, Elizabeth, and Sam Roberts. 2019. "Rachel Held Evans, Voice of the Wandering Evangelical, Dies at 37." *New York Times*, May 4, 2019. https://www.nytimes.com/2019/05/04/us/rachel-held-evans.html

Diefendorf, Sarah. 2018. "What US Evangelical Voters Really Want in Politics" *Scholars Strategies Network*, November 6, 2018. https://scholars.org/brief/what-us-evangelical-voters-really-want-politics.

Djupe, Paul, and Ryan L. Claassen (eds). 2018. *The Evangelical Crackup? The Future of the Evangelical-Republican Coalition.* Philadelphia: Temple University Press.

Dobson, James. "Dr. James Dobson on Donald Trump's Christian Faith." *Dr. James Dobson's Family Talk.* http://drjamesdobson.org/news/dr-james-dobson-on-trumps-christian-faith.

Dochuk, Darren. 2010. *From Bible Belt to Sunbelt: Plain-Folk Religion, Grassroots Politics, and the Rise of Evangelical Conservatism.* New York: W. W. Norton.

———. 2012. "Tea Party America and the Born-Again Politics of the Populist Right." *New Labor Forum* 21(1): 14–21.

———. 2019. *Anointed with Oil: How Christianity and Crude Made Modern America.* New York: Basic Books.

Dulk, Kevin, R. Den, and Robert J. Joustra. 2015. *The Church and Religious Persecution.* Grand Rapids, MI: Calvin College Press.

Echolls, Taylor. 2017. "The Evangelical Influence on the Bush Presidencies." September 17, 2017.https://classroom.synonym.com/the-evangelical-influence-on-the-bush-presidencies-12085971.html.

Edgell, Penny. 2016. "Seeing the White in Christian America." *The Society Pages*, December 15, 2016. www.thesocietypages.org/specials/seeing-the-white-in-christian-america/.

———. 2017. "An Agenda for Research on American Religion in Light of the 2016 Election." *Sociology of Religion* 78(1): 1–8.

Eisinger, Jesse. 2017. *The Chickenshit Club: Why the Justice Department Fails to Prosecute Executives.* New York: Simon and Schuster.

Elisha, Omri. 2008. "Moral Ambitions of Grace: The Paradox of Compassion and Accountability in Evangelical Faith-Based Activism." *Cultural Anthropology* 23(1): 154–89.

Emerson, Michael, and Christian Smith. 2000. *Divided by Faith.* New York: Oxford University Press.

Evans, Thomas. 2008. *The Education of Ronald Reagan: The General Electric Years and the Untold Story of His Conversion to Conservatism.* New York: Columbia University Press.

Faricy, Christopher G. 2015. *Welfare for the Wealthy: Parties, Social Spending, and Inequality in the United States.* New York: Cambridge University Press.

Fea, John. 2016. *Was America Founded as a Christian Nation? A Historical Introduction.* Louisville, KY: Westminster John Knox Press.

———. 2018. *Believe Me: The Evangelical Road to Donald Trump.* Grand Rapids, MI: Eerdmans.

Fehrenbacher, Don E. 2001. *The Slaveholding Republic: An Account of the United States Government's Relations to Slavery.* New York: Oxford University Press.

Fields, Barbara Jeanne. 1982. "Ideology and Race in American History." In J. Morgan Kousser and James M. McPherson (eds.), *Region, Race, and Reconstruction: Essays in Honor of C. Vann Woodward*, 143–77. New York: Oxford University Press.

Finkelman, Paul. 2018. *Supreme Injustice: Slavery in the Nation's Highest Court.* Cambridge, MA: Harvard University Press.

Fitzgerald, David Scott. 2019. *Refuge beyond Reach: How Rich Democracies Repel Asylum Seekers.* New York: Oxford University Press.

Fligstein, Neil. 2001. *The Architecture of Markets: An Economic Sociology of Twenty-First Century Capitalist Societies.* Princeton, NJ: Princeton University Press

Fligstein, Neil, and A. Goldstein. 2015. "The Emergence of a Finance Culture in American Households, 1989–2007." *Socioeconomic Review.* doi: 10.1093/ser/mwu035.

Fligstein, Neil, and Taekjin Shin. 2003. "The Shareholder Value Society: A Review of the Changes in Working Conditions and Inequality in the US, 1976–2000." Institute and Research on Labor Employment, IRLE Working Paper No. 88-03. http://irle.berkeley.edu/workingpapers/88-03.pdf.

Foner, Eric. 1970. *Free Soil, Free Labor, Free Men: The Ideology of the Republican Party before the Civil War.* New York: Oxford University Press

Formisano, Ronald P. 2015. *Plutocracy in America: How Increasing Inequality Destroys the Middle Class and Exploits the Poor.* Baltimore: Johns Hopkins University Press.

Forrester, Katrina. 2019. *In the Shadow of Justice: Postwar Liberalism and the Remaking of Political Philosophy.* Princeton, NJ: Princeton University Press.

Foster, Gaines M. 1987. *Ghosts of the Confederacy: Defeat, the Lost Cause, and the Emergence of the New South.* New York: Oxford University Press.

———. 2002. *Moral Reconstruction: Christian Lobbyists and the Federal Legislation of Morality, 1865–1920.* Chapel Hill: University of North Carolina Press.

Fox, Cybelle. 2012. *Three Worlds of Relief: Race, Immigration, and the American Welfare State from the Progressive Era to the New Deal.* Princeton, NJ: Princeton University Press.

Fraser, Nancy. 2016. "Expropriation and Exploitation in Racialized Capitalism: A Reply to Michael Dawson." *Critical Historical Studies* 3, no. 1 (Spring): 163–78.

Fraser, Nancy, and Rahel Jaeggi. 2018. *Capitalism: A Conversation in Critical Theory.* Cambridge: Polity.

Fredrickson, George M. 1981. *White Supremacy: A Comparative Study in American and South African History.* New York: Oxford University Press.

Froud, J., S. Johal, A. Leaver, and K. Williams. 2006. *Financialization and Strategy: Narrative and Numbers.* Abingdon, UK: Routledge.

Frymer, Paul. 2017. *Building an American Empire: The Era of Territorial and Political Expansion.* Princeton, NJ: Princeton University Press.

García, María Cristina. 2004. "Exiles, Immigrants, and Transnationals." In *The Columbia History of Latinos in the United States since 1960,* ed. David Gutiérrez, 146–86. New York: Columbia University Press.

Gerbner, Katharine. 2018. *Christian Slavery Conversion and Race in the Protestant Atlantic World.* Philadelphia: University of Pennsylvania Press.

Gerson, Michael. 2017. "'Trump is Evangelicals' 'Dream President.' Here's Why." *Washington Post.* May 15, 2017.https://www.washingtonpost.com/opinions/trump-is-evangelicals-dream-president-heres-why/2017/05/15/77b1609a-3996-11e7-a058-ddbb23c75d82_story.html.

Gerstle, Gary. 2017. *American Crucible: Race and Nation in the Twentieth Century.* Princeton, NJ: Princeton University Press.

———. 2018. "Civic Ideals, Race, and Nation in the Age of Obama." In *The Presidency of Barack Obama: A First Historical Assessment,* edited by Julian Zelizer, 261–80. Princeton, NJ: Princeton University Press.

Gillette, William. 1979. *Retreat from Reconstruction, 1869–1879.* Baton Rouge: Louisiana State University Press.

Glaude, Eddie J. 2017. "The 'Trump Effect' and Evangelicals." *Harvard Divinity School Bulletin.* http://bulletin.hds.harvard.edu/articles/springsummer2017/trump-effect-and-evangelicals/.

Glickman, Lawrence B. 2019. *Free Enterprise: An American History.* New Haven, CT: Yale University Press.

Gloege, Timothy. 2018. "#Itsnotus: Being Evangelical Means Never Having to Say You're Sorry." January 3, 2018. *Religion Dispatches.* http://religiondispatches.org/itsnotus-being-evangelical-means-never-having-to-say-youre-sorry/.

Golash-Boza, T. (2015). *Deported: Policing Immigrants, Disposable Labor and Global Capitalism.* New York: New York University Press.

Goldstein, Adam. 2012. "Revenge of the Managers." *American Sociological Review* 77(2): 268–94.

Goldstone, Lawrence. 2011. *Inherently Unequal: The Betrayal of Equal Rights by the Supreme Court, 1865–1903*. New York: Walker.

González, Gabriela. 2018. *Redeeming La Raza: Transborder Modernity, Race, Respectability, and Rights*. New York: Oxford University Press.

González, Manuel G. 2009. *Mexicanos: A History of Mexicans in the United States*. Bloomington: Indiana University Press.

Greenhouse, Steven. 2019. *Beaten Down, Worked Up: The Past, Present, and Future of American Labor*. New York: Knopf.

Grem, Darren E. 2016. *The Blessings of Business: How Corporations Shaped Conservative Christianity*. New York: Oxford University Press.

Gribben, Crawford. 2015. "Holy Nation: America, Born Again." *American Interest* 11 (4). https://www.the-american-interest.com/2015/11/22/holy-nation-america-born-again/.

Griswold, Eliza. 2018. "Evangelicals of Color Fight Back against the Religious Right." *New Yorker*, December 26, 2018. https://www.newyorker.com/news/on-religion/evangelicals-of-color-fight-back-against-the-religious-right.

———. 2019. "The Radically Inclusive Christianity of Rachel Held Evans." May 6, 2019. *New Yorker*. https://www.newyorker.com/news/postscript/the-radically-inclusive-christianity-of-rachel-held-evans.

Gushee, David P. 2007. "Evangelicals and Politics: A Rethinking." *Journal of Law and Religion* 23(1): 1–14.

Gutiérrez, David G. 2013 "An Historic Overview of Latino Immigration and the Demographic Transformation of the United States." Washington, DC: National Park Service, US Department of the Interior. https://www.nps.gov/heritageinitiatives/latino/latinothemestudy/immigration.htm.

Guyatt, Nicholas. 2016. *Bind Us Apart: How Enlightened Americans Invented Racial Segregation*. New York: Basic.

Hacker, Jacob, and Paul Pierson. 2010. *Winner-Take-All Politics: How Washington Made the Rich Richer—And Turned Its Back on the Middle Class*. New York: Simon & Schuster.

Hackett, Conrad, and Brian J. Grim. 2011. "Global Christianity: A Report on the Size and Distribution of the World's Christian Population." *Pew Research Center*. https://assets.pewresearch.org/wp-content/uploads/sites/11/2011/12/Christianity-fullreport-web.pdf.

Haddigan, Lee. 2010. "The Importance of Christian Thought for the American Libertarian Movement: Christian Libertarianism, 1950–71." *Libertarian Papers* 2(14): 1–31. https://mises.org/library/importance-christian-thought-american-libertarian-movement-christian-libertarianism-1950-71.

Harvey, David. 2005. *A Brief History of Neoliberalism*. New York: Oxford University Press.

Haselby, Sam. 2015. *The Origins of American Religious Nationalism*. New York: Oxford University Press.

Hernandez, Kelly Lytle. 2010. *Migra! A History of the US Border Patrol*. Berkeley: University of California Press.

Higham, John. 1955. *Strangers in the Land: Patterns of American Nativism, 1860–1925*. New Brunswick, NJ: Rutgers University Press.

Hochschild, Arlie Russell. 2016. *Strangers in Their Own Land: Anger and Mourning on the American Right*. New York: The New Press.

Holilnger, Dennis, and David P. Gushee. 2000. "Evangelical Ethics: Profile of a Movement Coming of Age." *The Annual of the Society of Christian Ethics* 20: 181–203.

Huang, Jon, Samuel Jacoby, Michael Strickland, and K. K. Rebecca Lai. 2016. "Election 2016: Exit Polls." *New York Times*, November 8, 2016. www.nytimes.com/interactive/2016/11/08/us/politics/election-exit-polls.html.

Hunter, James Davidson. 1984. "Religion and Political Civility: The Coming Generation of American Evangelicals." *Journal for the Scientific Study of Religion* 23(4): 364–80.

Hutton W. 1996. *The State We're In*. London: Vintage.

Ignatiev, Noel. 1995. *How the Irish Became White*. New York: Routledge.

Ingersoll, Julie J. 2015. *Building God's Kingdom: Inside the World of Christian Reconstruction*. Oxford: Oxford University Press.

Iyengar, Shanto, Yphtach Lelkes, Matthew Levendusky, Neil Malhotra, and Sean J. West-
wood. 2018. "The Origins and Consequences of Affective Polarization in the United
States." *Annual Review of Political Science* 22: 129–46.
Jackson, Robert H. 2000. *From Savages to Subjects: Missions in the History of the American
Southwest.* New York: M. E. Sharpe.
Jacobs, Elisabeth. 2017. "Everywhere and Nowhere: Politics in *Capital in the Twenty-First
Century*." In *After Piketty: The Agenda for Economics and Inequality*, edited by Heather
J. Boushey, J. Bradford DeLong, and Marshall Steinbaum, 512–42. Cambridge, MA:
Harvard University Press.
Jenkins, Jack. 2017a. "How Trump's Presidency Reveals the True Nature of Christian Na-
tionalism." *ThinkProgress*, September 13, 2017. https://thinkprogress.org/christian-
nationalism-religion-research-b8f9ccdc16239/.
———. 2017b. "Why Christian Nationalists Love Trump." *ThinkProgress*, August 7, 2017.
https://thinkprogress.org/trumps-christian-nationalism-c6fe206e40cc/.
———. 2019. "'Nones' Now as Big as Evangelicals, Catholics in the US." March 21, 2019.
Religion News Service. https://religionnews.com/2019/03/21/nones-now-as-big-as-
evangelicals-catholics-in-the-us/.
Jensen, Tom. 2017. "Trump Holds Steady after Charlottesville; Supporters Think Whites,
Christians Face Discrimination." *Public Policy Polling*, August 23, 2017. http://www.
publicpolicypolling.com/main/2017/08/trump-holds-steady-after-charlottesville-
supporters-think-whites-christians-face-discrimination.html.
Johnson, Emily S. 2019. *This Is Our Message: Women's Leadership in the New Christian
Right.* New York: Oxford University Press
Jones, Daniel Stedman. 2014. *Masters of the Universe: Hayek, Friedman, and the Birth of
Neoliberal Politics.* Princeton, NJ: Princeton University Press.
Jones, Jennifer, and Hana Brown. 2019. "American Federalism and Racial Formation in
Contemporary Immigration Policy: A Processual Analysis of Alabama's HB56," *Ethnic
and Racial Studies* 42(4): 531–51.
Jones, Robert P. 2016. *The End of White Christian America.* New York: Simon & Schuster.
———. 2018. "White Evangelical Support for Donald Trump at All-Time High." *PRRI*,
April 18, 2018. https://www.prri.org/spotlight/white-evangelical-support-for-donald-
trump-at-all-time-high/.
Jones, Robert P., Daniel Cox, Rob Griffin, Maxine Najle, Molly Fisch-Friedman, and Alex
Vandermaas-Peeler. 2018. "Partisanship Trumps Gender: Sexual Harassment, Woman
Candidates, Access to Contraception, and Key Issues in 2018 Midterms." *PRRI*, October
3, 2018. https://www.prri.org/research/abortion-reproductive-health-midterms-trump-
kavanaugh.
Jones-Rogers, Stephanie E. 2019. *They Were Her Property: White Women as Slave Owners
in the American South.* New London, CT: Yale University Press.
Keith, Tamara. 2017. "How 'Positive Thinking' Helped Propel Trump to the Presidency."
National Public Radio, January 19, 2017. http://www.npr.org/2017/01/19/510628862/how-
positive-thinking-helped-propel-trump-to-the-presidency.
Kelkar, Kamala. 2017. "How a Shifting Definition of 'White' Helped Shape U.S. Immigra-
tion Policy." *PBS NewsHour*, September 16, 2017. https://www.pbs.org/newshour/nation/
white-u-s-immigration-policy
Kellner, Douglas. 2007. "Bushspeak and the Politics of Lying: Presidential Rhetoric in the
'War on Terror.'" *Presidential Studies Quarterly* 37(4): 622–45.
Kendi, Ibram X. 2016. *Stamped from the Beginning: The Definitive History of Racist Ideas in
America.* New York: Nation Books.
Kerber, Linda K. 1997. "The Meanings of Citizenship." *Journal of American History* 84, no.
3 (December): 838–43.
Kessell, John L. 2002. *Spain in the Southwest: A Narrative History of Colonial New Mexico,
Arizona, Texas, and California.* Norman: University of Oklahoma Press.
Kiely, Eugene. 2017. "Trump's Tax Plan and 'the Rich.'" *FactCheck.org* 14 September. http:/
/www.factcheck.org/2017/09/trumps-tax-plan-rich/.

Knuckey, Jonathan. 2005. "Racial Resentment and the Changing Partisanship of Southern Whites." *Party Politics* 11(1): 5–28.

Korrol, Virginia Sanchez. 1994. *From Colonia to Community: The History of Puerto Ricans in New York City.* Berkeley: University of California Press.

Kotz, David M. 2015. *The Rise and Fall of Neoliberal Capitalism.* Cambridge, MA: Harvard University Press.

Kousser, J. Morgan, and James McPherson (eds). 1982. *Region, Race, and Reconstruction: Essays in Honor of C. Vann Woodward.* New York: Oxford University Press.

Krippner Greta R. 2005. "The Financialization of the American Economy." *Socioeconomic Review* 3: 173–208.

———. 2011. *Capitalizing on Crisis: The Political Origins of the Rise of Finance.* Cambridge, MA: Harvard University Press.

Kruse, Kevin. 2015. *One Nation under God: How Corporate America Invented Christian America.* New York: Basic Books.

Labberton, Mark. 2018. *Still Evangelical? Insiders Reconsider Political, Social, and Theological Meaning.* Downers Gove, IL: InterVarsity.

Lafer, Gordon. 2017. *The One Percent Solution: How Corporations Are Remaking America One State at a Time.* Ithaca, NY: ILR.

Langone, Alix. 2018. "The 10 Richest People in America." *Money,* January 16, 2018. http://money.com/money/5095574/the-10-richest-people-in-america/.

Larner, W. 2000. "Neoliberalism: Policy, Ideology, Governmentality." *Studies in Political Economy* 63: 5–26.

Layman, Geoffrey C., Kerem Ozan Kalkan, and John C. Green. 2014. "A Muslim President? Misperceptions of Barack Obama's Faith in the 2008 Presidential Campaign." *Journal for the Scientific Study of Religion* 53(3): 534–55.

Lee, Erika. 2019. *America for Americans: A History of Xenophobia in the United States.* New York: Basic.

Lee, Jennifer, and Min Zhou. 2015. *The Asian American Achievement Paradox.* New York: Russell Sage Foundation.

Lesser, Gabriel, and Jeanne Batalova. 2015. "Central American Immigrants in the United States." *Migration Policy Institute,* August 15, 2019. http://www.migrationpolicy.org/article/central-american-immigrants-united-states.

Lew-Williams, Beth. 2018. *The Chinese Must Go: Violence, Exclusion, and the Making of the Alien in America.* Cambridge, MA: Harvard University Press.

Lewis, Andrew R. 2018. *The Rights Turn in Conservative Christian Politics: How Abortion Transformed the Culture Wars.* Cambridge, UK: Cambridge University Press.

Lewis, Andrew R., and Dana Huyser De Bernardo. 2010. "Belonging without Belonging: Utilizing Evangelical Self-Identification to Analyze Political Attitudes and Preferences." *Journal for the Scientific Study of Religion* 49(1): 112–26.

Lienesch, Michael. 1996. *Redeeming America: Piety and Politics in the New Christian Right.* Chapel Hill: University of North Carolina Press.

Lin, Ken-Hou, and Donald Tomaskovic-Devey. 2013. "Financialization and U.S. Income Inequality, 1970–2008." *American Journal of Sociology* 118(5 March): 1284–329.

Lindsay, D. Michael. 2007. "Ties that Bind and Divisions That Persist: Evangelical Faith and the Political Spectrum." *American Quarterly* 59(3): 883–909.

Lipka, Michael. 2016. "Evangelical Increasingly Say It's Becoming Harder for Them in America." *Pew Research Center,* July 14, 2016. http://www.pewresearch.org/fact-tank/2016/07/14/evangelicals-increasingly-say-its-becoming-harder-for-them-in-America/.

LiPuma, Edward. 2017. *The Social Life of Financial Derivatives: Markets, Risk, and Time.* Durham, NC: Duke University Press.

Litwack, Leon. 1961. *North of Slavery: The Negro in the Free. States, 1790–1860.* Chicago: University of Chicago Press.

Liu, Joseph. 2011. "The Tea Party and Religion." *Pew Research Center's Religion & Public Life Project,* February 22, 2011. www.pewforum.org/2011/02/23/tea-party-and-religion/

Lockett, James D. 1991. "Abraham Lincoln and Colonization: An Episode That Ends in Tragedy at L'Ile à Vache, Haiti, 1863–1864." *Journal of Black Studies* 21, no. 4 (June): 428–44.

Loewen, James W. 2005. *Sundown Towns: A Hidden Dimension of American Racism.* New York: The New Press.

Luxenberg, Steve. 2019. *Separate: The Story of* Plessy v. Ferguson, *and America's Journey from Slavery to Segregation.* New York: Norton.

Lynerd, Benjamin T. 2014. *Republican Theology: The Civil Religion of American Evangelicals.* New York: Oxford University Press.

Machado, Daisy L. 2003. *Of Borders and Margins: Hispanic Disciples in Texas, 1888–1945.* New York: Oxford University Press.

Macias-Rojas, Patrisia. 2016. *From Deportation to Prison: The Politics of Immigration Enforcement in Post-Civil Rights America.* New York: New York University Press.

MacLean, Nancy. 1994. *Behind the Mask of Chivalry: The Making of the Second Ku Klux Klan.* New York: Oxford University Press.

———. 2017. *Democracy in Chains: The Deep History of the Radical Right's Stealth Plan for America.* New York: Viking.

Maffly-Kipp, Laurie F. 1994. *Religion and Society in Frontier California.* New Haven, CT: Yale University Press.

Maggor, Noam. 2017. *Brahmin Capitalism Frontiers of Wealth and Populism in America's First Gilded Age.* Cambridge, MA: Harvard University Press.

Magness, Phillip W., and Sebastian N. Page. 2011. *Colonization after Emancipation: Lincoln and the Movement for Black Resettlement.* Columbia: University of Missouri Press.

Mahler, Sarah J., and Katrin Hansing. 2005. "Toward a Transnationalism of the Middle: How Transnational Religious Practices Help Bridge the Divides between Cuba and Miami." *Latin American Perspectives* 32, no. 1 (January): 121–46.

Marsden, George M. 2006. *Fundamentalism and American Culture: The Shaping of Twentieth-Century Evangelicalism, 1870–1925.* New York: Oxford University Press.

Martí, Gerardo. 2005. *A Mosaic of Believers: Diversity and Innovation in a Multiethnic Church.* Bloomington: Indiana University Press.

———. 2008. *Hollywood Faith: Holiness, Prosperity, and Ambition in a Los Angeles Church.* New Brunswick, NJ: Rutgers University Press.

———. 2010. "Ego-affirming Evangelicalism: How a Hollywood Church Appropriates Religion for Workers in the Creative Class." *Sociology of Religion* 71(1): 52–75.

———. 2015. "Religious Reflexivity: The Effect of Continual Novelty and Diversity on Individual Religiosity." *Sociology of Religion* 76 (1): 1–13.

———. 2016. "'I Was a Muslim, but Now I Am a Christian': Preaching, Legitimation, and Identity Management in a Southern Evangelical Church." *Journal for the Scientific Study of Religion* 55 (2): 250–70.

———. 2017. "The Global Phenomenon of Hillsong Church: An Initial Assessment." *Sociology of Religion* 7 (4): 377–86.

———. 2018. "*Maranatha* (O Lord, Come): The Power/Surrender Dynamic of Pentecostal Worship." *Liturgy* 33 (3): 20–28.

———. 2019. "The Unexpected Orthodoxy of Donald J Trump: White Evangelical Support for the 45th President of the United States." *Sociology of Religion: A Quarterly Review* 80 (1): 1–8.

———. 2020. "The Legitimation of White Christian Libertarianism: Uncovering the Cultural Pillars of the Trump Presidency." In *Religion Is Raced: Understanding American Religion in the 21st Century*, edited by Grace Yukich and Penny Edgell. New York: New York University Press.

Martí, Gerardo, and Gladys Ganiel. 2014. *The Deconstructed Church: Understanding Emerging Christianity.* New York: Oxford University Press.

Martin, Isaac William. 2013. *Rich People's Movements: Grassroots Campaigns to Untax the One Percent .* New York: Oxford University Press.

Martin, Rachel, and Steve Inskeep. 2017. Interview with David Greene. "Trump's First 100 Days: Tax and Economic Policies." *National Public Radio*, April 24, 2017. https://www.npr.org/2017/04/24/525359256/trumps-first-100-days-tax-and-economic-policies.

Martínez, Jessica, and Gregory A. Smith. 2016. "How the Faithful Voted: A Preliminary 2016 Analysis." *Pew Research Center*. November 9, 2016. https://www.pewresearch.org/fact-tank/2016/11/09/how-the-faithful-voted-a-preliminary-2016-analysis/.

Martínez, Monica Muñoz. 2018. *The Injustice Never Leaves You: Anti-Mexican Violence in Texas*. Cambridge, MA: Harvard University Press.

Masci, David. 2017. "Almost All U.S. Presidents, Including Trump, Have Been Christians." *Pew Research Center*, January 20, 2017. http://www.pewresearch.org/fact-tank/2017/01/20/almost-all-presidents-have-been-christians/.

Massey, Douglas S., and Karen A. Pren. 2012. "Unintended Consequences of US Immigration Policy: Explaining the Post-1965 Surge from Latin America." *Population and Development Review* 38(1): 1–29.

Mathews, Mary Beth Swetnam. 2017. *Doctrine and Race: African American Evangelicals and Fundamentalism between the Wars*. Tuscaloosa, AL: University of Alabama Press.

Maxwell, Angie, and Todd Shields. 2019. *The Long Southern Strategy: How Chasing White Voters in the South Changed American Politics*. New York: Oxford University Press.

McAdam, Doug, and Karina Kloos. 2014. *Deeply Divided: Racial Politics and Social Movements in Post-War America*. New York: Oxford University Press.

McRae, Elizabeth Gillespie. 2018. *Mothers of Massive Resistance: White Women and the Politics of White Supremacy*. New York: Oxford University Press.

Mealer, Bryan. 2018. "'I'm Not Anti-Trump, I'm Just Pro-Jesus': The Evangelicals Stumping for the Democrats." *Guardian*, October 31, 2018. https://www.theguardian.com/global/2018/oct/31/trump-democrats-evangelicals-pro-jesus-republicans.

Menchaca, Martha. 2001. *Recovering History, Constructing Race: The Indian, Black, and White Roots of Mexican Americans*. Austin: University of Texas Press.

Miller, Steven P. 2016. *The Age of Evangelicalism: America's Born-Again Years*. New York: Oxford University Press.

Minian, Ana Raquel. 2018. *Undocumented Lives: The Untold Story of Mexican Migration*. Cambridge, MA: Harvard University Press.

Mirowski, P., and D. Plehwe (eds). 2009. *The Road to Mont Pelerin: The Making of the Neoliberal Thought Collective*. Cambridge, MA: Harvard University Press.

Mitchell, Travis. 2016. "Evangelicals Rally to Trump, Religious 'Nones' Back Clinton." *Religion & Public Life Project*, Pew Research Center. July 13, 2016.https://www.pewforum.org/2016/07/13/evangelicals-rally-to-trump-religious-nones-back-clinton/.

Mitchell, William L. 1962. "The Cuban Refugee Program." *Social Security Bulletin* 25: 3 (March).

Montejano, David. 2010. *Anglos and Mexicans in the Making of Texas, 1836–1986*. Austin: University of Texas Press.

Moore, Joseph S. 2016. *Founding Sins: How a Group of Antislavery Radicals Fought to Put Christ into the Constitution*. New York: Oxford University Press.

Moreno, Paul D. 2008. *Black Americans and Organized Labor: A New History*. Baton Rouge: Louisiana State University.

Mulder, Mark T., and Gerardo Martí. 2020. *The Glass Church: Robert H. Schuller, the Crystal Cathedral, and the Strain of Megachurch Ministry*. New Brunswick, NJ: Rutgers University Press.

Mulder, Mark T., Aida I. Ramos, and Gerardo Martí. 2017. *Latino Protestants in America: Growing and Diverse*. Lanham, MD: Rowman & Littlefield.

Nau, Michael David. 2011. "Financialization, Wealth, and Income Inequality." Paper presented at the American Sociological Association Annual Meeting, Las Vegas, NV, 2011.

———. 2013. "Economic Elites, Investments, and Income Inequality." *Social Forces* 92(2): 437–61.

Neiwert, David. 2017. *Alt-America: The Rise of the Radical Right in the Age of Trump*. London: Verso.

Newman, Simon P. 2007. "One Nation under God: Making Historical Sense of Evangelical Protestantism in Contemporary American Politics." *Journal of American Studies* 41(3): 581–97.

Nicolaisen, Peter. 2003. "Thomas Jefferson, Sally Hemings, and the Question of Race: An Ongoing Debate." *Journal of American Studies* 37, no. 1 (April): 99–118.

Noll, Mark A. 2008. *God and Race in American Politics: A Short History.* Princeton, NJ: Princeton University Press.

Okrent, Daniel. 2019. *The Guarded Gate: Bigotry, Eugenics and the Law That Kept Two Generations of Jews, Italians, and Other European Immigrants Out of America.* New York: Scribner.

Ostler, Jeffrey. 2019. *Surviving Genocide: Native Nations and the United Sates from the American Revolution to Bleeding Kansas.* New Haven, CT: Yale University Press.

Painter, Nell Irvin. 2010. *The History of White People.* New York: Norton.

Palley, Thomas. 2008. "Financialization: What It Is and Why It Matters." In *Finance-Led Capitalism: Macroeconomic Effects of Changes in the Financial Sector,* edited by Eckhard Hein, Torsten Niechoj, Heinz-Peter Spahn, and Achim Truger, 29–60. Marburg, Germany: Metropolis.

———. 2012. *From Financial Crisis to Stagnation: The Destruction of Shared Prosperity and the Role of Economics.* New York: Cambridge University Press.

Parker, Christopher S., and Matt A. Barreto. 2014. *Change They Can't Believe In: The Tea Party and Reactionary Politics in America.* Princeton, NJ: Princeton University Press.

Patten, Eileen. 2015. "How American Parents Balance Work and Family Life When Both Work." *Pew Research Center,* November 4, 2015. https://www.pewresearch.org/fact-tank/2015/11/04/how-american-parents-balance-work-and-family-life-when-both-work/.

Peck J. 2010. *Constructions of Neoliberal Reason.* Oxford, UK: Oxford University Press.

Perlmann, Joel. 2018. *America Classifies the Immigrants: From Ellis Island to the 2020 Census.* Cambridge, MA: Harvard University Press.

Phillips-Fein, Kim. 2009. *Invisible Hands: The Making of the Conservative Movement from the New Deal to Reagan.* W. W. Norton.

Piketty, Thomas. 2014. *Capital in the Twenty-First Century,* translated by Arthur Goldhammer. Cambridge, MA: Harvard University Press.

Pistor, Katharina. 2019. *The Code of Capital: How the Law Creates Wealth and Inequality.* Princeton, NJ: Princeton University Press.

Putnam, Robert D., and David E. Campbell. 2012. *American Grace: How Religion Divides and Unites Us.* New York: Simon & Schuster.

Ramos, Aida I., Gerardo Marti, and Mark T. Mulder. 2018. "The Growth and Diversity of Latino Protestants in America." *Religion Compass* 12 (July): 7.

———. Forthcoming. "Latino/a Protestantisms: Historical and Sociological Overviews." In *Oxford Handbook of Latino/a Christianities in America.* New York: Oxford University Press.

Rampell, Catherine. 2017. "Opinion: Who Wins Biggest in the GOP Tax Plan? The Lazy Rich." *Washington Post,* November 6, 2017. https://www.washingtonpost.com/opinions/who-wins-biggest-in-the-gop-tax-plan-the-lazy-rich/2017/11/06/0d010482-c337-11e7-84bc-5e285c7f4512_story.html?utm_term=.60d93fbc302e.

Renaud, Myriam. 2017. "Myths Debunked: Why Did White Evangelical Christians Vote for Trump?" The Martin Marty Center for the Public Understanding of Religion, The University of Chicago Divinity School. January 19, 2017. https://divinity.uchicago.edu/sightings/myths-debunked-why-did-white-evangelical-christians-vote-trump.

Roels, Shirley J. 1997. "The Business Ethics of Evangelicals." *Business Ethics Quarterly* 7(2): 109–22.

Rosenthal, Brian M., and Sheryl Gay Stolberg. 2017. "Man Charged after White Nationalist Rally in Charlottesville Ends in Deadly Violence." *New York Times,* August 12, 2017. https://www.nytimes.com/2017/08/12/us/charlottesville-protest-white-nationalist.html.

Rosenwald, Brian. 2019. *Talk Radio's America: How an Industry Took Over a Political Party That Took Over the United States.* Cambridge, MA: Harvard University Press.

Ross, Brian, and Rehab El-Buri. 2008. "Obama's Pastor: God Damn America, US to Blame for 9/11." *ABC News*, March 13, 2008. http://abcnews.go.com/Blotter/DemocraticDebate/story?id=4443788.

Ross, E. A. 1901. "The Causes of Race Superiority." *Annals of the Institute for Political Science* 18: 67–89.

Rothstein, Richard. 2017. *The Color of Law: A Forgotten History of How Our Government Segregated America.* New York: Liveright.

Rush, Nayla. 2018. "Refugee Resettlement Admissions in FY 2018." *Center for Immigration Studies*, October 1, 2018. https://cis.org/Rush/Refugee-Resettlement-Admissions-FY-2018.

Ruotsila, Markku. 2015. *Fighting Fundamentalist: Carl McIntire and the Politicization of American Fundamentalism.* London: Oxford University Press.

Sandel, Michael J. 1996. *Democracy's Discontent: America in Search of a Public Philosophy.* Cambridge, MA: Harvard University Press.

Schalch, Kathleen. 2006. "1981 Strike Leaves Legacy for American Workers." *NPR*, August 3, 2006. www.npr.org/2006/08/03/5604656/1981-strike-leaves-legacy-for-american-workers.

Schlozman, Daniel. 2015. *When Movements Anchor Parties: Electoral Alignments in American History.* Princeton, NJ: Princeton University Press.

Schlozman, Daniel, and Sam Rosenfeld. 2019. "The Long New Right and the World It Made, Version of January 2019." Paper prepared for the American Political Science Association meetings. Boston, Massachusetts, August 31, 2018. https://static1.squarespace.com/static/540f1546e4b0ca60699c8f73/t/5c3e694321c67c3d28e992ba/1547594053027/Long+New+Right+Jan+2019.pdf.

Schwadel, Philip, and Gregory A. Smith. 2019. "Evangelical Approval of Trump Remains High, but Other Religious Groups Are Less Supportive." *Pew Research Center*, March 18, 2019. https://www.pewresearch.org/fact-tank/2019/03/18/evangelical-approval-of-trump-remains-high-but-other-religious-groups-are-less-supportive/.

Shapiro, Thomas M. 2017. *Toxic Inequality: How America's Wealth Gap Destroys Mobility, Deepens the Racial Divide, and Threatens Our Future.* New York: Basic.

Shellnutt, Kate. 2017. "Young, Female, and Pro-Trump: How White Evangelical Millennials Are Defying Political Predictions." *Christianity Today*, July 26, 2017. http://www.christianitytoday.com/women/2017/july/young-female-and-pro-trump.html.

Shupe, Anson. 1989. "The Reconstructionist Movement on the New Christian Right." *Religion Online*, October 4, 1989.https://www.religion-online.org/article/the-reconstructionist-movement-on-the-new-christian-right/.

Silverman, Gary. 2017. "How the Bible Belt Lost God and Found Trump." *Financial Times*, April 13, 2017.https://www.ft.com/content/b41d0ee6-1e96-11e7-b7d3-163f5a7f229c.

Slobodian, Quinn. 2018. *Globalists: The End of Empire and the Birth of Neoliberalism.* Cambridge, MA: Harvard University Press.

Smith, Christian. 1998. *American Evangelicalism: Embattled and Thriving.* Chicago: University of Chicago Press.

Smith, Gregory A. 2016. "Many Evangelicals Favor Trump because He Is Not Clinton." *Pew Research Center*, September 23, 2016. http://www.pewresearch.org/fact-tank/2016/09/23/many-evangelicals-favor-trump-because-he-is-not-clinton/.

———. 2017. "Among White Evangelicals, Regular Churchgoers are the Most Supportive of Trump." *Pew Research Center*, April 26, 2017. https://www.pewresearch.org/fact-tank/2017/04/26/among-white-evangelicals-regular-churchgoers-are-the-most-supportive-of-trump/.

Smith, Gregory A., and David Masci. 2016. "Exit Polls and the Evangelical Vote: A Closer Look." *Religion & Public Life Project, Pew Research Center*, March 14, 2016.https://www.pewresearch.org/fact-tank/2016/03/14/exit-polls-and-the-evangelical-vote-a-closer-look/.

Solow, Robert M. 2017. "Piketty Is Right." In *After Piketty: The Agenda for Economics and Inequality*, edited by Heather J. Boushey, Bradford DeLong, and Marshall Steinbaum, 48–59. Cambridge, MA: Harvard University Press.

Stampp, Kenneth M. 1965. *The Era of Reconstruction, 1865–1877*. New York: Alfred A. Knopf.

Stewart, Evan, Penny Edgell, and Jack Delehanty. 2018. "The Politics of Religious Prejudice and Tolerance for Cultural Others." *The Sociological Quarterly* 59(1): 17–39.

Stokes, Bruce. 2017. "What It Takes to Truly Be 'One of Us'" *Pew Research Center*, February 2017. https://www.pewresearch.org/global/wp-content/uploads/sites/2/2017/02/Pew-Research-Center-National-Identity-Report-FINAL-February-1-2017.pdf.

Stolberg, Sheryl Gay, and Brian M. Rosenthal. 2017. "Man Charged after White Nationalist Rally in Charlottesville Ends in Deadly Violence." *New York Times*, August 12, 2017. https://www.nytimes.com/2017/08/12/us/charlottesville-protest-white-nationalist.html.

Sullivan, Amy. 2017. "America's New Religion: Fox Evangelicalism." *New York Times*, December 15, 2017. https://www.nytimes.com/2017/12/15/opinion/sunday/war-christmas-evangelicals.html.

Sullivan, Patricia. 2006. *Days of Hole: Race and Democracy in the New Deal Era*. Chapel Hill: University of North Carolina Press.

Sutton, Matthew Avery. 2014. *American Apocalypse: A History of Modern Evangelicalism*. Cambridge, MA: Belknap.

Telles, Edward M., and Vilma Ortiz. 2008. *Generations of Exclusion: Mexican-Americans, Assimilation*. New York: Russell Sage Foundation.

Tesler, Michael. 2016. *Post-Racial or Most-Racial? Race and Politics in the Obama Era*. Chicago: University of Chicago Press.

Tichenor, Daniel J. 2002. *Dividing Lines: The Politics of Immigration Control in America*. Princeton, NJ: Princeton University Press.

Tisby, Jemar. 2019. *The Color of Compromise: The Truth about the American Church's Complicity in Racism*. Grand Rapids, MI: Zondervan.

Tomaskovic-Deveya, Donald, and Ken-Hou Lin. 2011. "Income Dynamics, Economic Rents, and the Financialization of the US Economy." *American Sociological Review* 76(4): 538–59.

Trachtenberg, Alan. 1982. *The Incorporation of America: Culture and Society in the Gilded Age*. New York: Hill and Wang.

Trotter, Joe William Jr. 2009. *Workers on Arrival: Black Labor in the Making of America*. Berkley: University of California Press.

Trump, Donald J. "Donald J. Trump Presidential Campaign Announcement Full Speech." *CSPAN*, June 16, 2015.https://www.youtube.com/watch?v=apjNfkysjbM.

Vecoli, Rudolph J. 1996. "The Significance of Immigration in the Formation of an American Identity." *The History Teacher* 30, no. 1(November): 9–27.

Vorenberg, Michael. 1993. "Abraham Lincoln and the Politics of Black Colonization." *Journal of the Abraham Lincoln Association* 14, no. 2(Summer): 22–45.

Wacker, Grant. 2014. *America's Pastor: Billy Graham and the Shaping of a Nation*. Cambridge, MA: Harvard University Press.

Wadhia, Shoba Sivaprasad. 2019. *Banned: Immigration Enforcement in the Time of Trump*. New York: New York University Press.

Warren, Robert. 2019. "US Undocumented Population Continued to Fall from 2016 to 2017, and Visa Overstays Significantly Exceeded Illegal Crossings for the Seventh Consecutive Year." *Center for Migration Studies*, January 16, 2019. https://doi.org/10.14240/cmse-sy011619.

Wasem, Ruth E. 2009. "Cuban Migration to the United States: Policy and Trends." *Library of Congress Congressional Research Service*. https://digital.library.unt.edu/ark:/67531/metadc689389/m1/1/high_res_d/R40566_2009Jun02.pdf.

Weber, Max. 1968. *The Protestant Ethic and the Spirit of Capitalism*. New York: Scribner.

———. 1978. *Economy and Society*. Berkeley: University of California Press.

White, Richard. 2018. "Utopian Capitalism." Pp 119-139 in *American Capitalism: New Histories*, edited by Sven Beckert and Christine Desan. New York: Columbia University Press.

———. 2017. *The Republic for Which It Stands: The United States During Reconstruction and the Gilded Age, 1865–1896*. New York: Oxford University Press.

————. 2019. "Utopian Capitalism." In *American Capitalism: New Histories*, edited by Sven Beckert and Christine Desan, 119–39. New York: Columbia University Press.

Whitehead, Andrew L., and Samuel L. Perry. 2020. *Taking America Back for God: Christian Nationalism in the United States*. New York: Oxford University Press.

Whitehead, Andrew L., Samuel L. Perry, and Joseph O. Baker. 2018. "Make America Christian Again: Christian Nationalism and Voting for Donald Trump in the 2016 Presidential Election." *Sociology of Religion* 79(2): 147–71.

Whitman, James Q. 2017. *Hitler's American Model: The United States and the Making of Nazi Race Law*. Princeton, NJ: Princeton University Press.

Wilde, Melissa J., and Sabrina Danielsen. 2014. "Fewer and Better Children: Race, Class, Religion, and Birth Control Reform in America." *American Journal of Sociology* 119(6): 1710–60.

Williams, Daniel K. 2012. "Richard Nixon's Religious Right: Catholics, Evangelicals, and the Creation of an Antisecular Alliance." In *The Right Side of the Sixties: Reexamining Conservatism's Decade of Transformation*, edited by Laura Jane Gifford and Daniel K. Williams, 141–58. New York: Palgrave Macmillan.

————. 2016. *Defenders of the Unborn: The Pro-Life Movement before Roe v. Wade*. New York: Oxford University Press.

Williams, Linda Faye. 2003. *The Constraint of Race: Legacies of White Skin Privilege in America*. University Park: Pennsylvania State University Press.

Wilson, Charles Reagan. 2009. *Baptized in Blood: The Religion of the Lost Cause, 1865–1920*. Athens: University of Georgia Press.

Wolfe, Patrick. 2006. "Settler Colonialism and the Elimination of the Native." *Journal of Genocide Research* 8(4): 387–409.

Wolin, Sheldon S. 2004. *Politics and Vision: Continuity and Innovation in Western Political Thought*, expanded edition. Princeton, NJ: Princeton University Press.

Wong, Janelle. 2018. *Immigrants, Evangelicals, and Politics in an Era of Demographic Change*. New York: Russell Sage.

————. 2019. "We Are All Evangelicals Now." *Religion & Politics*, January 22, 2019. https://religionandpolitics.org/2019/01/22/we-are-all-evangelicals-now-race-politics/.

Wong, Tom K. 2017. *The Politics of Immigration: Partisanship, Demographic Change, and American National Identity*. New York: Oxford University Press.

Wormald, Benjamin. 2015. "Religious Landscape Study." *Religion & Public Life Project, Pew Research Center*, May 11, 2015. www.pewforum.org/religious-landscape-study/.

Worthen, Molly. 2017. "A Match Made in Heaven." *Atlantic*, April 18, 2017. http://www.theatlantic.com/magazine/archive/2017/05/a-match-made-in-heaven/521409/.

Yourish, Karen, and Troy Griggs. 2018. "8 U.S. Intelligence Groups Blame Russia for Meddling, but Trump Keeps Clouding the Picture." August 2, 2018. https://www.nytimes.com/interactive/2018/07/16/us/elections/russian-interference-statements-comments.html.

Zaw, Khaing, Jhumpa Bhattacharya, Anne Price, Darrick Hamilton, and William Darity Jr. 2017. "Women, Race & Wealth." *Research Brief Series* 1 (January). http://www.insightcced.org/wp-content/uploads/2017/01/January2017_ResearchBriefSeries_WomenRaceWealth-Volume1-Pages-1.pdf.

INDEX